Academically Gifted
American Male C
Students

Academically Gifted African American Male College Students

Fred A. Bonner II

Foreword by Kofi Lomotey

Afterword by Donna Y. Ford

 PRAEGER

AN IMPRINT OF ABC-CLIO, LLC

Santa Barbara, California • Denver, Colorado • Oxford, England

Copyright 2010 by Fred A. Bonner II

All rights reserved. No part of this publication may be reproduced, stored in a retrieval system, or transmitted, in any form or by any means, electronic, mechanical, photocopying, recording, or otherwise, except for the inclusion of brief quotations in a review, without prior permission in writing from the publisher.

Library of Congress Cataloging-in-Publication Data
Bonner II, Fred A.
  Academically gifted African American male college students /
Fred A. Bonner II; foreword by Kofi Lomotey; afterword by Donna Y. Ford.
    p. cm.
  Includes bibliographical references and index.
  ISBN: 978-0-89789-857-7 (print : alk. paper) ISBN: 978-0-313-38723-4 (ebook)
  1. African American men—Education (Higher)   2. African American male college
students   3. African Americans—Scholarships, fellowships, etc.   I. Title.
  LC2781.B56   2010
  378.1'982996073—dc22   2009043476

14   13   12   11   10   1   2   3   4   5

This book is also available on the World Wide Web as an eBook.
Visit www.abc-clio.com for details.

Praeger
An Imprint of ABC-CLIO, LLC

ABC-CLIO, LLC
130 Cremona Drive, P.O. Box 1911
Santa Barbara, California 93116-1911

This book is printed on acid-free paper ∞

Manufactured in the United States of America

Contents

Foreword

Fred Bonner has produced a creative and important book addressing the unique circumstances of African American male gifted and talented college students. As Bonner points out, many of these students are successful in precollegiate and higher education institutions; yet, little is written about their challenges or their successes. This book begins the process of addressing this oversight in the literature.

The key question that Bonner raises in this book is what are the perceptions of African American male gifted and talented college students relative to the support they receive from their institutions. It is one thing to be gifted and talented. It is another thing to be supported by one's institution. Clearly, the lack of such support can be devastating to students.

This book, as Bonner indicates, is important because (1) African Americans, in general, and African American males, in particular, are underrepresented in gifted and talented classrooms—elementary, secondary and tertiary; (2) limited research has been conducted on gifted and talented students in higher education; and (3) even less research has been done on African American male gifted and talented students in higher education.

The challenges with regard to African Americans in gifted and talented programs begin in elementary school. As Bonner points out, teachers are generally the first providers of referrals for gifted and talented programs. Herein lies another illustration of the limitations of many teacher education programs in the United States.

We continue to prepare teachers to teach one particular type of student—white Anglo-Saxon Protestant males—a type that no longer exists in large numbers, particularly in major urban centers. Teachers, then, are baffled by the rapidly increasing number of students who do not fit into this category—students they have not been prepared to teach. The result is that teachers do what they can to avoid interacting with these "different" students. They place them in the back of the room; they send them to the principal's office; they recommend them for expulsion, special education or suspension; or they just ignore them. This is not an indictment of teachers but, instead, is an indictment of many of our teacher training programs. What, you might ask, does this have to do with gifted and talented education? Everything, I would respond. Just as teachers are not prepared to teach culturally different students, they are ill-equipped to identify culturally different gifted and talented students. Hence, culturally different gifted and talented students, as Bonner points out, go unidentified at alarmingly high rates.

As Gail Kofsky indicates, cited herein, there are at least five reasons why African Americans are underidentified for and, subsequently, underrepresented in gifted and talented programs: (1) wrong criteria used, (2) biased screening employed, (3) erroneous referral processes implemented, (4) ignorance of diversity issues, and (5) poor teacher training.

In this book, Bonner reports on two case studies: one of an African American male gifted and talented student at a predominantly white college and another of an African American male gifted and talented student at a historically Black university. While this is a descriptive study rather than an empirical study, Bonner seeks, in part, to address the myth that the best African American students attend predominantly white colleges and universities. Indeed, we know that many African American students who have been highly successful in high school—as evidenced by standardized achievement test scores and high school grade point average—do, in fact, attend historically Black colleges and universities (HBCUs). Another goal of Bonner is to delve into the issue of the focus on academic excellence at predominantly white schools as compared to that which is observed at HBCUs. Some evidence is uncovered—though it is not generalizable from a descriptive study—indicating that academic excellence is indeed stressed at predominantly white institutions and at HBCUs.

The limitations of a descriptive study are obvious; however, they play a key role in setting up future theory-testing explorations. In this instance, Bonner has opened the door for a plethora of studies, a door that I hope he and others will go through. Some of these future studies and research inquiries might look at questions such as the following:

- What is the relative benefit of predominantly white colleges and universities versus HBCUs in addressing the needs of African American male gifted and talented students? What are the strengths of each type of institution in this regard?
- Given the limitations of standardized tests, how might we better identify students who are gifted and talented? Might theories such as Gardner's theory of multiple intelligences offer some insights?
- What is the role of culturally responsive teaching in identifying culturally different gifted and talented students and in bringing about the overall academic success of African American students? Is it important for teachers to be knowledgeable about cultural differences of students and of the implications for teaching?

- What roles do factors such as peer groups, families, and faculty play in bringing about the success of African American male gifted and talented college students? How can they detract from or facilitate their success?
- What is the relative importance of selected factors (e.g., class size, potential relationships with faculty, institutional size, and geographic location) for African American male gifted and talented students when they go about selecting a college or university? Relatedly, what is the impact of such factors on the ultimate success of these students?
- How important is the mission of an HBCU (or a traditionally White institution) in addressing the needs of African American male gifted and talented students?
- To what degree does the description of the HBCU in this study reflect other HBCUs, in terms of being supportive, collaborative, and validating?

This is an important book that Bonner has put together. He gives us information about the experiences of African American male gifted and talented college students, he proposes ideas for critical future research, and he shows us more. What more has Bonner shown us?

- Teacher training, when addressing gifted and talented students—as in so many other areas—is critically important.
- Understanding learning styles is imperative for all teachers.
- Understanding the relationships that African American males who are gifted and talented engage in while in college will better prepare us to retain and graduate them.
- African American males who are gifted and talented suffer a double whammy: (1) they are discriminated against because of the color of their skin (and are, therefore, inadequately supported); and (2) they are not supported in ways that other gifted and talented students are.
- African American male gifted and talented students can be successful and supported at HBCUs.
- Not all African American gifted and talented students emphasize their talents; many view such behavior as "acting White."

Enjoy.

Kofi Lomotey
Southern University and A & M College

Acknowledgments

To my friend, mentor, advisor, and dissertation chair (the comfortable chair) James Swartz, who has been with me every step of the way in the development of my research agenda, I want to say that your guidance has not only led me to the completion of this book but also led me to receive two awards and a million dollar grant from the National Science Foundation (NSF). From the long hours discussing the intricacies of phenomenology and grounded theory and who we thought to be the best contemporary jazz artists, I have learned so much from you and owe you a profound debt of gratitude. You were the lightning rod helping me not only to frame my work in such a way as to give "voice" to these gifted African American males but to tell a story—a story that spoke of the assets that these men brought to higher education contexts as opposed to the deficits that the literature tended to convey.

To John W. Murry, my mentor-friend who encouraged me to pursue my passion and engage in research and scholarship that was not for the purpose of just completing a degree but for the goal of changing society, I want to say that we started off together—you as an assistant professor and me as a "green" graduate student, and you have always been there as a guiding light. I have used your mentoring and guidance as a model for how I interface with my students. We speak of modeling and scaffolding key mentoring behaviors—you have done just that!

Susan Johnsen, it was in your class that this little research light of mine began to shine. I consistently tell the story of how my research project in your course on giftedness, loosely titled "Cultivating Giftedness among African American Male Populations: A Study of HBCUs and PWIs," was where it all began. You are the quintessential mentor. Although my study was typical of novice level research, you made me feel as if it was the most important study in the world Thank you for all that you have done and continue to do for students, for the field, and for me.

Marcia Imbeau, Gordon Morgan, and Suzanne Gordon were a part of my dissertation "dream team." Marcia, you provided such a wealth of knowledge when it came to responding to my queries related to giftedness and the gifted literature. Gordon Morgan, it was because of you that I chose to focus my hours outside of the Higher Education Administration program in sociology—you truly are a University of Arkansas legend. And finally, Suzanne Gordon, your editorial expertise and the amazing tone that you set at the beginning of my dissertation defense—"This is an amazing piece of work, don't we all agree?"—gave me the confidence to hang in there and fight the dissertation defense hydra that day—I won!

Stephen James and Trey Williams, the two brilliant, creative, outstanding, talented, and gifted African American men who participated in this study, you are the hope and inspiration for generations to come. I thank you for allowing me into your lives to gain perspective on and tell a different narrative about academically gifted African American men, who too are worthy of our attention, but who often go unnoticed. Your stories that were shared some ten years ago are still instructive today for those who seek viable strategies and sage wisdom on how to frame higher education contexts that are supportive of high-achieving brothers like you. Beyond being gifted, you two are "just good people."

Donna Ford, whom I refer to as my "shero," thanks for all the work that you do on populations of color in gifted education. You read and provided key feedback on the very first article that I wrote as a graduate student and have been a tremendous source of support throughout my career in academe. Elizabeth Potenza, my editor at Praeger Publishers was always calm, cool, and collected during our many phone conversations; when I got off the phone with you, somehow I just knew that everything was going to be all right. I appreciate your kindness and patience throughout this process.

Dorothy Bonner, beyond being a supportive mom and key confidante, you are my mother-friend. Thanks so much for your patience and the use of your living room during the holiday breaks to work on this book. Alonzo Flowers, my graduate assistant, you are an invaluable source of support. What would I do without your keen transcription and organizational skills in nudging this book along? And last but not least, Melvin C. Terrell, my mentor, thanks for your encouragement to keep moving—thanks for keeping me focused by asking, "So, when is the book coming out?"

Introduction

WHAT CAN A STUDY CONDUCTED 10 YEARS AGO TELL ME ABOUT GIFTED AFRICAN AMERICAN MALES NOW?

Perhaps the best response to the question posed in the heading is to invoke the use of the old proverb, "The more things change, the more they stay the same." Given the ten-year time lapse since my initial interview with the two academically gifted African American males, a legitimate query is *how relevant and applicable are these findings in a very contemporary context?* In essence, do the experiences and narratives shared by these two men a decade ago have any salience today? As much as I would like to say that many of the challenges these men articulated have lost their savor and have been completely replaced by more affirming and positive engagements, such has not been the case.

Invariably the stories that these men shared, along with the experiences I was able to chronicle through observations and the collection of written documents, highlight a number of recurrent patterns. For example, the themes that were uncovered in the initial research study included relationships with faculty, peer relationships, family influence and support, factors influencing college selection, self-perception, and institutional environment. A survey of the current literature (Bonner & Evans, 2004; Cuyjet and Associates, 2006; Fashola, 2005; Ginwright, 2004; Hughes & Bonner, 2006; Kershaw, 2001; Kunjufu, 2005; Shujaa, 1994; White & Cones, 1999) focusing on African American males in secondary as well as postsecondary settings reveals many of the same maladies that existed since the initial study was conducted. A focus on the literature (Bonner, 2001; Bonner & Jennings, 2007; Bonner, Jennings, Marbley, & Brown, 2008; Ford, 1995; Ford, Grantham, & Harris, 1998; Ford, Harris, Tyson, Frazier-Trotman, 2002; Fries-Britt, 1998; Fries-Britt & Turner, 2002; Harper, 2005; Hebert, 1998; Hebert, 2002) highlighting academically gifted African American males in particular reveals similar problems that this cohort continues to face.

Thus, the goal of this book is to not only highlight the problems but also offer alternative ways to look at the issues that continue to threaten the achievement of African American males in general and those academically gifted African American males in particular who seek to be successful in our higher education enclaves in this country. Whether it is the historically Black college and university (HBCU) environment or the predominantly White institution (PWI) setting, understanding the potential factors that contribute to the oftentimes arrhythmic experiences that these men have with academe is critical.

I implore the reader to consider each statement and problematize all the themes in an effort to determine more effective ways to frame our higher education settings to be more conducive to the learning, growth, and development of academically gifted African American males. While this book, based on qualitative research traditions, eschews any attempts at generalization, it is more than appropriate for the reader to use the narrative accounts and empirically derived findings to determine what aspects of these men's experiences are transferable to their specific contexts. Yes, in the 10 years since I conducted the initial study, we have witnessed many positive changes; not the least of which includes the emergence of a new and vocal generational cohort—the Millennials—and the election of the nation's first African American president. However, we have also witnessed change that has not been quite as positive. For example, increasing numbers of Black and brown children with concomitant decreases in the number of Black and brown teachers; the *overinclusion* of students of color in special education and the *underinclusion* of these students in gifted and talented programming; and a retrenchment in key funding for those who are in the direst need if higher education is to be an option. So, what this book will offer and what Trey and Stephen's experiences will provide you with some ten years later is a window to look out on the past and a door to open up to opportunities in the future. These gifted African American males are ready to talk—are you ready to listen?

ACADEMICALLY GIFTED AFRICAN AMERICAN MALES IN COLLEGE: SUCCESS IN THE HISTORICALLY BLACK COLLEGE AND UNIVERSITY (HBCU) AND PREDOMINANTLY WHITE INSTITUTION (PWI) CONTEXT

I try to be creative. I like being spontaneous. I don't like it when people know my next move. I never let my left hand know what my right hand is doing. Because, when people have got you figured out, they can do a lot of things to you and I don't like that.

—Trey Williams

I think you could have many interpretations of that word—gifted. Yes, I think you could call me gifted.

—Stephen James

"You're interested in studying whom?—academically gifted African American males? You know the greater academic community doesn't believe this being exists!" These words spoken by a trusted friend and colleague rang out in my mind like the synchronized chimes in a clockmaker's repair shop. Was my graduate school comrade aware of some writ that unbeknownst to me would lead my dissertation process to result in the sequel to the Never-Ending Story? Had I stumbled upon a research topic that would prove to be the bane of my doctoral existence? Were the pundits within academe ready to focus on students of a caramel, chocolate, ebony, or mocha hue, particularly if this focus cast the light in a direction away from the alabaster and ivory stalwarts who traditionally occupied center stage? All these questions swirled around in my head as I contemplated conducting research highlighting the experiences of the academically gifted African American male collegian within the historically Black college and university (HBCU) as well as the traditionally White institution (TWI) context.

Although I had never attended a historically Black college or university, I am fortunate to have parents and a grandparent who are alumni of these institutions. The vivid stories they shared with me regarding their college days have allowed me to vicariously experience the HBCU. My mother attended Prairie View Agricultural and Mechanical University (PVAMU), an institution located in Prairie View, Texas, a small town outside of Houston. She received both a bachelor's and a master's degree from the institution. My father received his bachelor's degree from Paul Quinn College. Paul Quinn College at the time was a private Methodist institution of approximately six hundred students located in Waco, Texas. The campus has since moved to Dallas, Texas. My father later attended PVAMU, where he received his master's degree. My grandmother received her bachelor's degree from Bishop College, a small Baptist school. Bishop College at that time was located in Marshall, Texas. It has since moved to Dallas and been reorganized as a new institution—Paul Quinn College, my father's alma mater.

My parents' experiences heightened my interest in HBCUs, but I must also attribute a great deal of my interest in these institutions to several of my undergraduate and graduate program experiences. As an undergraduate at the University of North Texas, I received the University Intercultural Award. This award is presented to the highest-ranking (i.e., in terms of grade point average) African American and Hispanic student in each class. I received this coveted prize for two consecutive years. Although I was elated to be honored for what the university community recognized as academic prowess, I was somewhat pensive regarding the real meaning of this award. Would I have excelled in this manner had I chosen to attend an HBCU? Were the standards of educational excellence the same at HBCUs and TWIs? Did highest-ranking African American student mean more at a TWI?

This litany of questions piqued my curiosity to investigate academic achievement and scholarly excellence, both generally as these issues were found to impact African American male populations and specifically as they impacted academically gifted African American male collegiate populations. My initial work in this area started during my graduate school experience at Baylor University. I completed an assignment in a master's level course on gifted and talented education entitled "Which Institution Is More Effective at Cultivating Giftedness among African American Males: The Historically Black College or the Traditionally White Institution?" I interviewed two African American male undergraduate students, one attending Baylor University and the other attending Prairie View Agricultural and Mechanical University. Both men had been identified while matriculating in public school as academically gifted. Although this study was not the soundest piece of scholarship in terms of research methodology, it did provide me with a viable framework on which to build a more elaborate investigation of this topic in the future. And that is exactly what I did: as a doctoral student at the University of Arkansas, I was afforded the opportunity through my dissertation research to expand and recast this initial study.

Why Study Giftedness?

Giftedness is a concept that has fascinated, perplexed, and even infuriated many. A cursory glance at the literature in this area will reveal our nation's bifurcated view on this topic. Both Nicholas Colangelo and Gary Davis, two higher education scholars who study gifted populations, assert, "On the one hand, we applaud the individual who has risen from a humble background. . . . On the other hand, as a nation, we have a strong commitment to egalitarianism, as reflected in that mighty phrase 'All men are created equal'" (Colangelo & Davis, 2003). Yet, throughout history, and some assert even prior to records being kept, we have always been interested in what Joseph Renzulli (1981) calls "people of superior ability."

Although the interest in giftedness has continued, there has not been widespread interest in identifying giftedness among individuals representing minority populations. If we look at the information reported by the College Board as well as the *Carnegie Quarterly* we find facts and statistics that provide quite disparaging reports: that is, findings from these two sources suggest that African American students, particularly males, are three times as likely to be placed in classes for the educable mentally retarded as are White students, but only half as likely to be placed in classes for the gifted or talented. Juwanza Kunjufu (1991), in an *Education Week* article that looked at Detroit's male academies, found high levels of underachievement among African American male students; while this group comprised a mere 8.5 percent of the total U.S. school population, its members were found to represent 36 percent of the U.S. special education population. Further, it was Donna Ford (1994, p. 1), professor of education, who uncovered in her review of the literature on gifted African Americans that only 2 percent of the articles and scholarly publications she reviewed focused attention on gifted minority learners in general, and even fewer focused specifically on African American students (the largest U.S. minority population). These studies represent only the tip of the iceberg when it comes to a lack of viable research and scholarship focusing on gifted minority children.

The limited amount of literature highlighting the gifted African American student has primarily focused on students within elementary and secondary settings. The focus on giftedness during the K-12 experience is not unique to the African American student population; most gifted programming initiatives are primarily implemented at these levels. Unfortunately, gifted literature highlighting collegiate student populations remains very limited. Barring the work of a few scholars, including the likes of Donna Ford, Sharon Fries-Britt, Tarek Grantham, Shaun Harper, Thomas Hebert, and my own research, the experiences of the gifted African American collegian remain unnoticed. And perhaps what makes this population even more invisible is the fact that the research we conduct is often relegated to academic journals that typically fail to reach beyond the walls of college and university libraries. Hence, this book represents an attempt to reach the broader population in an effort to bring some attention to this cohort of students, who represent an important aspect of our national resources.

A growing body of literature has focused on the psychosocial (developmental) issues African American students experience during their college-going years, with a particular emphasis on the situations (academic and nonacademic) these students encounter relative to the type of institutions they attend. Prime examples include various studies showing the relative impact predominantly African American and predominantly White institutions have on the academic as well as the social experiences of African American students. Still other studies lend credence to the argument that African American students attending historically Black institutions experience a greater degree of person-environment congruence—meaning their sense of "fit" with the institution often stems from a close association between the student's espoused worldview and the institutions' espoused mission and goals.

Although most of the research in this area represents an array of achievement levels among the African American collegiate population, it is unclear as to what the particular institutional factors are that contribute to the success of these students. A primary reason why we should focus on these students is what Ford, Webb, and Sandidge (1994) call a "spilling over" of the issues confronting them at the K-12 level into the collegiate setting. In addition, the tried and true measures that colleges and universities traditionally employ lack potency when used as a means to assess the needs of the academically gifted African American male.

The overriding question this book seeks to answer is the following: What are the perceptions of academically gifted African American males attending historically Black colleges or universities and academically gifted African American males attending traditionally White institutions concerning their relationships with their respective institutions in cultivating their academic giftedness? More pointedly, are there identifiable factors influencing the success of the academically gifted African American male collegian, and if so, are these factors specific to the type of institution attended? This book reveals these factors, uncovered as themes in a qualitative research investigation of two students, both young, gifted, African American, and male. Although these case studies are not representative of all academically gifted and talented African American males, they do serve as a viable medium to initiate dialogue concerning these two particular experiences, which may in turn transfer to other postsecondary contexts involving similar actors. In addition, this book offers a wealth of information to faculty, staff, and administrators within higher education settings, and also to parents and students themselves who are concerned about the conditions that are necessary to promote the success of these students.

A Look at the History of Giftedness and Gifted Theorists

The study of giftedness and the manifestation of the concept is not a modern phenomenon. What some have termed a "universal fascination" with individuals who possess extraordinary mental abilities has continued to serve as grist for the discussion mill surrounding this topic. Jane Piirto, in *Talented Children and Adults: Their Development and Education* (1999), reported that from Plato to Gardner, from the patriarch Moses to the matriarch grandma Moses, society has struggled with developing viable definitions to deal with individuals who stand out by virtue of their abilities. Piirto goes on to assert that in Plato's Republic, Socrates asserted that "ideal leaders must be soldiers and philosophers, and must be good in 'the contemplation of numbers,' or mathematics, for 'natural reckoners are by nature quick in virtually all their studies'" (p. 15). Clearly, Socrates recognized that some people possessed more of a natural affinity for intellectual pursuits—"some people have 'gifts' of nature such as a 'certain keenness for study'"—hence the early identification of a special class of people we have come to refer to as "the gifted."

Giftedness as a concept was also highly debated among the warring classes of ancient Sparta. Gary Davis and Sylvia Rimm, in their text *Education of the Gifted and Talented* (1989), reported that military acumen and skill were highly valued among classes of young boys. Beginning at age seven, these boys received training in the arts of combat and warfare. Many of these young males, those who lacked physical ability and military acuity, were at best relegated to lower-class status in society, and at worst were killed, with many being flung from the side of a cliff.

In addition to the importance placed on the gifted during the Hellenistic period, particularly in terms of gifts manifested by way of military prowess, Davis and Rimm (1989) also report on the value the Chinese as well as the Japanese placed on highly intelligent children and youth. The Chinese during the Tang Dynasty in the seventh century A.D. are particularly noted for their efforts at cultivating the talents of these individuals. The Japanese during the Tokugawa period (1604–1868) supported schools of various clans that tracked Samurai children differently than the children of commoners.

Thus, although the sociohistorical contexts that have framed the way the term gifted is defined are quite diverse, the term has always meant *exceptional ability* or *extraordinary talent*. And the term has served as a major means of separating the wheat from the chaff—the wheat representing those possessing outstanding abilities and the chaff representing those who are far less adroit. Additionally, during the historical periods mentioned above, we see the early rumblings of a system that has often served as the bane of our existence in education: namely, we see the very first signs of a tracking system. While the Chinese and Japanese may not have taken such drastic measures as flinging their young citizens who did not display exceptional talents and abilities from the side of a cliff like the Spartans, they did relegate these children to a lower status in life (Davis & Rimm, 1989; Meyer, 1965). Hence, death for children in these cultures was inevitable: for the Spartan child a quick and sudden death, and for the Japanese child a slow and enduring death—a death that lasted a lifetime.

GIFTED EDUCATION THEORISTS AND INFLUENCES

In early America, concern for the education of gifted and talented children was not a high priority item on the national agenda. Some gifted youth were accommodated in the sense that attending secondary school and college was based on both their academic abilities and their ability to pay. Several individuals as well as national and world events sparked the development of the gifted education movement. Individuals such as Francis Galton, Alfred Binet, Lewis Terman, and Leta Hollingsworth from ages past exerted a major influence on the field. In contemporary contexts, individuals such as Howard Gardner (1983), Joseph Renzulli (1986), and Robert Sternberg (1985) have made major contributions to this evolutionary process. Beyond each of these theorists, myriad other influences have made a major mark on gifted education—Sputnik, formal definitions, standardized testing, teacher nominations, and learning style preferences. The relative contribution of each theorist and source of influence will be treated in turn.

Sir Francis Galton

English scientist Sir Francis Galton (1822–1911), "a younger cousin of Charles Darwin" (Davis & Rimm, 1989, p. 9), is noted as one of the earliest theorists who conducted research and wrote on intelligence and intelligence testing. Galton was highly influenced by his cousin Charles's book, *On the Origin of Species* (1859); from his study of this text, he reasoned that individuals who had acute senses and who could sense approaching danger and find viable food sources would be favored from an evolutionary standpoint. In essence, Galton was creating a variation on Charles Darwin's theme; instead of the classic mantra "Only the strong survive," Galton asserted, "Only the smart survive." It was his view that those individuals possessing visual and auditory as well as tactile skills were those deemed to be the most intelligent—hence, able to survive.

What Galton's theory did was to establish what has been characterized as the hereditary basis of intelligence—meaning that individuals who were recognized or distinguished by their intelligence appeared to come from successive generations within particular families. Galton's conclusions were published in his most noted work, *Hereditary Genius* (1869). Although Galton's intelligence tests failed to consider key contextual factors such as access to resources, family background, and privilege, his emphasis on heredity as a means of determining intelligence is still widely used today and is shared by many individuals within and outside of the field of gifted education; however, this view is widely disputed by individuals who point to a variety of learning and environmental factors that influence intelligence.

Alfred Binet

According to J. A. Plucker in *Human Intelligence: Historical Influences, Current Controversies, and Teaching Resources* (2003), after receiving a law degree in 1878, Alfred Binet initiated studies in science at the Sorbonne. Although he did not have any formalized graduate study in psychology, he is probably one of the most frequently acknowledged contributors to the field. Modern intelligence testing can trace its roots back to the work that Binet completed in France during the 1890s. Plucker goes on to report that in 1904, as a member of La Société Libre pour l'Etude Psychologique de l'Enfant, Binet accepted the challenge to devise a test that would identify "dull youth" in the community—a project that was completed for the French government. Along with his colleague T. Simon, he developed what has been referred to as the Binet-Simon scale, a measure that tested students' abilities at various ages. Binet's tests proved to be somewhat inconclusive and were later labeled as failures. It was found that the measures used to determine differences in abilities between normal students and dull students—tests such as hand speed, hand squeezing strength, pressure to the forehead before pain ensued, detecting differences in hand-held weights, and reaction time to sounds or in naming colors—were not particularly conclusive.

Yet, despite the seeming failure of Binet's tests, a term that has had major implications for the study of intelligence emerged from his work: the concept of mental age, the notion that children grow in intelligence and that any given child could be potentially ahead of or behind the intellectual stage for his or her actual age. Colangelo and Davis (2003) pointed out that at any given chronological age, children who appear to be more academically capable are partly due to greater intelligence.

Lewis W. Terman

Lewis W. Terman accomplished some of the most influential research in the field of giftedness. As a psychologist at Stanford University, "Terman supervised the modification and Americanization of the Binet-Simon tests, producing what has served as the model for the development of intelligence testing in the country" (Davis & Rimm, 1989, p. 6). Additionally, Terman's study of gifted children, through his project entitled the Stanford Studies of Genius, brought together a group that has been recognized as the most studied group of gifted individuals in the world. Joanne Whitmore, in her text *Giftedness, Conflict, and Underachievement* (1980), noted that Terman's work was initiated with populations of individuals scoring above 140 on the Stanford-Binet IQ test. Whitmore went on to report that his findings contradicted previous studies that portrayed the gifted as being prone to insanity with an accompanying host of compensatory weaknesses; contrastingly, Terman's research presented the gifted as an elite class possessing an extensive range of abilities.

Although Terman's work was groundbreaking, apparently clarifying many misconceptions surrounding the gifted, a new problem quickly developed. Terman's research, which advanced the notion of identifying giftedness through standardized testing, has caused the field to solely focus on this form of identification. Many view the strict reliance on this unitary measure as a form of bias and discrimination against the culturally different or the economically disadvantaged.

Leta Hollingsworth

Leta Hollingsworth, as one of the first researchers to study high-ability children, was able to underscore critical aspects of the development of this cohort. Applying virtually the same IQ criterion as Terman in identifying gifted children, Hollingsworth was able to design a number of experimental courses that allowed her to design, teach, and evaluate these novel curriculum approaches. She suggested in her book *Children above 180 IQ* (1975) that high-ability children have five general conduct problems that they must grapple with at some point during their development:

1. To find enough hard and interesting work at school.
2. To suffer fools gladly.
3. To keep from becoming negativistic toward authority.
4. To keep from becoming hermits.
5. To avoid the formation of habits of extreme chicanery.

Hollingsworth's study of children with IQs of 180 and above remains one of the most definitive works in the field. In 1931, she remarked: "It is the business of education to consider all forms of giftedness in pupils in regard to how many individuals may be trained for their own welfare and that of society at large." Hollingsworth referred to gifted children as the "original thinkers" of their generations, who required focused attention on instructional processes that would assist them in developing to their fullest potential.

Sputnik

The launch of Sputnik on October 4, 1957, exerted a profound influence on national political, military, and educational fronts. For many individuals in the nation, Sputnik represented defeat—the Soviet Union had amassed scientific talent that had far outpaced the efforts put forth in this area by the United States. Several reports ensued that disparaged the American educational system and spoke candidly about the nation's lack of prowess in fields such as science and mathematics. Also, there was an outcry by many who asserted that those individuals showing great intellectual promise, namely, gifted youth, were not being challenged in school systems across the nation. In essence, the cultivation of the gifts and talents of high-achieving youth in our schools was at best haphazard and at worst nonexistent.

Sputnik's influence on talent mobilization in the nation was nothing short of revolutionary. School officials and governmental pundits began to pay closer attention to the curriculum offered in schools. According to a 1959 report by the first official U.S. education mission to the USSR, the typical Russian high school graduate had completed 10 years of math, 5 years of physics, 4 years of chemistry, 1 year of astronomy, 5 years of biology, and 5 years of a foreign language (Davis & Rimm, 1989). A flurry of dialogue that spoke to the rigors of an American education versus a Soviet education ensued. Ability grouping and accelerated course formats were but two of the measures taken to promote a renewal in curriculum.

Howard Gardner

Perhaps most noted for his multiple intelligences (MI) theory presented in collaboration with his colleagues at Harvard Project Zero, an educational research group, Howard Gardner has made significant contributions to the field of gifted education. Gardner's theory, first presented in his work *Frames of Mind* (1983), challenges many of the assumptions regarding general intelligence, or g, according to which most models of intelligence tests are framed.

Gardner's theory challenged the narrow view of intelligence as residing solely in linguistic and logical-mathematical abilities, the abilities that most intelligence tests tended to measure. What Gardner suggested was that giftedness should be measured in the natural contexts in which it emerged; traditional IQ tests would be ineffective in capturing the nuances of this elusive concept. The eight intelligences Gardner presented include the following: linguistic, logical-mathematical, spatial, musical, bodily-kinesthetic, interpersonal, intrapersonal, and naturalistic. What Gardner's theory has helped promote is a more inclusive definition of giftedness, one that takes on a more pluralistic view of intelligence. Fortunately, MI theory has served to include more diverse individuals among the ranks of the gifted, particularly people of color and women.

Robert J. Sternberg

Another highly regarded scholar who has made critical contributions to the field of gifted education is Robert J. Sternberg. Sternberg's conception of intelligence is based on his *Beyond IQ: A Triarchic Theory of Intelligence* (1985). It is the interaction of what he refers to as three subtheories (i.e., componential, experiential, and contextual) that are presented to explain human intelligence. The componential subtheory involves human analytical abilities, best measured through various psychometric tests or the completion of various academic exercises. The experiential subtheory reveals how individuals are able to think creatively and apply these creative thought processes to new and novel situations. Finally, the contextual subtheory provides some plausible means of viewing how individuals operate on a day-to-day basis, how they deal with mundane everyday tasks. These three subtheories are respectively labeled as analytical, creative, and practical.

Sternberg's theory is viewed as being novel in its approach to identifying intellectual giftedness, particularly among populations of color or those who are otherwise underrepresented. According to Sternberg, intelligence is not a single thing; it comprises myriad skills, both cognitive and noncognitive (Sternberg, 2007).

Joseph Renzulli

A model that has been central to the evolution of gifted education has been Joseph Renzulli's "three-ring conception of giftedness" (1986). Renzulli divided giftedness into two categories: the first category was defined as *schoolhouse giftedness*—displayed through test taking abilities and high performance on standardized tests. The second category is *creative-productive giftedness*, evidenced by individuals who are capable of creating or developing novel products to fit the needs of various contexts and constituents. Renzulli asserts that it is the interaction between these two categories that essentially contribute to giftedness.

These two categories, especially the second category Renzulli outlined, contributed to the development of his three-ring conception of giftedness. According to this model, giftedness is composed of the interaction of three basic clusters of human traits: above-average ability, task commitment, and creativity; hence, Renzulli's model offers yet another approach to studying giftedness from a multifaceted perspective.

Abraham Tannenbaum

Abraham Tannenbaum's (1983, 1997) psychosocial view of giftedness is presented via his five-factor model. The factors in this model include the following: (1) a "sliding scale of general intelligence, (2) exceptional special aptitudes, (3) nonintellective factors, (4) environmental factors, and (5) chance or luck" (as cited in Piirto, 1999, p. 25). The model is typically displayed as a five-pointed star with each factor connected at the various points. According to Tannenbaum, each factor has static and dynamic characteristics that work in concert to yield exceptional performances or outstanding products.

One of Tannenbaum's major concerns about the way giftedness was identified is that precocity along with various contextual and environmental factors could potentially be overlooked. Tannenbaum states: "Those who have the potential for succeeding as gifted adults require not only the personal attributes often mentioned in definitions of giftedness, but also some special encounters with the environment to facilitate the emergence of talent" (as cited in Gross, Merrick, Targett, Chaffey, MacLeod, & Bailey, 2005, p. 16).

In addition to presenting his five-factor model, Tannenbaum spoke very candidly about how giftedness and talent are part and parcel of the times in which they are realized. He identified four talents: scarcity talents, those of people who make ground-breaking discoveries in some field of endeavor; surplus talents, those of people who add to the beauty of the world through art, music, or literature; quote talents, those of people who have the skills to provide needed goods and services; and anomalous talents, those people who have skills within practical domains (e.g., cooking, oratorical skills, trivia).

Francoys Gagné

To distinguish between giftedness and talent, Gagne developed what he called the differentiated model of giftedness and talent. According to Gagné (1990), he called talent "the developmental product of an interaction between aptitudes and intrapersonal and environmental catalysts" (as cited in Piirto, 1999, p. 27). There are five aptitudes or gifts domains specified in his model: intellectual, creative, socio-affective, sensorimotor, and "others" (e.g., extrasensory perception, the gift of healing, etc.). Through developmental processes that are essentially shaped through learning, training, and practicing, individuals, specifically children, are able to transform these aptitudes into skills specific to various fields; in essence they are able to transform these aptitudes into various talents.

In 1995, Gagne also asserted that the field of gifted education can be made more democratic—i.e., inclusive—by three means: reexamining the threshold for defining giftedness, that is, by lowering the recognized IQ score of 130 to 115; developing more qualitatively based categories to recognize other forms of talent; and identifying talent among fields (cooking, popular music, gardening, electrical work) outside the traditionally recognized areas (law, medicine, engineering), in which talent also becomes manifest (Piirto, 1999).

Martin D. Jenkins

Martin D. Jenkins, a Howard University–trained engineer who spent the majority of his career in higher education administration as dean, registrar, and ultimately college president, is to be credited with much of the early focus on giftedness among African American populations. Jenkins's doctoral dissertation, which focused on 103 high-ability African American children who attended school on Chicago's South Side, was completed in 1935.

Robinson and Clinkenbeard (2008) reveal in their book chapter "History of Giftedness: Perspective from the Past Presage Modern Scholarship" that most notable among Jenkins' research is the study he conducted that highlighted 26 African American students in grades three through eight across seven Chicago public schools. This study included students who initially scored 120 or above on the McCall Multi-Mental Scale and who subsequently scored 140 or above on the Stanford-Binet. Perhaps the most intriguing finding from this study was a nine-year-old girl, whom Jenkins' identified and referred to as "B." "B," with her identified IQ score of 2000, became the focus of a case study and publication that Jenkins entitled "The Case of B—A Gifted Negro Girl." What Jenkins was able to capture very early on and clarify particularly as it related to giftedness among African American populations is illuminated in his statement about the gifted African American case study participants he was investigating:

> These cases bring into sharp focus the limitations which our society places on the development of the highly gifted Negro. These children are nurtured in a culture in which racial inferiority of the Negro is a basic assumption. Consequently, they will experience throughout their lives, educational, social and occupational restrictions which must inevitably affect achievement and motivation. Wide individual differences, of course, are to be anticipated in reaction to this condition. Some of these individuals will meet frustration and draw away; others will go on to careers of high usefulness and accomplishment. (Jenkins, as cited in Robinson and Clinkenbeard, 2008, p. 20)

DEFINING GIFTEDNESS

Giftedness is a concept that has multiple meanings and therefore can be quite elusive in terms of attempts to explain how it is operationalized. A number of "official" definitions of giftedness have been developed over the years—in 1972, 1978, and 1993. The 1972 definition, presented by the commissioner of the U.S. Office of Education, Sidney Marland, to Congress, asserted that

> Gifted and talented children are those identified by professionally qualified persons who by virtue of outstanding abilities are capable of high performance. These are children who require differentiated educational programs and/or services beyond those normally provided by the regular school program in order to realize their contribution to self and society. Children capable of high performance include those with demonstrated achievement and/or potential ability in any of the following areas, singly or in combinations: (1) general intellectual ability, (2) specific academic aptitude, (3) creative or productive thinking, (4) leadership ability, (5) visual and performing arts ability, and (6) psychomotor ability. (parentpals.com)

The Marland report went on to state that the gifted comprised 3–5 percent of the school-going population, while the talented made up 11–15 percent of this group.

Although the definition of giftedness offered in the report provided multiple areas in which gifts and talents were assessed, it was viewed by many as problematic. Joseph Renzulli provided the most pointed discussion regarding the weaknesses inherent in the definition. He reported that the definition had three distinct problems: first, it failed to include nonintellective (motivational) factors; second, it failed to address the nonparallel nature of the six categories—creativity and leadership do not exist apart from a performance area to which they can be applied; and third, it treated each category as if it were an exclusive entity.

The 1978 definition of giftedness offered what Donna Ford (1994) advanced as an encouraging move for the field of gifted education and how giftedness was subsequently identified. This definition, outlined in the Gifted and Talented Children's Act of 1978, went a step further, to include the "potentially" gifted; thus, students who for various reasons had yet to manifest their gifts and talents did not go unrecognized. Yet this definition still did not accomplish the task of increasing the diversity among the ranks of the gifted; nor did it provide much variation in the areas primarily viewed as comprising gifted behavior, namely, academic and intellectual prowess on standardized intelligence measures.

The most recent federal definition of gifted was offered by the U.S. Department of Education (1993) in their *National Excellence: A Case for Developing America's Talent* report. According to this definition,

> Children and youth with outstanding talent perform or show the potential for performing at remarkably high levels of accomplishment when compared with other of their age, experience, or environment. These children and youth exhibit high performance capacity in intellectual, creative, and/or artistic areas, and unusual leadership capacity, or excel in specific academic fields. They require services or activities not ordinarily provided by the school. Outstanding talents are present in children and youth from all cultural groups, across all economic strata, and in all areas of human endeavor. (p. 3)

Giftedness and the P-12 African American Student

African Americans have historically faced widespread underrepresentation in gifted and talented programs in our nation's schools. Data collected by the Carnegie Corporation (1984/1985) and the College Board (1985) revealed the overinclusion of African American students in special education classes and the underinclusion of these same students in gifted and talented courses. A question that I asked in an article in the *Journal of Black Studies* (2000) was, "Why do we continually fail to recognize gifted and talented African American students?" (p. 643).

Attempts to address the problems associated with African American giftedness have often resulted in a "Catch-22" scenario of sorts: parents attribute the problems of underidentification to the schools, the schools attribute the problem to the coordinators of gifted students, and the coordinators attribute the problem to the various testing agencies. The outcome of this is that often nothing is accomplished and the problem of under- or nonidentification of these cohorts continues to escalate. Perhaps a good place to start in addressing this problem is with the individual child. L. Rhodes, in his (1992) article, "Focusing Attention on the Individual in Identification of Gifted Black Students," says that gifted and talented coordinators must draw their attention away from Black children in the aggregate and focus on them as individuals. In this way, the unique needs of these students are considered and examined for their influence not only on their chances of academic success but also on their potential inclusion in gifted and talented programs.

This chapter, with its focus on giftedness among African American students at the P-12 level, will highlight many of the common issues that have impacted these students and in many ways led to their underrepresentation in gifted and talented programs. These issues include standardized testing, teacher nomination procedures, learning style preferences, family and peer influences, screening and identification, and gifted underachievement. The chapter will conclude with a brief discussion of alternative theories that may be used in the identification of gifted African American students as well as a discussion regarding the relevance of including multicultural education in teacher preparation programs, particularly for teachers who will be involved with gifted and talented students and programming for them.

STANDARDIZED TESTING

The standardized test has served as the primary tool in the identification of gifted students. In many ways, these tests are a major roadblock for students who are not privy to the ways in which the individuals who construct these tests think. Asa Hilliard (as cited in Bonner, 2000, p. 646) said that there are two fundamental questions that are asked by assessors (or tests), and these two questions represent two fundamentally different approaches to the assessment of human behavior:

1. Do you know what I know?
2. What is it that you know?

The first approach is what most standardized tests measure. The language, culture, and experiences of the individuals who construct these tests become the prevailing benchmarks by which success is measured. The tests then become a measure of which students have a better grasp of White, middle-class patriarchy, not what knowledge and information they have acquired. Hilliard went on to state that these standardized assessments are limited in scope; they are convergent and therefore unable to deal with divergent or novel thinking, expression, or problem solving. These tests are unable to deal with what Robert Sternberg and Carol Davidson (1986) refer to as "nonentrenched" measures of exceptional intelligence—those measures that require information processing outside of people's ordinary experience.

The sole reliance on traditional assessment measures such as standardized tests runs the risk of putting African American students at a great disadvantage. Yet, it is important to note that attempting to ameliorate these disadvantages by lowering standards and "cut-off" scores or by adding points to the scores received by these students obfuscates the true problem—the actual standardized test itself. It is important to recognize that standardized tests have some usefulness as assessment instruments, but they should never be used as the sole indicator of such a complex and multifaceted concept such as giftedness. It is important for those who design these assessment measures to construct them in such a way that real differences are not obliterated and real similarities are not overlooked.

TEACHER NOMINATIONS OF GIFTED AFRICAN AMERICAN STUDENTS

Identifying potentially gifted and talented students is a task that is often initiated by a classroom teacher. Although coordinators of gifted and talented students are trained to identify and recognize the manifestation of giftedness, Rhodes (1992) found that traditional classroom teachers are not typically the beneficiaries of such training. Due to their lack of training, teachers make judgments and recommendations based on their own preconceived ideas of what characteristics a gifted student should exhibit. Unfortunately, this mode of identification has proven to be at best inconsistent and at worst completely ineffective, in many instances further exacerbating the problem of underidentification of African American students.

White, middle-class society often serves as the template upon which teacher nominations of gifted and talented students are based. Students who are essentially out of "cultural sync" with their teachers often go unidentified, regardless of their intellectual abilities and prowess. For African American students, initiation into the ranks of gifted and talented programs typically begins with the realignment of their cultural behavior to fit the mold of what the teacher deems as acceptable and appropriate conduct. Many times, this realignment process means the total relinquishment of the cultural nuances that would identify the student as a member of a particular racial group. This "guilt by association" implies that African American students must somehow demonstrate to their teachers that the negative behaviors and stereotypes that are generally associated with their racial cohort do not represent them. Jacqueline Irvine in her book *Black Students and School Failure* (1990) alluded to this issue when she said that the imposed denial and refutation of one's cultural background and heritage are directly associated with the manifestation of self-hatred, lowered self-esteem, heightened anxiety, and lower academic achievement among African American students.

The literature has revealed that when African American students behave in ways that are different from or contrary to teacher expectations of cultural norms, these students are treated more like individuals. When students behave in a manner that supports teachers' preconceived notions, these students are often branded and summarily tracked into classes that teachers feel can more appropriately deal with their behavior. namely, vocational or special education courses. One of the teachers who participated in Gouldner's study of an all-African American high school said,

> A good class has children who learn to sit quietly at their desks, raise their hands before talking, wait patiently for the bell to ring before leaving their seats, stand in line with their partners in an orderly way, and when in school repress any expression of anger, frustration, or exuberance. (p. 29)

This teacher's comments closely parallel N. D. Feshbach's (1969) findings from a study of the pupil behaviors that student teachers preferred: they preferred behaviors indicating rigidity, conformity, orderliness, dependence, passivity, and acquiescence rather than behaviors indicating flexibility, nonconformity, untidiness, independence, activity, and assertiveness. Yet we know that these behaviors are more typical for gifted students than others, and that embracing a very narrow view of the gifted student profile means that underidentification of students, especially African American students, will continue.

Teachers must be properly trained if they are to continue to serve as the primary gatekeepers for gifted and talented programs. They should be trained on the uses and misuses of standardized assessment measures as well as the importance of diverse learners and learning styles and multiculturalism. E. Paul Torrance (1973; Torrance & Reynolds, 1978), formerly professor educational psychology at the University of Georgia, accurately asserts that if educators are really interested in identifying gifted and talented students within minority groups, they must be willing to direct their searches to those characteristics that are valued by these groups and not a self-imposed template that assumes one size will fit all. Without a focus on the training of teachers, Donna Ford (1994) reveals, the probability of gifted and talented African American students being identified and placed in these programs decreases two-fold.

LEARNING STYLE PREFERENCES

Developing some capacity to understand student learning styles is a necessary precursor to determining the most effective instructional methods and tools to use in the classroom. This becomes increasingly important when we consider how gifted students learn—an important variable in effective teaching. However, the pioneers in the field of learning style preferences, Rita Dunn and Kenneth Dunn (1992), contend that we have given scant attention to the impact that learning style preferences have in the classroom teaching and learning context.

Several definitions are used to describe *learning style,* a term often used interchangeably with *cognitive style* or *learning ability.* One definition of learning styles was advanced by Bernice McCarthy (1990), who defined the term as meaning approaches to cognitive, affective, and psychological factors that function as relatively stable indicators of how individuals concentrate on, perceive, interact with, and respond to learning environments. Additionally, Torrance and Reynolds (1978) have indicated that individuals exhibit different styles of learning and processing information not only through their preferences but also through the efficiency with which they utilize one or the other style and through their knowledge of when to utilize primarily one style or the other.

The classroom teaching and learning environment often proves to be a formidable place for gifted African American students. This environment presents several challenges, many stemming from the lack of congruence between the school culture and students' individual learning styles. Affective aspects of the environment and the relationship with the teacher are important aspects of the learning context for African American students. Hilliard (1976) goes so far as to state that schools in their approach to curriculum and instruction adopt an analytical style as opposed to the relational cognitive style that many students of color embrace. The literature defines the relational nature of African American students—namely, they are predisposed to learning that is characterized by freedom of movement, variation, creativity, divergent thinking approaches, inductive reasoning, and a focus on people. Schools, on the other hand, emphasize an analytical style, or learning characterized by rules and restriction of movement, standardization, conformity, convergent thinking approaches, deductive reasoning, and a focus on things.

In "Making It" Black Family Style: "Building on the Strengths of the Black Family" (1981), M. F. Peters noted that when African American lower-class children attend school at age four or five, they discover that the behavioral rules have changed. Although there are attractive things to explore, there are new rules and expectations; there is now an emphasis on sitting still. Play and interaction with others are confined to particular times during the day; music is heard only during music time; and physical activity, body movement, and expression that is not tied to cognitive learning are relegated to activity or play periods or physical education class. In turn, these children are lost, punished, or put down.

As with Hilliard's study, Barbara Shade's 1982 research on African American cognitive style suggested that differences in social cognition for these student populations was determined by recognition patterns that emphasized affective rather than physical characteristics, and that African American children preferred a variety of stimuli in their learning environments as well as a variety of teaching methods and materials. With regard to perceptual style, Shade's work closely mirrored the research of Herman Witkin and Carol Moore (1975), who found that African Americans tend to exhibit a field-dependent rather than a field-independent cognitive style. Table 2.1 highlights these two cognitive styles. Field-independent individuals have a more global and interrelated approach to visual information and are thus unable to distinguish the necessary parts for problem solving. The opposite approach, field independence, is characteristic of people who are able to isolate the necessary parts from distracting elements in order to solve problems.

For many gifted African American students, this "line item" incongruousness of teaching and learning styles, coupled with a foreign classroom environment, can potentially present a problem. Thus, the use of a multifaceted approach to instruction as well as some form of learning style assessment could greatly enhance the

Table 2.1   Field-Dependent and Field-Independent Teaching Strategies

Field-Dependent	Field-Independent
1. Focuses on needs, feelings, and interests of students	1. Focuses on task
2. Acts as a consultant or supervisor in the classroom	2. Fosters modeling and imitation
3. Uses an informal approach and elicits classroom discussion	3. Uses a formal, lecture-oriented approach
4. Uses personal rewards	4. Uses impersonal rewards
5. Encourages group achievement	5. Encourages individual achieve
6. Narrates and humanizes concepts	6. Emphasizes facts and principles
7. Identifies with class	7. Remains emotionally detached

educational experiences of these students. Recognizing cultural differences does not imply that a hierarchical relationship between Eurocentric (analytical) and Afrocentric (relational) style has to exist. Yet it does call attention to the fact that teachers and schools tend to use a unitary method of instruction—analytical—and to ignore relational methods as a viable approach. This focus on analytical styles in turn privileges nonminority students and at the same time disadvantages students of color and female students.

FAMILY AND PEER INFLUENCES

Gifted African American students face many challenges within and outside of school settings. Some of the most formidable challenges are experienced within family and peer circles. In many instances, for gifted African American children to gain acceptance by family and peers, they are required to mask their abilities or conceal their talents in order to fit in with the group. Unlike their gifted White counterparts, these students learn that they must navigate two cultures, home and school, and that often these two environments are quite different. Performance at a level befitting their gifted designation is what schools expect of these African American students, while at home they are expected to act in a manner that conforms to the social norms and traditions of the family and community.

The literature in the area of African American student achievement and success supports the fact that many African American children hide their academic abilities or attempt to shroud their giftedness by becoming class clowns, dropping out, or suppressing their efforts in order to avoid being perceived as "acting White" or as being *raceless*. The possibility that African American students will employ these behaviors, often circumventing their chances of academic success, is an alarming and disturbing prospect not only for their advancement in P-12 systems but also for their inclusion in gifted and talented programs.

Educators and gifted and talented coordinators find it unbelievable that these students would sabotage their chances at success to retain their position "off the radar screen" that would identify them as academically talented, but these actions have been documented by several researchers in both education and psychology. One such noted researcher, Lisa Whitten (1992), used the term *survival conflict* to explain this behavior. Survival conflict is a reaction these students have when they surpass the accomplishments of family and/or peers. It is in many ways a fear of being successful or, as one researcher stated, "Anticipation of negative consequences from competitive striving" (Horner, 1972). This behavior can essentially manifest itself in one or several responses: guilt, ambivalence, anxiety, and depression. The manifestation of these feelings is frequently subconscious and can be debilitating if they are not addressed and handled appropriately; hence, self-sabotage, procrastination, decreased productivity, and devaluation of one's self-concept, accomplishments, and ambitions can likely ensue.

Most families are supportive of the achievements of the gifted and talented African American student, while some are more ambivalent due to jealousy, competitiveness, or a fear of being abandoned or belittled by the achiever. The nonsupportive family often creates an environment that fosters survival conflict, directly or indirectly, in a student who otherwise may or may not have experienced these reactions. Perhaps the most troubling aspect about the views expressed by family and peers concerning this phenomenon is that individuals possessing strong intellectual abilities and giftedness are a seen as "sell outs" and their behaviors are referred to as "acting White." This advances the notion that academic prowess and intellectual ability are characteristics and traits that are nonindigenous to African American populations.

SCREENING AND IDENTIFICATION

The nomination process for gifted and talented programs should begin with a thorough understanding of the limitations of the theoretical frameworks associated with the identification process; this would provide a good start in making these programs more inclusive. It was Sternberg and Davidson (1986) who said that if we are to maximize the potential of gifted and talented individuals in the nation, it is imperative to take into account the multiplicity of forms in which giftedness and talents can be found.

Several studies highlight factors that have been found to contribute to the non-identification of African American students for gifted and talented programs. Gail Kofsky (1992) listed these factors as (a) the criteria used to determine eligibility, (b) the screening process, (c) problems in the student referral process, (d) lack of understanding of cultural diversity, and (e) the lack of in-service training. It is the second factor that has proven to be one of the most powerful in the nonidentification of African Americans for gifted programs; the identification tools used for screening have also been proven inadequate in identifying students with handicapping conditions, young children, and girls.

Rating scales and teacher checklists are used in tandem with standardized test scores as the primary screening measures schools have traditionally employed in the screening and identification of students who seek entry into gifted programs. According to several researchers, the problem of identifying African American gifted students is largely an issue of finding viable ways to integrate information from a set of multiple criteria into a conventional screening and identification process.

A lack of teacher training and user-friendly assessment instruments has unfortunately increased the ambiguity in the screening and identification process. Assessment instruments are many times poorly worded, are esoteric, or lack validity in adequately describing or providing an authentic view of the student population under consideration: so much so that Carl Pegnato and Jack Birch in their research (1959) found that teachers were able to identify only 45 percent of the gifted children in their junior high school classes—a figure that drops to 10 percent for kindergarten teachers. Thus, it is readily apparent that without proper training, teachers will continue to refer only those students who fit their preconceived ideas about who the gifted student is and what behaviors these students should exhibit. In essence the outcome of this continued cycle of ascribing such a narrow and fixed view of giftedness is that many students who by the current definition show gifted potential will be overlooked.

GIFTED UNDERACHIEVEMENT

Underachievement among student populations in our P-12 systems is a problem that crosses cultural/ethnic, racial, and socioeconomic boundaries. This issue becomes even more problematic among gifted populations, particularly when African American cohorts are considered. According to Diane Whitmore (1986),

> Lack of motivation to excel is usually a result of a mismatch between the student's motivational characteristics and opportunities provided in the classroom. Students are typically highly motivated when (a) the social climate of the classroom is nurturant, (b) the curriculum content is relevant to the student's personal interests and is challenging, and (c) the instructional process is appropriate to the students' natural learning style. (p. 423)

All too often, African American students lack a "goodness of fit" with all three factors listed above. Several researchers have attributed the problem of underachievement to the combination of psychological, social, and cultural forces. Still others have suggested that the identification of gifted students through intelligence tests early in their school careers is a barrier for many African American students. This can be partially attributed to the manifestation of underachievement behaviors by African American students during their first-, second-, and third-grade levels, the time when screening for inclusion in gifted programs takes place. Poor performance on intelligence tests in conjunction with myopic views of giftedness that are based on faulty psychometric assumptions often means that a vast majority of African American students go unidentified as gifted, as underachieving, or both.

Sternberg and Davidson (1986) advanced the notion that standardized tests only work for some of the people some of the time—not for all of the people all of the time—and that some assumptions that we make in our use of tests are, at best, correct only for a segment of the tested population and, at worst, correct for none at all. To further support this point, Hilliard (1976) found that to be successful on standardized tests, students' language, vocabulary, general experience pool, and basic approach to the solution of problems must coincide with the very limited experiences of the individual or individuals who actually framed the questions for the test.

If we rely on the old adage, that intelligence is "what intelligence tests measure," identifying African American students for gifted programs will continue to be a problem. It is important to note that the vast majority of our most productive citizens are not those who happen to score at the 95th percentile or above on standardized intelligence tests; nor were these individuals necessarily straight "A" students who, as Renzulli (as cited in Bonner, 2000, pp. 653–654) said, "discovered early on how to play the lesson-learning game." Therefore, the intelligence test that has been viewed as sacrosanct in assessing giftedness must make room for various other modes of assessment and models that will expand our understanding of the term. Chapter 1 highlights a number of the contemporary theorists who have provided alternative means of assessing as well as defining giftedness.

The idea of expanding the boundaries and seeking greater flexibility in the ways we look at giftedness should not be viewed as the precipice overlooking the demise of gifted and talented programming. A common ground on which the relaxation and modification of rigid nomination and identification procedures needs to be reached; thus, a more globalized view of what it means to be gifted can emerge and the problems associated with underidentification can be eradicated for all groups.

GENDER DIFFERENCES AND GIFTED AFRICAN AMERICAN MALES

Any discussion of the experiences of African American males in the school context would be incomplete if it failed to consider some of the unique challenges that the members of this population face when compared to their African American female counterparts. Too often, by aggregating the engagements of African American males and females, particularly in educational settings, nuances endemic to the African American male experience become "washed away" or essentially ignored. An article co-authored by Wood, Kaplan, and McLoyd (2007), "Gender Differences in the Education Expectations of Urban, Low-Income African American Youth: The Role of Parents and the School," states that

> Despite considerable gains of African Americans over the past 30 years across a broad spectrum of achievement indices, males have made less progress than females, particularly with respect to participation in postsecondary education. Education-related gender disparities exist for African Americans of all income levels, but are especially striking for individuals of low socioeconomic status (SES): For example, in 1992, among low-income African Americans, only 32% of male high school graduates immediately entered postsecondary institutions, as compared to 51% of females (King, 2000). In 2001–2002, although men in all racial/ethnic categories earned 45% of bachelor's degrees awarded, African American men earned only 34% of bachelor's degrees awarded to African American undergraduates (Peter & Horn, 2005). (p. 417)

What these figures underscore is a growing problem that will only worsen if a more thoughtful approach to addressing the ever-widening gap between African American males and females is not addressed. One point of departure in beginning to address the complexities of this problem involves the schooling experiences and educational expectations that are conveyed to this population. Offered as a hypothesis in the article by Wood and colleagues (2007) is what they describe as a "strong empirical and theoretically" based view that the characteristics often used to describe African American males (e.g., lazy, violent, athletic and not intellectual) create negative expectations of these individuals that are at best difficult and at worst impossible to overcome. Hudley and Graham (2002) added to this point in their research by uncovering data that showed African American female adolescents possessing more advanced levels of *achievement striving* than their male African American male peers. As a result of these varying levels of achievement striving, stereotypes are created. As a consequence, Wood and colleagues state that "These stereotypes favor African American girls, girls' self-beliefs about the potential for completing college should be enhanced, whereas those of boys should be diminished" (p. 419).

If the data are disaggregated and a focus on the underrepresentation of African American males in particular is advanced, a more dire narrative of the participation of this group in gifted programming is realized. The differences between African American males and females are readily observed in the data collected by the Office of Civil Rights (2002). According to these data, representation in gifted programming across the nation includes the following:

- 7.64% of all students in such programming are Asian/Pacific Islander students,
- 72.59% are White students,
- 8.43% are African American students,
- 10.41% are Hispanic/Latino students, and
- 0.93% are American Indian/Alaskan American students.

For African American students, males represent roughly 3.65% of the 8.43 percent cited above. So, less than half of the African American students, who in total represent less than 10 percent of the total population of gifted students in the country, are African American males. Thus, to say that alternative strategies and nuanced interventions are warranted in an attempt to meet the needs of this cohort is an understatement. Gilman W. Whiting in his article "From At Risk to At Promise: Developing Scholar Identities among Black Males" states that "although educators are justifiably seeking the most effective ways to identify giftedness and potential in all students, this need seems most pressing for Black males" (2006, p. 223).

ALTERNATIVE THEORIES IN THE IDENTIFICATION PROCESS

The pathway leading toward the almost unitary point of view from which we define giftedness was cleared many years ago by Lewis Terman through the development of the Stanford Binet Intelligence Test. Giftedness and the standards on which giftedness was based was determined by the attainment of high scores on IQ tests—tests much like the Stanford Binet. Unfortunately, the problem with these assessments is that there is no single measure or "one size fits all" test that

can be readily utilized. Giftedness is defined, shaped, structured, and operationalized in a societal milieu and not solely inside a person's head; societal influences
exert a profound influence on behavior. Consequently, tests that attempt to reduce
these behaviors into a readily assessable form are often found to be too general and
overly simplistic.

The intersection of culture and individual behavior must be considered in the
application of theory and definitions used to identify gifted learners. A number
of theorists have recognized the importance of considering the unique characteristics that each gifted learner brings to the table. One such theorist, Joseph
Renzulli (1986), with his three-ring conception of giftedness, attempts to describe
giftedness from a wider perspective. Giftedness is identified as three interlocking clusters (rings). These rings consist of above average (although not necessarily
superior) ability, task commitment, and creativity. Renzulli states that it is critical
to note that no single cluster makes giftedness but it is the interaction among the
three clusters that research has shown to be the necessary ingredient for creative-
productive accomplishment.

Howard Gardner's (1983) theory of multiple intelligences has offered a comprehensive framework from which a different set of approaches to and solutions
of the gifted identification process can be implemented. Gardner's expansion on
his original theory now includes eight intelligences, which he has identified as linguistic, logical-mathematical, spatial, musical, bodily-kinesthetic, interpersonal,
intrapersonal, and naturalistic. He is convinced that these eight intelligences are
highly independent and that nearly all children and adults show certain distinctive
profiles of strength and weakness in these areas. Additionally, Gardner asserts that
the development of high-level competence requires innate capacity, motivation,
and opportunity, with the environment, cultural context, and language potentially
serving as influences.

Sternberg's (1985) triarchic theory of intelligence is another set of theories,
containing three subtheories that act as the governing bases for understanding
extraordinary intelligence:

> The first subtheory relates intelligence to the internal world of the individual, specify-
> ing the mental mechanisms that lead to more and less intelligent behavior. The second
> subtheory specifies those points along the continuum of one's experience with tasks
> or situations that most critically involve the use of intelligence. The third subtheory
> relates intelligence to the external world of the individual, specifying three classes of
> acts—environmental adaptation, selection, and shaping—that characterize intelligent
> behavior in the everyday world. (p. 223)

This brief list of theories and theorists is in no way exhaustive; it is merely provided as a means of revealing how a more globalized view of giftedness, one in
which a unitary standard such as intelligence tests is not the sole means of assessment, is possible. The theorists discussed above also recognize the importance of
social and cultural influences in the expression of gifted behavior. Renzulli has
said that at the very least, attributes of intelligent behavior must be considered

within the context of cultural and situational factors. Gardner has implied that culture, language, and environment do not determine whether an individual will be gifted but that these factors influence the specific ways in which giftedness is expressed. Sternberg found that exceptional intelligence cannot be fully understood outside a sociocultural context, and it may in fact differ for a given individual from one culture to the next. These theorists with their reconceptualized approaches to identifying gifted students provide a greater sense of hope for all learners.

TEACHERS AND MULTICULTURAL EDUCATION

Student learning, growth, and development are directly influenced by the curriculum and the instructional materials teachers select, which exert a powerful influence on the type of education learners receive. Thus, the messages schools convey should support both democracy and inclusion. Multicultural education has played an important part in accomplishing this goal.

The emergence of multicultural education in schools is an indicator of the changing student demographic profile and needs. Researchers Donna M. Gollnick and Peter C. Chinn (1990) state that multicultural education is the educational strategy in which students' cultural backgrounds are viewed as positive and essential in developing classroom instruction and school environments. It is designed to lend support and extend the concepts of culture, cultural pluralism, and equality into the formal school setting. The American Association of Colleges for Teacher Education (AACTE), among others states that

> Multicultural education is education that values cultural pluralism. Multicultural education affirms that schools should be oriented toward the cultural enrichment of all children and youth through programs rooted to the preservation and extension of cultural diversity as a fact of life in American society. (Hunter, 1974, cited in Arnez, 1993. p. 510)

Why is multicultural education important to gifted African American students? These students, like other students of color who are not in gifted programs experience, racism and discrimination at the hands of classroom teachers. Harvard University professor Sarah Lawrence Lightfoot (1978) says that teachers, like all of us, use the dimensions of class, race, sex, and ethnicity to bring order to their perception of the classroom context. Rather than gaining a more in-depth and holistic understanding of children with the passage of time, teachers tend to reify stereotyped perceptions, with the result that children become caricatures of their discriminatory vision.

Multicultural education will increasingly become a key component in education and must not be viewed as merely ancillary to teacher training programs. All teachers should be exposed to a curriculum that focuses on relevant diversity and multicultural issues in the classroom. A dangerous precedent is set when schools make the assumption that this type of training is only relevant for White teachers; teachers of color also need this information. It is incorrect to assume that all minority teachers are effective instructors of minority children and that all White teachers are ineffective in this same regard. Yet it is correct to assume that teachers who are culturally incongruent with their students can benefit from multicultural education.

Tearing down many of the cultural barriers found to exist through the provision of multicultural education means that gifted African American students will have fewer obstacles to overcome as they seek to be academically successful. Beginning with teacher training and the curriculum, the classroom can become a stimulating place for all students, particularly gifted African American students, regardless of their cultural backgrounds and experiences.

Giftedness and the Collegiate African American Student

Chapter 2 has highlighted the major issues found to influence gifted K-12 African American populations. To reiterate Donna Ford's statement on giftedness, "Less than 2% of the articles and scholarly publications focus attention on gifted minority learners in general, and even fewer focus specifically on African American students" (at the time of her research, the largest U.S. minority population). A search of the existing literature reveals wide gaps in research and studies conducted with African American K-12 students, but when this search is extended to postsecondary populations, the literature almost becomes nonexistent. To explain the postsecondary gifted African American collegian requires the synthesis of literature from a number of different areas: K-12 gifted and talented, retention, collegiate honors, counseling, and college student development. It is unfortunate that these gaps exist or that giftedness becomes subsumed under other areas such as honors that may or may not adequately address giftedness as a construct.

In speaking to the issues impacting the gifted African American collegian, my research and the research of others who have studied these populations reveals some interesting findings; for example, the issues found to impact the general African American student population are not only the same issues that are found to impact the gifted African American student population but are these same issues often in more extreme forms. In an empirical investigation for the National Research Center on the Gifted and Talented (NRC-GT), based on my dissertation research, I found that six factors were most significant when I attempted to shed light on the experiences of the African American males I studied. These emergent factors included relationships with faculty, peer relationships, family influence and support, factors influencing college selection, self-perception, and institutional environment.

This chapter, with its focus on giftedness among African American students at the postsecondary level, will highlight each of the factors just mentioned and will serve as scaffolding for the next five chapters that focus specifically on the two African American gifted males who participated in my dissertation research study—Trey Williams and Stephen James (these are pseudonyms). More information about these two men will be shared in subsequent chapters. Each factor will serve as a framework to fully address the impact it has on the manifestation of giftedness for these two African American males. Additionally, two different contexts will be considered, with the historically Black college and university (HBCU) and traditionally White institution (TWI) serving as the backdrops for discussion.

RELATIONSHIPS WITH FACULTY

The importance of the relationship between college student and faculty member cannot be understated, with this relationship taking on even more significant meaning when race is factored into the equation. It was Deryl Smith et al. (1997) who found that students of color, particularly African American students, who elected to attend TWIs described their in- and out-of-classroom experiences as "chilly," unwelcoming, and inhospitable. African American collegians reported their collegiate experiences as running the gamut between virtually being ignored in critical conversations and dialogue to essentially being sought after to serve as the spokespersons for their entire race. Revealing an additional burden, it was the work of William Sedlacek (1993) that uncovered the unequal treatment of African American students and their nonminority peers in the classroom teaching and learning environment by faculty, with faculty providing significantly less praise to African American students.

African American males are particularly at risk in these academic environments in which they are unable to establish key relationships with faculty members. The higher education literature consistently cites the establishment of these relationships as the most critical factor in successful matriculation. The work of Sharon Fries-Britt and Bridget Turner (2002) revealed that 100 percent of the African American males in their study reported a "proving process" as being required in the classroom setting before faculty perceived that they possessed the intellectual capital to be academically successful. This proving process serves as yet another obstacle these students must overcome. Perceptions that gaining entrance to the institution was solely based on Affirmative Action mandates or that race and not academic merit were the standards used for admission are other barriers that have been documented as powerful countervailing forces in the college-going experiences of these students.

In a chapter I contributed to Michael Cuyjet and associates' book, *African American Men in College* (Bonner & Bailey, 2006), I cited the work of Anthony D'Augelli and Scott L. Hershberger (1993), who found that African American men (1) are perceived by society to have poor academic socialization and low expectations for their academic achievement, (2) are less likely to seek out faculty for assistance, and (3) assume they will be subjected to some form of mistreatment by faculty. This research is important in that it reveals the negative perceptions that African American males possess regarding relationships with faculty. Before academe can begin to address issues such as student achievement and success and academic and socialization processes, these negative perceptions must first be addressed. A prime example of this need to focus on these perceptions concerns the widespread use of mentoring programs to assist with various aspects of college student development. If African American males feel disconnected from and discounted by faculty, programs of this nature are destined for failure.

Establishing viable relationships between student and faculty is particularly important for gifted African American male college students. Perhaps the most important aspect of the gifted student's experience in the college setting is having a guide or mentor who focuses attention on honing the collegian's abilities. The need to foster the gifts and talents of students who show great promise in academic disciplines or areas of endeavor by providing mentorship and training cannot be circumvented. Academe commonly makes the erroneous assumption that these students, due to their academic prowess, do not need assistance. A common refrain is, "He is smart, and he doesn't need my help." Yet we know that the gifted student, oftentimes at levels higher than those of their nongifted peers, require guidance and nurturing to be academically successful. In *When Gifted Kids Grow Up: Counseling Gifted College Students Requires an Understanding of Their Special Needs,* Ford, Webb, and Sandidge (1994) argues that

> the psychological, cultural, and social issues confronting gifted college students have received only scant attention. One of the more plausible explanations for this paucity is the myth that gifted college students have no problems, or that their problems disappear once they leave formal schooling. Thus, we know little about what happens when the gifted go on to college. (p. 36)

PEER RELATIONSHIPS

Peer relationships and their importance to the undergraduate student experience in academe are highlighted across the extant literature. According to J. Carroll's (1998) research, the evidence is quite clear that both the frequency and quality of students' interactions with peers and their participation in extracurricular activities are positively associated with persistence (that is, remaining at the institution). Peer groups comprise an important source of support for African American college students attempting to simultaneously negotiate the unfamiliar terrain of the college and university context as well as the new growth and development challenges they face regarding their own identity. As I have stated (2001), "Peer groups are important in that they often expose students to viable social circles of similar achievement-oriented peers, thereby reifying these students' aspirations and goals" (p. 21).

The peer group serves as the community in which African American male collegians can safely test assumptions or create and forge new identities without the fear of judgment or reprisal. These communities are akin to "safe zones" where the individual is able to simply be himself. Several scholars have talked about the peer group and its relationship to such important factors as academic and social integration, retention, and even leadership development. White and Cones (1999), in *Black Man Emerging: Facing the Past and Seizing a Future in America*, have said that the peer group "meets the needs for belonging, feedback, and new learning experiences" (p. 214) for African American male cohorts. Each of these needs becomes even more pervasive when African American males are placed in nonminority contexts, environments in which they are expected to establish some sense of agency and essentially develop without role models, individuals, or visible symbols that support their cultural and ethnic frame of reference.

What the peer group has been found to primarily address the need for belonging for these postsecondary African American male students. When the student feels that he belongs or "matters," using the term that higher education scholar Nancy Schlossberg (1989) coined, the student is much more likely to remain at the institution—in essence the student is more likely to persist. Alexander Astin (1993), professor of higher education at the University of California Los Angeles, supports this point in stating that both the frequency and the quality of student interactions in peer group clusters are found to be positively associated with persistence. Additionally, we know that the sociocultural influences provided within these groups have been shown to be an even more powerful indicator of persistence than the academic influence these groups promote.

For the gifted African American male college student, the peer group becomes an important means of navigating multiple and intersecting identities in the higher education setting. Not only are these students required to deal with their status as African Americans in a predominantly White setting, but they are also required to deal with their status as high-achieving students in a context that many times responds negatively to high scholastic achievement. Establishing peer groups in which gifted African American males can connect to other gifted African American students, especially other males, is critical for the range of issues and factors previously cited in regard to their nongifted peers. Promoting these student peer groups enables African American males to see other gifted males who are successfully navigating their way through the academy. They are also afforded the opportunity to see positive representations of giftedness among students who like them are both African American and "smart."

FAMILY INFLUENCE AND SUPPORT

The family unit is identified in the literature as serving as a primary source of influence and support for the African American male college student. Serving as the earliest and primary unit in which notions about identity and self are developed, the family plays a valuable role. Research has documented the impact of the family on the psychosocial and social development of African American students and has also revealed the impact on their academic potential. Much has also been said about the influence of family on such varied areas as racial identity development, resilience, and self-esteem. These are all very important areas, with the development of positive self-esteem being paramount in enabling these individuals to survive the rigors of academe.

Perhaps the most significant role the family plays is serving as a sounding board for the collegian to talk about the opportunities and challenges of being African American and male in the higher education setting. Depending on the educational level of members within the family unit, some may not have had the experience of going to college; yet it is the moral support that these individuals provide that is so critically necessary for students to be successful. Again, in my chapter in Michael Cuyjet and associates' book, I argue that "The familiar refrains 'hang in there' and 'you can do it' often provide the extra push to spur these students on to academic success" (p. 29). Recapitulating a familiar theme, oftentimes it is not the academic matter that provides the greatest source of angst for African American male college students but the nonacademic matter; as William Sedlacek (1993) reports, the *noncognitive* aspects of the institution tend to be the most difficult for students to deal with.

The college-going process for the African American male collegian and his family is often a collective endeavor in which both the family and the student become involved. Other actors that can play a part in this process are the church and other key members in the community who become invested in the process. Thus, institutions are well served in their efforts to retain these students by strategically including family members in their policy and programming efforts. As I previously reported, "Institutions can serve as coauthors in the development of the student's voice, not trying to supplant the efforts of the family nor trying to short-circuit their responsibility for assisting in this process" (Bonner & Evans, p. 16).

Support from the family unit is critically important for gifted children during their experiences in both elementary and secondary school. Very early on, the family begins to occupy a central place and play an important role in the education of the gifted child. According to Jane Piirto (1994), gifted children are likely to follow a path of learning, growth, and development that their parents endorse—ultimately a path in which at least one parent has some interest. In chapter 2, I discussed the diverse set of issues, standardized testing, gifted underachievement, learning style preferences, and teacher nominations, that gifted African American male populations face in schools. Many of the same issues this group faces in K-12 become manifest at the postsecondary level—several in the very same forms. Therefore, the role that the family plays becomes even more important in college; although the role shifts from being more oriented toward advocacy to a greater focus on active listening.

FACTORS INFLUENCING COLLEGE SELECTION

Choosing a college or university to attend is a complex process that combines affective as well as cognitive decision-making processes. For most adolescents, this is typically a time full of angst and excitement, representing the ending of one chapter and the beginning of another. The old chapter with its order and structure, rules and regulations, is replaced by a new chapter that is much more fluid and laissez faire. Depending on parents to day-to-day structure is now no longer possible. The concerned classroom teacher is replaced by the distant and at times unconcerned college professor. This time presents even more challenges for students of color. Decisions to go on to college are intertwined with such concerns as leaving family behind, being academically successful in the new college setting, and handling potentially inhospitable social environments.

College-bound African American males have many of the same concerns about college success as others bound for college; these concerns quite often become amplified when difficulties associated with race and ethnicity are considered. Thus, finding an institutional context in which African American males perceive that they are not only encouraged to be successful but are also allowed to experience success firsthand is critical. Contributing to their perceptions are the stories and reports they receive from others who are informed about college settings and who have in some way previously experienced them. Whether it is a brother or sister or neighborhood friend who attended an institution under consideration, reports of incivility and hostility can serve as factors that negatively impact college selection decisions. Louis Attinasi's (1989) study of the college-going experiences of Mexican American students closely approximates the experiences of African American students. Thus, he talks about factors such as initial expectation engendering and role modeling, two of the factors influencing college selection.

The decisions that go into the college selection process for the gifted African American male are not necessarily different from the decisions that are made by their nongifted peers. As noted in previous discussions, these students' status as both African American and gifted places them in a unique position, requiring them to make strategic decisions in their selection processes. A fair question is: "What does it mean to be African American and high achieving in at this particular institution?" The problem then becomes one of identifying an institution that will provide the necessary challenge but in turn will provide the required level of support to succeed. Additionally, selecting an institution becomes dependent on issues such as finding viable mentors and role models who are invested in gifted African American male students and concerned about their social as well as their academic development. Even teaching and learning styles must be considered by these African American male students. Neil Daniel, in a 1985 article in the *Roeper Review*, noted that

> Many college professors, admissions counselors, program directors see the pool of gifted and talented students only as a recruitment resource. They look on honors students, Merit Scholarship Finalists, and other able learners as potential members of the

Pre-Med Program, or the Honors Program. They may not go on to the next step, making sure that their special programs are particularly suited to the abilities and learning styles of the superior students. (p. 236)

SELF-PERCEPTION

Understanding the African American male experience in our nation's schools requires a vigorous discussion of topics such as self-perception, self-esteem, and racial identity. Colleges and universities must become aware of the various challenges that African American males often confront during their K-12 experiences, primarily because these experiences, whether negative or positive, are transferred to the postsecondary environment. Author and public intellectual bell hooks in *We Real Cool: Black Men and Masculinity* (2004) asserts that African American men, more than any other group of men in our society, have been described and viewed as possessing a paucity of intellectual capital. She pointedly asserts that "African American men have been stereotyped via racism and sexism as being more body than mind" (p. 33). What this characterization tends to do very early on is to establish the perception that African American males can thrive only in areas that promote kinesthetic ability.

In my chapter "Assessing the Academic Climate for African American Men" (2006), I argue that "Researchers have identified several environmental conditions that can explain why African American males perform poorly in elementary and secondary schools: academic *disidentification*, lack of academic resilience, stereotype threat, and cool pose." Without going into a detailed discussion of these conditions, what each reveals is that student academic success and self-perception share a powerful relationship. How these males are made to feel in the educational setting predicts not only how they will perform academically but also how they construct their views of self.

All of the complexities associated with self-perception and self-esteem are confounded by expressions of giftedness among African American male populations. First, using the terms "gifted," "African American," "male," and "college" in combination produces very few "hits" in literal spaces such as library databases and in figurative places such as the "minds" of those who interface with these individuals in higher education contexts. For some, the gifted African American male student represents at best a walking anomaly and at worst a major exception to the rules governing their stereotypical views about such an individual. Again, bell hooks (2004) notes: "The curiosity that may be deemed a sign of genius in a White male child is viewed as trouble making when expressed by Black boys" (p. 36).

INSTITUTIONAL ENVIRONMENT

Clearly, if the retention of African American males is important to institutions of higher education, then the way these individuals interface and connect with the campus culture and environment must be considered. Considered as the foundation, the cornerstone of student development theory is Kurt Lewin's (1936) interactionist paradigm (B = f(P*E)). This equation, read as behavior is a function of the person times the environment, reveals how behavioral outcomes are determined by the interaction of the individual and the environmental context. Unfortunately, it is the environmental variable in this equation that has often provided African American males with the greatest challenges. The higher education environment described by African American males, particularly those who attend predominantly White institutions, has been viewed as at best chilly and at worst downright hostile.

If we look across institutional types, that is, if we specifically look at the variations found to exist in the environments African American males experience on HBCU campuses as opposed to predominantly White campuses, we find some major variations. According to Joseph Berger and Jeffrey Milem (2000), African American males who attend HBCUs are afforded the opportunity to develop positive self-concepts, as defined by psychosocial wellness, academic ability, and achievement orientation. Those who attend White institutions struggle with such complexities as academic and social integration as well as the negative perceptions and stereotypes that many within the campus community associate with African American males. An additional burden is that of having to prove that they are academically competent and that they have gained admission to the institution based on ability and merit and not based on an Affirmative Action mandate. Jacqueline Fleming, in her landmark book *Blacks in College* (1984), was resolute in her argument that predominantly White institutions have not done a good job of ensuring a positive matriculation experience for African American students.

Gifted African American males require an environment that supports both their African American and gifted statuses. The difficulties associated with being an African American male articulated above are often compounded by these students' academic prowess. In a predominantly White institution, these students find that they are further isolated and disconnected from other African American students when they elect to participate in honors colleges or programs designated for high academic achievers. From the establishment of study groups to the identification of viable role models, these males often find that their choices do not include African Americans or people of color. Perceptions of inferior academic abilities and Affirmative Action largesse become even more formidable hurdles when coveted spots in honors programs or on student research teams are at stake. The gifted African America male can find himself locked outside of the African American community, which does not relate to him at an academic level, and the White community, which does not relate to him at a cultural level—a virtual academic purgatory.

The Gifted African American Male College Student: A Study

To set the stage for the remainder of the book, this chapter provides background information on a previous study I conducted that looked at giftedness and the African American male college student. The next five chapters focus specifically on this study—chronicling and explicating the experiences of two gifted collegiate African American males—one in an HBCU setting and the other in a TWI context. Chapter 3 highlighted the six factors (relationships with faculty, peer relationships, family influence and support, factors influencing college selection, self-perception, institutional environment) that emerged from this study and provide a framework to structure the remaining discussions. Without providing a pedantic and exhaustive discussion of the research methods employed in this investigation, this chapter will provide a cursory overview of the salient aspects of the study design. Chapters 5, 6, 7, and 8 will specifically address the experiences of the two males participating in the study, while chapter 9 will provide critical recommendations and conclusions.

STUDYING GIFTED AFRICAN AMERICAN MALES IN COLLEGE

The question that I sought to answer in this study was the following: What are the perceptions of an academically gifted African American male undergraduate student attending a historically Black college or university (HBCU), and what are the perceptions of an academically gifted African American male undergraduate student attending a traditionally White institution (TWI), concerning his relationship with the institution in the cultivation of his academic giftedness? In addition to this question, I asked a number of subquestions in an attempt to truly get at how these individuals experienced giftedness in these two different institutional contexts. I also asked the following: What academic support systems were in place to facilitate the transition from high school to college? What services did the institutions provide to address the unique social and cultural needs of the African American student? Also, did the institution acknowledge and promote giftedness among its student populations through special policies and programming initiatives?

As stated earlier, it was the paucity of literature on gifted minority learners that prompted my interest in this topic. Information on gifted minority students, particularly gifted collegiate African American males, at the time I was conducting my study was virtually nonexistent. The scant data that was available tended to highlight the experiences of gifted students in elementary and secondary settings. It was the work of Donna Ford that sparked my interest in focusing on giftedness beyond the rigidly imposed K-12 parameters that continued to dominate discussions in the field. Ford (1992) argued that due to the myriad issues confronting school-age gifted learners, it would be careless to ignore the critical importance of their implications for gifted learners of all ages—especially gifted college learners.

I conducted two case studies in an attempt to address the questions that I had generated related to gifted African American male college students. The first case study was completed at East Texas State University (ETSU), a TWI now known as (and referred to throughout the rest of the book) Texas A&M University—Commerce (TAMUC). TAMUC is a public, four-year, coed, liberal arts university founded in 1889. The 140-acre campus is located in Commerce, Texas (population: 10,000), a small rural East Texas community located approximately 60 miles northeast of Dallas, Texas.

The *1996 Higher Education Directory* (Rodenhouse & Torregrosa, 1995) reported the enrollment of the institution to be 7,952 students. TAMUC was classified as a Doctoral University I according to the 1994 Carnegie classification system for postsecondary institutions. The composite American College Test (ACT) scores reported for the TAMUC freshman class were as follows: 2 percent of enrolled freshmen scored above 30, 24 percent scored 24–29, 48 percent scored 18–23, and 26 percent scored 12–17. The student body composition was as follows: 1 percent Asian American, 12 percent African American, 3 percent Hispanic, 1 percent Native American, 81 percent White, and 2 percent classified as other. The student faculty ratio was reported as 19:1. Seventeen percent of the students that were enrolled in the institution lived on campus. The majority of students who attended TAMUC were from the Southeast and Southwest regions of the country, as reported in the 1995 edition of *Lovejoy's College Guide* (Straughn & Straughn, 1995).

A second case study was conducted at an HBCU, Grambling State University (GSU). GSU is a public, four-year, coed, liberal arts university established in 1901. The 340-acre campus is located in Grambling, Louisiana, approximately five miles from Ruston, Louisiana (population 20,000). The student faculty ratio was reported as 12:1.

The 1996 *Higher Education Directory* (Rodenhouse & Torregrosa) reported the enrollment of the institution to be 7,956 students; the institution was designated as Masters I by the Carnegie classification; however, this institution offered the doctorate. The composite ACT scores reported for the GSU freshman class were as follows: 3 percent of enrolled freshmen scored 24–29, 16 percent scored 18–23, and 80 percent scored 12–17. The student body composition was recorded as follows: 94 percent African American, 3 percent White, and 3 percent classified as other. The majority of students who attended GSU were from the Southeast, with 48 percent out-of-state residents.

TREY WILLIAMS AND MY FIRST CAMPUS VISIT

Trey Williams was the first case study participant I visited during my initial round of data collection. Prior to my visit to TAMUC, I asked Trey to complete a biographical questionnaire that included personal information as well as information related to his family members. Trey listed his age as 21 and identified a small East Texas town as his place of birth and the place where he spent his formative years. He graduated from a public high school in 1993 in a class of approximately 100 students. The total population of Trey's high school was 500 students in grades 9 through 12. His high school grade point average was 3.70 on a 4.00, scale and his combined SAT score was 880. Trey was involved in a number of extracurricular activities in high school: football, basketball, track, and National Honor Society, in which he served as treasurer.

Trey received a number of honors and awards at his high school graduation. He was awarded an academic jacket for consistently maintaining an "A" average, as well as being recognized for his outstanding scholastic performance in Spanish and anatomy and physiology. Trey continued to excel academically in the collegiate setting, where he maintained a 3.4 GPA in his selected major—chemistry. Two of his other noteworthy achievements at the postsecondary level were the award of an American Chemical Society scholarship and a Dallas-Fort Worth Section Scholar Award. He was also named to the TAMUC Dean's List in three semesters. Trey's organizational memberships included his recognition as a student affiliate of the American Chemical Society and membership in one of the historically Black Greek letter organizations (HBGLOs). Trey informed me that he pledged the Greek organization during the summer 1996 term.

A Trip to Commerce, Texas

Trey and I spoke a number of times by telephone prior to our initial meeting. I found him to be easy to converse with and quite enjoyed our discussions. We discovered that we had several areas of commonality in our backgrounds, primarily stemming from our developmental years spent in northeast Texas. Additionally, we were able to commiserate about the challenges of majoring in one of the hard sciences. I explained what my dissertation data collection process would entail, in order to get Trey's comments and commitment to the study. I wanted to be clear about the number of campus visits, the nature of the questions, the identification of individuals who would participate, and the time investment required to complete the study. Trey spoke enthusiastically about his selection and assured me that he was looking forward to participating.

Approximately one week prior to my first visit to Commerce, Texas, I called Trey. I informed him that the first visit would be structured to provide us with time to talk and to get better acquainted. We would also conduct a standardized open-ended interview. We agreed on the time and place to conduct the interview—his place of residence was selected as the best site to complete this process.

I arrived in Commerce and stopped at a shopping center directly across the street from the TAMUC campus. Being somewhat familiar with the area, I decided that this was a good central location. I phoned Trey and he informed me that he lived in an apartment directly behind the shopping center and would drive around to meet me. While I waited for him to arrive, I inserted a new set of batteries into my tape recorder and conducted a test to insure that it was functioning properly. Just as I was attempting to conduct a second test of the equipment, a dark blue sports car pulled into the parking lot with an African American male driver who was alone in the car. The driver parked approximately 20 yards away, exited his vehicle, and proceeded to walk in my direction. I quickly decided that this individual had to be Trey Williams; I then placed the tape recorder in my backpack, exited my vehicle, and headed in his direction.

My suspicions were confirmed; he introduced himself as Trey Williams. Trey's personality seemed even livelier in person. My initial first impressions of Trey were that he appeared to be very down-to-earth and seemed extremely comfortable with the idea of participating in the study. It was Trey's apparent comfort level about the process that allayed many of my fears—in a sense, we were both novices.

Trey led and I followed him to his apartment, which as he previously reported was directly behind the shopping center. He invited me in and introduced me to his roommate—his brother Carl. The three of us shared stories about East Texas, football, and our respective hometowns. After about 20 minutes of laughter and sharing, Carl retreated to his room to allow us time to set up and conduct the interview. Trey was reminded of the measures I would employ to insure his confidentiality as well as the numerous member checks—a qualitative research method used to assist in the trustworthiness of data—to solicit his feedback on data findings. Chapter 5 includes a detailed discussion of Trey's interview.

Interviews with Trey and "Critical Others" at TAMUC

Trey Williams' standardized open-ended interview was conducted on September 24, 1996. Standardized open-ended interviews were also conducted over the course of the fall 1996 academic semester with friends, instructors, and administrators Trey interacted with on the university campus. The interview consisted of 39 questions, with the standardized open-ended format being selected due to the uniformity in questions posed to each participant. A standardized open-ended format minimized the variation in questions that I posed to the participants, which later assisted in analyzing participant responses across the data.

The questions posed in the interview were designed to elicit responses from Trey as well as the other participants highlighting their academic, social, and psychosocial experiences at the institution. Responses would then be used to make meaning of how Trey viewed his relationship with the institution and its impact on his academic success. The same standard-open ended interview questions posed to Trey were also posed to Trey's friends. The friends selected to participate in the study were also academically gifted African American males. I employed the same criteria in choosing these individuals as I did in choosing Trey. The friends' responses were used essentially to validate or possibly invalidate Trey's responses.

Two of Trey's friends were selected to respond to the interview. Both friends were African American males who were identified as academically gifted based on the criteria I used to make this determination. I have identified and will refer to these two individuals as Friend 1 and Friend 2. Friend 1 was a nontraditional-age (over 25 years old) undergraduate student majoring in chemistry. He was also Trey's laboratory research partner. Friend 1 had received a number of scholarships and awards for outstanding scholastic achievement in his major. Friend 2 was a traditional-age undergraduate mathematics major. Friend 2 had also received several awards and achievements for academic excellence.

The standardized open-ended interview was also used not only with Trey Williams and Friend 1 and Friend 2, but also with Trey's instructors. Before I posed the same set of interview questions to the instructors, I asked them to take a moment and consider a somewhat different approach in responding. I asked the instructors to respond in the manner in which they thought an academically gifted African American male would respond. One instructor said, "Oh, this is just like a role play." I informed the instructor that he could role play or use any images or ideas that came to mind in responding in the manner in which he perceived an academically gifted African American male would respond. Trey, Friend 1, and Friend 2 each responded from their own perspectives.

The instructors interviewed are identified as Teacher 1 and Teacher 2. Teacher 1 was a professor in the chemistry department. He also served as Trey's research advisor. Trey was currently enrolled in a biochemistry course taught by this professor. Teacher 2 was a professor in the biology department and had been identified by Trey as his mentor. At that time, Trey was enrolled in a cell biology course taught by this professor.

The final group of individuals I interviewed consisted of the handful of campus administrators that Trey interacted with on a regular basis. I used the same standardized open-ended interview instrument I had previously employed with Trey, his friends, and his instructors. The administrators were asked to respond in the same manner as the instructors, that is, their responses were to reflect the way in which they felt an academically gifted African American male would respond to the same set of questions.

The administrators are identified as Administrator 1, Administrator 2, Administrator 3, and Administrator 4. Administrator 1 was an African American female. She served as the campus director of Intercultural Services. Administrator 1 was very instrumental in assisting me with the search to identify participants for the study. She served as my primary campus contact. Administrator 2 was a White male. He was the head of the chemistry department at the time of my investigation. Administrator 2 at one time served as Trey's research advisor—Trey had previously been enrolled in one of his courses. Administrator 3 was a White male. He was the dean of the College of Arts and Sciences. He served as department head for the chemistry department prior to becoming dean. Administrator 3 was first introduced to Trey in a general chemistry course he taught. At one time, he also served as one of Trey's mentors. The final administrator, Administrator 4, was an African American male. He was the university's assistant dean of students. Administrator 4 had the least amount of direct contact with Trey, but he was able to provide a unique perspective on the experience of the academically gifted African American male on the TAMUC campus.

STEPHEN JAMES AND MY FIRST CAMPUS VISIT

Stephen James was the second case study participant I visited in my round of data collection. Prior to visiting Stephen at GSU, I asked him to complete the biographical questionnaire. Stephen listed his age as 21 and stated that he was born and grew up in a small town in South Louisiana. He graduated from a private Catholic high school in 1993 in a class of approximately 61 students. The total population of Stephen's high school was 200 students in grades 9 through 12. His high school grade point average was 3.14 on a 4.00 scale, and his combined ACT score was 18. Stephen was involved in a number of extracurricular activities, which included Beta Club, band, and the varsity basketball team.

Stephen received a number of honors and awards while in high school. He was a National English Merit Award winner and the recipient of his school's academic honor card recognizing his scholarly achievement. Stephen was also selected as outstanding bandsman by the school's music department. He continued to excel academically in the collegiate setting where he maintained a 3.50 GPA in his selected major—chemistry.

Additional achievements at the postsecondary level included the following: an Academic Merit Scholarship, a Ford Motor Scholarship, a National Collegiate Science Award, inclusion in Who's Who among American College Students, an All-American Scholar Award, inclusion on the National Dean's List, and a Richard Rayford Scholarship that recognized the highest-ranking junior chemistry major. For three semesters, Stephen was named to the GSU Honor Roll and University President's List. Stephen was involved in a number of campus organizations. He served as treasurer of the Golden Key National Honor Society and was also the vice-president of the GSU chapter of the National Association of Black Chemists and Chemical Engineers.

A Trip to Grambling, Louisiana

I spoke with Stephen by telephone, just as I had with Trey, prior to our initial meeting. Our conversations were typically short and direct; my first impressions were that Stephen was not a very gregarious individual and that I might have some difficulty in getting him to open up and talk. This somewhat heightened my trepidation about the data collection process; however, I decided to reserve judgment until we met face-to-face.

Prior to my trip to GSU, I shared with Stephen the data collection process and the level of involvement I needed from him to complete the study. He agreed to assist in any way possible. A week before my visit to Grambling, I contacted Stephen to determine the best time and place for our first interview. We agreed to meet in the chemistry department, located in the science building, to conduct the interview. Stephen gave me directions to the university as well as to the building.

I arrived on campus a bit early and decided to use this time to gather all of the materials necessary to conduct the interview and to test my tape recorder. After testing the equipment, I gathered my materials, placed them in my backpack, and headed off in the direction of the science building. Once inside the building, I climbed the stairs to the second floor and looked for the room number Stephen had provided during our conversation. It was not long before I found a door with a sign affixed that read, "Chemistry Department."

Upon entering the room, I noticed an African American woman sitting behind a desk. I informed her that I was there to meet a student in order to conduct an interview. Before she responded, another African American woman emerged from the office directly behind her and asked, "Are you here to meet Stephen?" I told her that indeed I was there to meet Stephen and to conduct an interview. She then told me that she was the head of the chemistry department and had been instrumental in helping me to identify a viable case study participant—Stephen. We spoke briefly and I retired to the adjoining conference room to prepare for the interview.

I sat in the conference room for approximately 10 minutes before Stephen arrived. My first impression of Stephen shattered all of my preconceived notions and previous apprehensions. He was warm and friendly and seemed to be completely invested in whatever role he could play to insure that my study would be a success. We laughed and talked about a range of topics—from majoring in chemistry to pursing a graduate education. I informed Stephen of the measures I would employ to protect his confidentiality as well as the numerous member checks I would conduct to solicit his feedback and input on findings. Chapter 7 includes a detailed discussion of Stephen's interview.

Interviews with Stephen and "Critical Others" at GSU

The same standardized open-ended interview I used to interview Trey Williams was used to interview Stephen James. The interview took place on October 8, 1996. Standardized open-ended interviews were also conducted over the course of the fall 1996 academic semester with friends, instructors, and administrators Stephen interacted with on the university campus. Again, the interview consisted of 39 questions, with the standardized open-ended format being selected due to the uniformity in questions posed to each participant. A standardized open-ended interview was used to minimize variation in participant responses.

The interview questions were designed to elicit Stephen's responses concerning his perception of how the institution cultivated his academic giftedness. The questions required Stephen to respond to academic, social, and psychosocial concerns. The same questions posed to Stephen were also posed to two of his friends, also identified as academically gifted African American males. The same criteria used to select Stephen for this investigation were employed to select his two friends. The friends' responses were used to validate or possibly invalidate Stephen's responses.

The two friends selected to respond to the interview are referred to as Friend 1 and Friend 2. Friend 1, like Stephen, was majoring in chemistry. At the time, Friend 1 was a fifth year senior and was working with Stephen as a research assistant in the department. Friend 1 was active on campus through his involvement in several organizations. Friend 2 was a nontraditional-age (over 25 years old) undergraduate student majoring in biology/pre-medicine. Friend 2 had transferred from a predominantly White junior college in the South. Friend 2 was classified as a senior. Stephen, Friend 1, and Friend 2 each responded from their own perspectives.

The second group that responded to the interview included Stephen's instructors. The instructors were asked to respond in the manner in which they thought an academically gifted African American male would respond. The instructors I interviewed identified as Teacher 1 and Teacher 2. Teacher 1 was an African American male professor in the chemistry department. He had previously served as one of Stephen's instructors. Teacher 2 was also an African American male professor in the same department. Stephen recommended that I interview Teacher 2. Teacher 2 served as one of Stephen's instructors in the chemistry program and was currently serving as his research advisor.

As a final interview group, I queried administrators that Stephen interacted with on campus, although these were limited interactions. I required each of the administrators, just as I had instructed both the administrators and instructors at TAMUC and the instructors at GSU, to respond to the questions in the manner in which they thought an academically gifted African American male would respond. The administrators were identified as Administrator 1 and Administrator 2. Administrator 1 is an African American female; she served as the assistant director of the Earl Lester Cole University Honors College. Administrator 1 was helpful in providing a general overview of the honors college experience on the GSU campus; Stephen was an inductee while the study was being conducted. Administrator 2 is also an African American female. At the time of the study, Administrator 2 was serving as the department head in chemistry—she also served as my primary contact in navigating the GSU campus administrative structure.

An Interview with Trey Williams

This chapter highlights Trey Williams's responses as well as the responses provided by the friends, instructors, and administrators he interacted with on the Texas A&M—Commerce (TAMUC) campus. Table 5.1 is a display depicting the six categories in the first row of the grid and the names of the participants in the first column. Statements made by each participant are included in the corresponding cells. According to Matthew Miles and A. Michael Huberman (1994), displays are useful tools in displaying through a visual format, information that can be systematically considered. The display I used is called a conceptually clustered matrix—it allowed me to look at both participants and their responses to each of the categories simultaneously.

These statements are related to each of the categories discussed in chapter 2. Each category was identified during the data analysis phase of the study through the use of an elaborate coding scheme. These emergent categories included relationships with faculty, peer relationships, family influence and support, factors influencing college selection, self-perception, and institutional environment. The statements included in the cells allowed me to make a number of observations from the perspective of each participant, essentially providing a cross-sectional view of the participants and their responses in each category. This chapter will provide a discussion of each category and summarize the responses provided by the participants as they relate to the guiding research question: What are the perceptions of an academically gifted African American male undergraduate student attending an HBCU, and what are the perceptions of an academically gifted African American male undergraduate student attending a TWI, concerning his relationship with the institution in the cultivation of his academic giftedness? Direct quotations from the respective interviews are used to provide depth to the respondents' expressed feelings.

Table 5.1 Conceptually Clustered Matrix: Case One Categories

Participants	Relationship With Faculty	Peer Relationships	Family Influence and Support	Factors Influencing College Selection	Self Perception	Institutional Environment
Case Trey Williams	I don't have personal contact as far as dinner or lunch. . . . I do call them and they know me on a first name basis.	I feel like that, uh, ... I need friends. I need friends because friends can pull a lot of strings for you and help you out.	I have a strong family bond and I have great ties with them.	Being in smaller classes so I could have more one-on-one type relationships with my professors.	I think I'm a kind soft-hearted person. . . . I really have a strong mind; I'm not a "groupie."	You can't help but feel that there is some type of competition when the professor is showing some type of favoritism.
Friends Friend 1	My research adviser basically comes in and more or less, I would classify it as a job setting, in a supervisory position.	There are a couple of people in the chemistry department that are like pseudo-friends.	My main driving force is my wife.	It was more of a matter of geographic location.	I'm basically an arrogant asshole.	It's more of a competition for us. Most of my classes if I'm not the only one in there, there is one other minority student and we are viewed as the outsider.

Friend 2	I might see a professor on the way to class, but it's not any type of personal contact.	I have a strong support group around here, you know, my frat and, uh, others . . . friends outside the fraternity.	I try to call my mother and we usually wind up praying.	Actually a friend of mine, who was my line brother. He talked to me over the telephone and we decided that I was going to come down here.	I have a lot to improve on. but I like myself.	When I first came here it was collaboration, but I think now it's a lot more competition.
Teachers Teacher 1	Perhaps I'd have some contact with faculty doing the sports thing. . . . but beyond that, probably not a lot.	I have uh, maybe one or two people I can talk to beyond the weather.	They were really involved with 1996, helping me out, to make sure that I found a college that was reasonably close to home.	Money, and it's close.	I do okay.	I've seen both of that—both competition and collaboration.
Teacher 2	He does have personal contact. He can interact with any of us.	I think he interacts with really fine people and he has a good bunch of friends.	I think he consults his family. I think he's the kind of person who does.	The distance from his home is probably the determining factor for choosing.	Excellent.	I don't think there's too much competition for a position.
Administrators Administrator 1	We deal a lot with, uh, the student affairs area . . . so, through that, it gives you an opportunity to dialogue with some faculty.	We pretty much work together, bond together, uh, socially . . . and we depend a lot on each other.	We are all, uh, pretty family oriented.	Basically geographics.	I'm the bomb!	The competition is a positive thing.

(*Continued*)

Table 5.1 Conceptually Clustered Matrix: Case One Categories (*Continued*)

Participants	Relationship With Faculty	Peer Relationships	Family Influence and Support	Factors Influencing College Selection	Self Perception	Institutional Environment
Administrator 2	Most of that has to do with the research that I'm doing in chemistry. There I see the faculty member, or in the laboratory.	I have a fair number of friends.	My family is probably my largest support, best support system.	It was close to home.	I sometimes question just how really smart I am.	It's very collaborative, but still you have to make your own grade.
Administrator 3	Uh, I do have contact with faculty outside the class.	I'm sure he does have some very close friends,	I think my gifts are having good, strong family support.	Because it was relatively close.	From time to time I feel a little bit insecure about myself.	There's always competition, but it's a friendly kind of competition.
Administrator 4	Uh, I have numerous contacts with professors both within my major and outside of my major	I can call some of my friends back at home for support.	I can pick up the phone and call them.	To see if my academic skills and achievements can match up with those of other races.	I'm more concerned about reaching out and being helpful to others. I don't like to dwell on myself.	I think definitely it's competition.

RELATIONSHIPS WITH FACULTY

In discussing his relationships with faculty, Trey revealed that these relationships were dualistic in nature. For example, although he viewed the faculty as being supportive of his academic endeavors, he perceived no relationship to exist beyond his engagements with them in the classroom setting. When describing his relationship with a professor he viewed as instrumental in assisting him to secure an academic scholarship, he stated:

> *He was instrumental in helping me and though we established a relationship, it was not a leisure or pleasure type of relationship . . . it was always academic. But then again, there was the barrier between just a regular student and someone he cared about and that barrier was broken.*

For Trey, clearly the academic aspects of the relationship are important, but so too are the more personal and social parts of these connections. Higher education scholar Michael Nettles (Nettles & Johnson, 1987) found that African American students were less likely than their White counterparts to experience frequent contact with faculty outside of the classroom. Yet the literature suggests that the impact of faculty on student norms, values, and attitudes, as well as faculty members' impact as role models, is enhanced when student-faculty interactions extend beyond the formal classroom setting.

Trey made additional references to his relationships with faculty. In speaking about his interactions with a particular professor in the chemistry department, he said:

> *I can say things that some other people can not say. . . . we have that type of relationship and he won't get mad as he would probably with somebody else that he didn't know. So that's the type of relationship I have had with that professor.*

Trey essentially shared with me that he had learned from his interactions with his professors that he could access them when needed. Yet, at the same time, he perceived that this access was limited to issues of academic importance—personal matters fell outside of acceptable discussion boundaries. His friends, Friend 1 and Friend 2, mentioned similar experiences regarding their relationships with faculty members.

Friend 1 described his contact with a faculty member, his advisor, as a "worker/supervisor relationship." In responding to an interview question asking if he thought his department was supportive of his academic endeavors, Friend 1 replied:

> *As far as my department, no! If you're Black and you're in chemistry, you're not supposed to be here.*

Later in the interview, Friend 1 responded to a question asking him to provide the advice he would give to an extremely high-achieving African American male thinking of attending TAMUC after high school graduation. Friend 1 said he would tell the individual that he found the professors "amenable." This statement could be viewed as contradictory to the previous statement he made about the professors in his department; however, I found that many of his responses did not refer to his major department (chemistry) but to another department on campus with which he felt some sense of affinity. When reporting on his relationships with this particular department, Friend 1 stated:

> *If they identify you with any kind of potential, they will pick you up and start you right down the lane because that group over there would like to see more minority students succeeding and trying to do their best.*

Hence, it appeared that Friend 1 reflected on his experiences with both departments when he responded not only to this question but also to other questions in the standardized open-ended interview. Again, a major concern here is the lack of positive interactions that this student had with his professors outside of the classroom. Although he viewed a particular department as being helpful and supportive of students of color, the relationships he established with the faculty in this unit were still primarily focused on his academic development.

Friend 2 perceived the faculty in his department as supportive:

> *I would have to say that they have been supportive, because, I mean, every time I see them they're asking me to make sure my classes are going well—things of that sort. I think that also has to do with the low percentage of Blacks who are in the program.*

Again, we see the support system intact as it relates to the student's academic needs. Yet there is no mention by Friend 2 of an equivalent social support system. When asked about the amount of contact he had with professors outside of the classroom, Friend 2 said, "I might see a professor on the way to class, but it's not any type of personal contact." Friend 2's statement is significant in the words he chose, describing his contacts with faculty as being devoid of any type of "personal contact."

The comments provided by both Friend 1 and Friend 2 closely paralleled Trey Williams's responses. The relationships students develop with faculty members are critical. Even for the student who possesses extraordinary academic abilities, these relationships remain essential. In a study focusing on student development, higher education scholar Marsha Baxter Magolda (1992) found that students at the highest level of complexity in intellectual development preferred a relationship with faculty that emphasized working together as colleagues.

Trey's instructors, labeled Teacher 1 and Teacher 2, also responded to the standardized open-ended interview—providing responses based on their perceptions of how an academically gifted African American male would respond. Teacher 1 asserted that the relationship between faculty and the academically gifted African American male student beyond the classroom was "not significant." As we see in Table 5.1, beyond occasionally attending a sporting event or on-campus program, the relationship between these parties was virtually nonexistent. Teacher 1 went on to share his background experiences with me—informing me that he had grown up in the North and considered himself to be deeply religious.

Teacher 1 perceived that he had a deeper appreciation and understanding of the African American student's plight on the traditionally White campus—noting that he too had experienced racism and prejudice in the higher education context. His comments were primarily based on his personal experiences with what he referred to as "intolerance" regarding his chosen religious practices. On faculty support, Teacher 1 said that he found some of the faculty supportive of students while others were not.

In responding to the question about faculty support, Teacher 1 offered the following description of a supportive faculty member:

> *A professor that was willing to answer my questions. I could go into his office whenever I want to, you know, call him up whenever I want to, and I'm not, well I don't feel like I'm getting in trouble or doing something terrible if I interrupt him. That's one example. There are other professors that are just plain jerks!*

Teacher 2 was a very strong supporter of Trey Williams and was forthright in informing me that he would be using Trey as a reference source in providing his responses to the interview questions—"I am going to respond in a way that I think Trey might respond." One of the first points Teacher 2 made was to state unequivocally that he believed significant relationships existed among students and faculty. In his response to the question regarding personal contact outside of the classroom between students and faculty, Teacher 2 answered:

> *He's interactive with me. He's been in my office several times talking with me and I wasn't his teacher at the time, so I know he's interactive with people outside of the classroom.*

All of the administrators I interviewed perceived that there was contact in some form between students and faculty outside of the classroom setting. This group was the furthest removed from the in-class/out-of-class interactions with students due to the status of their positions, yet they provided their comments. One of the first things I noticed about these respondents was their universal belief in a faculty support system that each student could access when needed. Trey had been previously enrolled in both Administrator 2 and Administrator 3's classes. Administrator 2 informed me that he thought the interactions between students and faculty were primarily confined to the academic setting, while Administrator 3 perceived these relationships as extending far beyond this context. Administrator 3 stated:

> *Well, I do have contact with faculty outside the class. In many cases it's to get additional help, but is some cases it's just to talk and to discuss the future, and what I might like to do. There was one faculty member who was encouraging me to pursue another major other than the one I was currently pursuing. As a matter of fact, there's more than one faculty member who has talked to me about this matter.*

Administrators 1 and 4 also perceived that there was an ongoing relationship between the students and the faculty members. I noted that both of these individuals worked within the Division of Student Affairs at TAMUC and found their comments were almost identical and reflective of the nature of their work—student centered and student focused. Thus, these two individuals were potentially influenced by their work and viewed student and faculty relationships through their own professional lenses. Administrator 1 identified key campus organizations and leadership positions within these organizations as the student's primary link to relationships with faculty outside of the classroom. In responding to the question based on his perceptions of how an academically gifted African American male would respond, he reported:

> *I think that being a part of outside organizations, being a part of the Student Government Association gives us a chance as students to work very closely with faculty.*

Administrator 4 commented:

> *One thing that I have discovered is that when you reach out to faculty members, and they begin to know you as a person, rather than by your social security number—when you need that extra assistance, they are willing to give it to you.*

Despite an array of responses across the administrators' interviews, they overwhelmingly believed that student/faculty contact and support did exist. Additionally, each administrator believed that relationships between academically gifted African American males and faculty existed.

Summary: Relationships with Faculty

Trey affirmed through his interview statements that he found the faculty supportive of his academic endeavors, but found that this support was not as readily available beyond the parameters of the classroom. In order to address the guiding research question, I analyzed Trey's responses to determine his perceptions of his relationships with faculty in regard to the institution's support of his giftedness.

Faculty members are an extension of the institution; one could even advance the idea that faculty members *are* the institution. Therefore, Trey's perception of the support he received from faculty is a direct indication of the support he received from the institution. The data indicated that he perceived the institution as meeting his expectations as far as his in-class needs were concerned, but beyond his in-class encounters, relationships with faculty were virtually nonexistent. The literature advances the importance of student relationships with faculty outside of the classroom. In Trey's case, the question was, "Could the university provide better support of his giftedness through increased student-faculty relationship which extended beyond the classroom?" A 1986 study by Walter Allen addressed this question—he found that relations with faculty proved to be a better predictor of student outcomes for African American students on White campuses than on Black campuses.

Although Trey had been and continued to be successful academically, meaningful relationships with faculty members within and outside of his department could have only served to enhance his collegiate experience and the cultivation of his giftedness. Relations with faculty provide a needed outlet, a support system for the African American student that is often missing in the predominantly White collegiate environment. I noted that the majority of faculty and administrators believed that some type of interaction between the academically gifted African American male student and faculty occurred beyond the classroom. The perceptions of both of Trey's friends and of Trey himself revealed just the opposite—that these relationships did not exist.

PEER RELATIONSHIPS

Trey spoke about the importance of peer relationships and the necessity of maintaining key friendships in his interview. In Table 5.1, I recorded a key statement he made about the importance of his peer connections. During the interview, Trey asserted that although he found friends to constitute an extremely important part of his life, he did not have an extensive circle of individuals whom he consulted or interacted with on a daily basis, other than his roommate, who happened to be his brother. In responding to the question of whether he found campus social relationships important, he stated:

> *Yeah, they are, but I don't just make it the biggest, most important thing like other people do. I don't rate it way up at the top as far as my list of priorities. . . . I'm basically centered around [sic] individuality. I believe that I have my family behind me and I have. . . . Well, I have God on my side and that's all I need. They are not that important . . . social relationships.*

Trey frequently commented about the relationship he had with his brother. His brother served as his friend and primary confidant. He also spoke about the close relationship he had with his laboratory partner, Friend 1, another African American male who was majoring in science. Additionally, members of his fraternity were also highlighted at certain times during our conversations. All of these individuals—from his biological brother to his laboratory partner and fraternity brothers—I determined were the individuals who comprised Trey's circle of friends.

Friend 1 talked about the difficulty in establishing true friendships with his peers on campus. He identified Trey as his closest friend and referred to the relationships he had with other peers on campus as "pseudo friendships." Friend 1 also talked about his status as a nontraditional student with a family and how this influenced the amount of time he spent socializing and the nature of the social relationships he established on campus.

Friend 2 identified his social group as consisting mainly of the members of his fraternity. When asked to describe his on-campus social support network, he said:

> *I would have to say that it is solely my fraternity. And, the role that they play, I mean, whenever there's a problem that arises, we're always there for each other and we just deal withy the problems as they come.*

Friend 2 also commented about his closest campus social relationship:

> *I wouldn't say that I had that social type of relationship with only one person. With everybody in my fraternity, I am able to say that if you know you have a problem, then we will work it out in the house. Or, whatever is dealt with in the house stays in the house.*

Friend 2's comments reflected more of an interdependent connection with his friendship networks than did the comments of Trey and Friend 1. Both Trey and Friend 1 talked about the importance of these systems but not to the same degree as Friend 2. Again, it was Trey's relationship with his brother that he perceived as reducing his need to establish relationships with others aside from his brother.

Administrator 1 described the peer relationships she believed an academically gifted African American male would establish on a traditionally White campus. She stated that these relationships, in her opinion, would consist mainly of other African American students:

> *Even though this is a pretty nice size school, there is still just about 11 or 12 percent African American students here. We pretty much work together and bond together socially. We depend a lot on each other, so a lot of it would depend on our association of friends.*

Administrator 1 also highlighted the importance for African American males of membership in certain campus organizations. Trey and Friend 2 were both involved in HBGLOs. They both cited these organizations as a positive force and source of peer support. Although Friend 1 was not a part of a campus organization other than the academic organization within his major, he said:

> *I would have liked to have had the time to socialize more. They [the university] have different organizations. I know that they have the NAACP here and I would have liked to have gotten into campus government and who knows I might become an attorney or something if I had the time, but I don't.*

The significance of peer relationships was reiterated throughout each interview. The levels of importance given to these relationships varied among participants. Yet even at the lowest level of peer interaction, the participants continued to report that these relationships were necessary to succeed in a traditionally White institution like TAMUC.

IN SUMMARY

Trey found that the relationships he maintained with peers were a critical part of his collegiate experience. These symbiotic relationships assisted him in numerous ways, from studying for important examinations to discontinuing a fraternity pledge process that he believed would have led to his academic demise.

Each relationship essentially shed light on the many aspects of the institution that could buttress or impede his academic progress. These relationships served as conduits that provided him with information he needed to determine how the institution would support his giftedness.

By establishing key peer relationships, Trey was able to develop some sense of community within his department, the chemistry department, which did not have a significant number of students of color. Although TAMUC, like most institutions, advances a mission that speaks to its efforts to meet the needs of every student, it is evident that some students fall between the cracks. Relationships with peers often serve to cover over these cracks and to pull these students back from the perils of attrition.

An Interview with Trey Williams—
Continued

This chapter is a continuation of chapter 5, in which Trey Williams's responses as well as the responses provided by the friends, instructors, and administrators he interacted with on the Texas A&M—Commerce (TAMUC) campus are highlighted. Please refer back to Table 5.1, which displays the six categories that emerged from this study; the names of the participants associated with the emergent categories are listed in the first column. Statements made by each participant are included in the corresponding cells.

The first two categories (relationships with faculty and peer relationships) were discussed in chapter 5. The present chapter will highlight the statements associated with the remaining four categories (family influence and support, factors influencing college selection, self-perception, and institutional environment). It is important to keep in mind the guiding research question for this investigation: What are the perceptions of an academically gifted African American male undergraduate student attending a historically Black college or university (HBCU) and what are the perceptions of an academically gifted African American male undergraduate student attending a traditionally White institution (TWI) concerning his relationship with the institution in the cultivation of his academic giftedness? Direct quotations from the interviews are used to provide depth to the respondents' expressed feelings.

FAMILY INFLUENCE AND SUPPORT

Familial influence and support was a major category found in each of the standardized open-ended interviews conducted with Trey and the other participants at TAMUC. Trey spoke quite freely about his relationship with his family and credited them with a major part in his academic success. Trey especially talked about the strong influence his mother exerted on his undergraduate experience. Trey's mother was a college-educated woman and exercised a strong influence on his higher education decision-making processes. Trey spoke of her involvement in his educational goal-setting processes during both his K-12 and postsecondary experiences. He made the following statement concerning his mother's influence:

> *I use the same patterns that she started me out with when I first got in school as far as kindergarten; I use the same ones up in college. I haven't changed. I was actually asked a question about that earlier last semester, and they asked me how do I make a GPA or why is it that I am so studious. It all goes back to my mother.*

Trey made a number of references to the role his mother played in his college selection process. In responding to the question about his reason for choosing TAMUC, Trey spoke about the impact his mother had on his decision to decline an offer from another institution he was considering attending:

> *I always discuss everything with my parents, especially my mother, and when I came back and told her about the UT campus and all that and what all the tour guides had to say, the one thing that really struck her was the class size. I told her how many and I think there were like 500 in some classes and she really didn't agree with that. She was more interested in me getting, like, a smaller, well, being in smaller classes so I could have more one-on-one type of relationships with my professors. So basically, she influenced me to come here because this was my second choice.*

Trey spent a great deal of time talking about the psychosocial and emotional support his family provided. He reported that he was in frequent contact with his family, citing telephone conversations with them as often as three times a week.

> *If things are going good then I tell them, "Yeah, I'm doing good, momma, things are going pretty good." But if things are going bad I might call them and say, "Something's wrong; things are not going right." But it's about three, I would say three times a week. They usually call me on, like, weekends.*

Six of the remaining eight interviewees made some reference to the importance of the mother, both as source of influence and as a source of support. Teacher 2 spoke directly about his past experiences with Trey and the role he perceived his family played, his mother in particular, during his college selection process.

> *They played a big role. I would like to meet his parents because I know he consults with them; he has already revealed that to me. He might confide with his mother because she is younger than his father, but I know he respects his father. I know they interact and they are a big, big part of what he's done and I know they will be a big part in his future.*

Administrator 3 identifies family support as an important component in the success of the academically gifted African American male undergraduate student (see Table 5.1). In addressing the question about the family's role in the college selection process, Administrator 3 stated:

> *My family wanted me to go to what they considered a good school, to reach a certain profession. They helped me select a college that was affordable but yet had the kind of academic training that I could use.*

Again, we note that both Trey's interview and Administrator 3's interview identified the active role the family unit plays in students' lives. The family's active role in the collegiate process translates into academic success and the ultimate cultivation of the student's academic gifts and talents. Family support and involvement in the student's collegiate experience can have widespread implications not only in the area of student success but in the relationship the institution maintains with the parents of these students.

Summary: Family Influence and Support

The category of familial influence and support was highlighted in several statements across the interview data that spoke to the importance of familial influence in supporting academically gifted African American males—particularly Trey Williams—during their undergraduate experience at TAMUC. Trey's relationship with his family impacted his collegiate experiences from the initial institutional selection processes he engaged in to his successful graduation from the institution.

Important to Trey's academic success was his ability to establish close and meaningful relationships with faculty on campus. It was his mother who very quickly recognized that her son's success would depend on his connections to faculty members who would assist him to navigate the academic system. She was convinced that his selection of a larger institution in the state would not provide him with these opportunities; therefore, she encouraged him to seek out a smaller, more close-knit postsecondary environment.

Additionally, Trey spoke of his mother's involvement across his educational career. It was her counsel and guidance that provided him with the basic skills and mindset to take on the challenges of higher education. The skills she imparted to her son shaped his perceptions and views of how the institution would support his giftedness: namely, through small classes, one-on-one relationships with faculty, and recognition for his academic achievement.

FACTORS INFLUENCING COLLEGE SELECTION

Trey cited smaller class sizes and one-on-one relationships that he perceived he could establish with faculty members as key factors in selecting an institution. His discussion and his logic around this process mirrored much of what he shared under the previous category, family influence and support, concerning the influence his mother had on his collegiate decision-making process. Trey spoke candidly about his choice of college in the interview:

> *Since I have been going here, I'm really glad I did because I am more able to understand the subject at hand as opposed to UT Austin. I had classmates go there, and they are way behind because they don't have any type of real reaction, I mean interaction with their professors. They are just basically numbers and I didn't think that would be good for me or my understanding of certain things.*

Although Trey cited the size of the institution as the key determining factor in selecting it, the prevailing factor for most of the remaining participants was related to geographic location. For example, Teacher 2 mentioned a number of factors that would impact the decision-making process but ultimately decided that geographic location was the main driving force behind any final decision. In providing a response he believed to be typical of that of an academically gifted African American male collegian, he said,

> *Probably I would think it would have something to do with it being near his home, the size, the quality of the school, the number of students compared to the teachers. . . . The distance from home is probably the determining factor.*

Friend 1, Teacher 1, Teacher 2, Administrator 1, Administrator 2, and Administrator 3 all highlighted geographic location as one of the main factors considered in the selection process. Teacher 1 also added another critical dimension to the selection process discussion—money. Teacher 1 believed that financial considerations played a major role in the selection of an institution; consequently, he asserted that an institution near home would be viewed as a more economical and cost effective option.

Another view on the factors associated with the college selection process was advanced by Administrator 4. Administrator 4 stated that the key reason an academically gifted African American male would choose to attend TAMUC would be to determine if his academic skills were comparable to those of other races. According to Administrator 4, a gifted African American male college student would select an institution primarily

> *to get an education, to get a feel of what it would be like to attend a predominantly White university, to see if my academic skills and achievements can match up with those of other races.*

Administrator 4's response was not atypical of what I heard not only from other administrators but also from African American male students. According to many of the discussions regarding selecting a college or university, especially if the decision is being made whether to attend a TWI or an HBCU, African American students will use their peers to set educational benchmarks and goals. A commonly held perception is that the benchmarks cannot be aptly measured in homogenous contexts: relative academic achievement and standing to be worthy of merit must be viewed in relationship to majority (White) students.

In Summary

The most frequently cited reason for selecting an institution among the participants in this study was geographic location. Although this was widely cited, Trey did not mention geographic location as a determining factor in his selection of an institution during his interview. Trey identified his ability to develop close and meaningful relationships with faculty, which was directly connected to class and institutional size, as the most significant factor in his decision-making process.

To address the guiding research question, I concentrated on the factors that influenced Trey's decision to attend TAMUC and how these factors molded his perception of the institution's support of his giftedness. Again, it was the accessibility and the support of family that molded and shaped Trey's college decision-making processes. According to Michael Sutton (2006) in his chapter "Developmental Mentoring of African American College Men" in Michael Cuyjet's book *African American Men in College,* relations with faculty are positively related to university grade point average, considerations of dropping out, and feeling a part of campus life. The importance of the relationships Trey established with faculty had widespread significance for his perceptions of how the university as a whole supported his giftedness. The relationships Trey established with faculty are basically the relationships he established with the institution; therefore Trey's giftedness was essentially supported through committed and meaningful liaisons with faculty.

A second critical determining factor in Trey's selection process had to do with the size of the institution. His perception of the impact of institutional size on his academic success also directly connects with how he perceived the institution would support his giftedness. Although the literature has been somewhat inconsistent in reports on institutional size and the subsequent impact on educational attainment, several researchers have found that when controlling for student pre-college characteristics and other institutional traits, attending a large institution exerted a negative influence on persistence and degree attainment.

SELF-PERCEPTION

Many inferences were made concerning self-perception, whether the respondents' own self-perception, the self-perception of friends, or the self-perception the teachers and administrators projected onto the image they held of academically gifted African American male undergraduates. Comments regarding self-perception ranged from "excellent" to "I do okay," with a number of variations mentioned in between. Trey talked openly about his own self-perception, and shared it during the interview, stating that he found himself to be an open and caring individual. He used terms such as *kind, gentle, soft-hearted, neat,* and *compassionate* in describing himself. He reported:

> *When people come to me and need help, I never turn my nose up or walk away. I know if I was in that same position, I know I would like help them. So I try to put my feet in other people's shoes as far as that is concerned.*

Trey spoke briefly about his own perceptions, his self-perceptions of his academic ability. Yet he was quick to share with me his reluctance to speak boldly or to brag about his scholarly prowess, choosing to allow his work and the accomplishments his work provided to speak for him. I expected Trey to spend a significant amount of time discussing his academic abilities and acumen, but found that he talked about these issues very little. Even when prompted to discuss his academic giftedness in an interview question, Trey immediately told me that he did not like to concentrate on his academic abilities. He stated that it was his perception that all individuals possessed gifts in certain areas. He went on to state that he perceived himself as an independent thinker who was unwilling to give up his academic successes for social gratification. He went on to state that he perceived himself as a very spontaneous person:

> *There's no type of influence from other people. I feel like I want to do it, I do it; if I don't, I just don't. A lot of people have gotten upset with me because of that.*

He went on to report:

> *I try to be creative. I like being spontaneous. I'm the type of person that I don't like for people to know my next move. I never let my left hand know what my right hand is doing. When people got you figured out they can do a lot of things and I don't like that.*

In responding to the request to provide what he believed to be his friend's perception of him, Trey's conversation turned to what he reported as very limited interactions with his peers on a social level and how many of them perceived him as overly studious.

> *When I do go out or anything, everybody is surprised to see me. Even my own frat brothers, my own line brothers, they are surprised to see me. I tell them, "I go out—not all of the time like y'all but I go out."*

He also commented:

> *They think that I have a book in my hand all the time, which is not a bad thing. I guess it's just someone on the outside looking in.*

Friend 1 exuded a self-assured presence and appeared to be quite comfortable in sharing with me his perceptions of himself as well as the perceptions he believed others had of him. When asked about his own self-perceptions, Friend 1 said:

> *I'm basically an arrogant asshole. I keep it like that to eliminate a lot of interactions with a lot of people.*

When questioned about the perceptions Friend 1 believed his friends had of him, he reported:

> *They think I'm an arrogant asshole, that I walk around with my head in the clouds all the time, which I do. I don't care. The people that are really close to me know that I'm not that way and that I'm a very beautiful person.*

It was easy to determine Friend 1's comfort level with me in his response to the questions that spoke to issues of self-perception. When asked about his response to someone describing him as gifted, his reply was "Definitely!" It appeared to me that Friend 1's status as a nontraditional student became manifest in his interview comments, revealing the mature level of confidence and assurance of who he was and how he perceived that others viewed him.

Friend 2 did not provide much detail concerning his self-perceptions. When asked to respond to the question, Friend 2 began to very quickly discuss his short-comings and need for improvement. He concluded his commentary by revealing that he liked the person he had become as a result of his self-improvement process:

> *I'm proud of myself because if I would have thought of myself, you know four years ago, that I would be where I am right now, then I would have said, "Man you're crazy."*

Friend 2 perceived that his friends thought of him as a good-natured person who would be there for them if they needed his assistance. When asked about his response if someone referred to him as gifted, Friend 2 replied that he would question the meaning of their reference, because he did not view himself as gifted:

> *I feel like in order to say I'm gifted means to say that I'm somewhere above the rest. I don't feel that the Lord has given me anything that He hasn't given anyone else—maybe just in a different area.*

When Teacher 2 was asked to identify the self-perceptions he believed an academi-cally gifted African American male would have of himself, he replied, "Excellent." Teacher 2 also stated that he believed this individual's peers would hold similar perceptions of the individual and hold him in very high regard. Again, it is impor-tant to note the close relationship Teacher 2 maintained with Trey Williams and his insistence that he use Trey as his model in responding to the interview questions.

I found the responses provided by Administrator 2 and Administrator 3 to be quite similar. Both of these respondents perceived that an academically gifted African American male might find reason at times to question his academic abili-ties. According to Administrator 3,

> *I, from time to time, feel a little bit insecure about myself. I'm not quite sure that I'm as good as other people seem to think I am.*

The statements provided by these administrators provided valuable insight regard-ing their views on the perceptions that African American males would have of themselves. None of the academically gifted African American males who were interviewed expressed reservations or concerns about the perceptions they believed their peers or other institutional officials had of them. Yet, we see that the admin-istrators' view of these students' self-perceptions reflect what they believed was a sense of insecurity that the students harbored. Additionally, the administrators were reluctant to refer to these students' academic abilities as giftedness, opting to advance notions of hard work and diligence as their tools for achieving success.

In Summary

The statements in this category provided the most diverse range of responses across the various interview participants. Trey's comments regarding self-perception primarily centered on statements about key affective attributes. It was Trey's depic-tion and description of himself as *soft-hearted* and *caring* as well as *creative* and *spontaneous* that seemed to elicit the greatest response from him. However, I found some incongruities in Trey's response to the question about how his self-perception related to his general view of how the institution supported his giftedness.

Trey perceived himself to be a creative and spontaneous person. When responding to the interview question that about the institution's provision for his creative abilities, he reported that he did not find the institution particularly supportive of his creativity or creative abilities. Trey indicated that he found the institutional context contrived and predetermined, and saw no real use of his creative insight or opportunities to advance it. Hence, I found that the institution was not thoroughly supporting Trey's giftedness as it related to the category of self-perception.

After interviewing Trey and the other participants at TAMUC, I returned to the literature to determine what impact a lack of support for Trey's creativity could potentially have on his long-term achievement. An article by Denise de Souza Fleith, Joseph Renzulli, and Karen L. Westberg (2002) was resolute in affirming the importance and need for developing appropriate stimulation and training for creative abilities. These authors went on to state that individuals responsible for special programming should be knowledgeable about strategies for reinforcing, nurturing, and providing appropriate resources to students at those times when creativity is displayed.

For Trey, the programming initiatives that Renzulli identified should have translated into programming (course structuring) within Trey's department. Whether creativity is addressed at the department, college, or university level, Trey should have perceived that his creativity was not only supported but developed through his academic relationship with the institution. According to Davis (2003), a logical place to begin any programming agenda that advances creativity should be the cultivation and awareness of this topic and the molding of attitudes, dispositions, and motivations.

INSTITUTIONAL ENVIRONMENT

Interview participants provided a range of responses related to their perceptions of the institutional environment. Trey's comments, captured in Table 5.1 were both insightful and interesting, especially his comments on the question that asked him to describe the institutional context as being either competitive or collaborative, as well as his response regarding the advice he would provide to another academically gifted African American male who was contemplating enrolling in the institution after graduating from high school. In responding to the latter question Trey said,

> I would tell him that you got to be on your p's and q's. You got to be 10 times as smart as anybody else, especially somebody White, because there is always going to be some type of favoritism or some type of leeway being given to them—or some type of break. So, you really, really got to prove yourself. I had to prove myself. It shouldn't come down to that, but yet still it happened to me.

Trey's comments about the institutional environment are worthy of note; they reflect his perceptions of an environment that was in many ways competitive and unequal in its treatment of some students. His views seemed to fall directly in line with the extant literature addressing this issue. Several studies have addressed these same issues as they relate to the African American student's perception of the institutional environment. One study in particular, by K. W. Jackson and L. A. Swan (1991), found that Black males in White institutions perceived the competition as more extremely intense than those who attended predominantly African American institutions.

What was unique in this particular case study, unlike several of the previous studies, was Trey's designation as being academically gifted. If his perception is one in which he views the institutional context as being competitive and non-collaborative, what is the perception of the African American male who is not academically gifted and finds himself on the academic margins of the institution? Trey is succeeding at the institution and is confident in his intellectual abilities, but what happens to the at-risk African American male who is barely achieving the minimum grade point average necessary to remain enrolled in the institution?

Teacher 1 identified the institutional environment as both competitive and collaborative:

> *I think it's a mixture. We're competing for grades, but we also, in the labs, we work together very often, and so I think I've experienced both.*

Teacher 1 and Administrator 2 both provided similar responses to the question about the institutional environment. Both saw the environment as competitive mainly in the area of grading, but collaborative in all other venues. Administrator 4, although he said that he found the institutional environment competitive, did not view this competition as counterproductive or negative with regard to the student's achievement:

> *I think definitely it's competition. Students are always striving to do the best they can academically, because doing their best is going to help determine the number of scholarships they're going to receive. And I don't look upon that competition as being something negative.*

Teacher 2 found the institutional environment to consist of very limited competition, and went on to say that the environment strongly supported collaboration. He stated that "campus interactions" he witnessed supported his claims. Teacher 2 did not explain what he meant by interactions; nor did he describe the parties involved in them.

In Summary

This category revealed a wide range of responses from interview participants, from competitive to collaborative to a mixture of both. Trey perceived the environment as extremely competitive. He also talked candidly about the inequities he believed to exist not only within his department but also across the institution. According to Trey, these inequities were often drawn along racial lines, as emphasized by his comment that in order to achieve academic success, he had to work twice as hard as his White counterparts.

Whether his perceptions were real or imagined, they constituted Trey's perceptions of the institutional environment. In relating Trey's perceptions of the institutional environment to the research question, I found that his giftedness was not supported within this category, closely paralleling what is cited in the literature. Findings by M. Hughes (1987) revealed that African American students perceived predominantly White postsecondary environments as intellectually oriented, achievement oriented, independence oriented, and competition oriented. Hughes went on to state that such orientations are least likely to produce the best environment for Black students, for whom socially oriented climates are crucial for their success.

Trey's perceptions regarding the institutional environment were also echoed by both of his friends, two other academically gifted African American males. Therefore, if the institution is to truly support the gifts and talents of Trey and other African American students on campus, it must first come to terms with the perceptions that these students have regarding the institutional environment. According to researchers, predominantly White colleges have not succeeded in combating African American students' social isolation, perceptions of classroom biases, and perceptions of hostile interpersonal climates. Trey's perceptions are not new, but the institution's interventions to address his perceptions should be.

An Interview with Stephen James

This chapter highlights Stephen James's responses as well as the responses provided by the friends, instructors, and administrators he interacted with on the Grambling State University (GSU) campus. Table 7.1 is a display depicting the six categories in the first row of the grid and the names of the participants in the first column. Statements made by each participant are included in the corresponding cells. The display used in this table is a conceptually clustered matrix—it allowed me to look at both participants and their responses to each of the categories simultaneously.

Statements in the matrix are related to each of the categories discussed in chapter 2. Each category was identified during the data analysis phase of the study through the use of an elaborate coding scheme. These emergent categories included relationships with faculty, peer relationships, family influence and support, factors influencing college selection, self-perception, and institutional environment. The statements included in the cells allowed me to make a number of observations from the perspective of each participant—essentially providing a cross-sectional view of the participants and their responses in each category. The chapter will provide a discussion of each category and summarizes the responses provided by the participants as they relate to the guiding research question: What are the perceptions of an academically gifted African American male undergraduate student attending an HBCU and what are the perceptions of an academically gifted African American male undergraduate student attending a TWI, concerning his relationship with the institution in the cultivation of his academic giftedness? Direct quotations from the respective interviews are used to provide depth to the respondents' expressed feelings.

RELATIONSHIPS WITH FACULTY

In discussing his relationships with faculty, Stephen revealed that he did not have a great deal of interaction with them, but he knew that he could call on

Table 7.1 Conceptually Clustered Matrix: Case Two Categories

Participants	Relationship with Faculty	Peer Relationships	Family Influence and Support	Factors Influencing College Selection	Self Perception	Institutional Environment
Case Stephen James	I don't really have direct interaction with the faculty outside the classroom. . . . I have their numbers: if I so need, I could call on them.	Well, I have many friends. . . . I guess I don't have like a "true friend."	I always call home for like, uh, mainly, even small problems. . . . I'm trying to get out of that.	Mainly because both of my parents are from—came here.	Okay, I think I am intelligent, ambitious, confident, devoted to what I would like to pursue.	It's just like a collaboration of many students working together.
Friends Friend 1	One teacher, we used to go with and play racquetball. Some of the teachers you may see at intramurals sometimes.	It's like a friend-mentor type of relationship. . . . I feel I can go to him with whatever and I know he will be there.	My aunt always supports me in a lot of aspects, so, and my foster parents definitely.	I liked the environment that Grambling had, the community environment, the togetherness and also, the people who were there—the instructors who were there.	Uh, I think I'm a pretty cool guy.	I think it would be more collaboration. . . . If we're going to get our grades, we're going to have to get together and study.
Friend 2	You do have access to the professors, you know, in terms that aren't necessarily traditional. . . . I've gone to their houses for different things. I've called them after hours.	I have a good friend who's also in my department. . . . We spend time studying together.	I have several aunts who, unlike my mother and father, have gone to college and they help out in terms of advising and stuff like that.	. . . I wanted to go to an HBCU.	I think I'm doing great.	It's definitely more of a collaborative effort. We might need a little more competition around here. It would be more healthy.

(Continued)

61

Table 7.1 Conceptually Clustered Matrix: Case Two Categories (*Continued*)

Participants	Relationship with Faculty	Peer Relationships	Family Influence and Support	Factors Influencing College Selection	Self Perception	Institutional Environment
Teachers Teacher 1	Well, on occasion, we have gatherings where we get together.	Well, I don't have a whole lot of friends, but I have friends. . . . They support me where it is necessary, where I allow them to support me.	I have relatives that attended Grambling and they suggested that I come here to get a well-rounded education, one where people would care whether or not I was successful.	I chose it because it's a small institution, it's an historically black institution, and I thought I would get more personal attention if I attended a smaller university like this—like Grambling.	I am a person who can be trusted—trustworthy—I am friendly once you get to know me.	If you asked whether there's competition or cooperation, I would say there is more coopera-tion than there is competition here at Grambling.
Teacher 2	I have a faculty mentor whom I get to talk to outside of regular class hours. . . . So, we get to talk about more than just what's going on in the classroom.	My closest relation-ship would be with my other colleagues, the other chemistry majors, because we spend a lot more time together.	Anytime there's something that leads me to a question I re-ally am not sure about, then I'll go to my parents for advice.	The best place to go would be with people who can understand me and be able to relate to me in more than one area.	I think that I am an open to suggestions; I am here to try to learn as much as I can, to do a good job, and to have good grades, and to, uh, prepare myself for the future.	Some of our upper-level classes are smaller. So, there's a competition component built into the smaller class. But, we collaborate as well, and especially within our research groups.

Administrators						
Administrator 1	Some faculty members will adopt you and take you into their home. That's just a part of Grambling.	It'll probably be someone in the science area, because, like I said . . . you start spending a lot of time over there.	I think that a student would counsel with their families.	The institution has a record of producing outstanding African American men and women.	I think there's a great determination there to succeed.	You have to collaborate and try to help each other, but you have to compete.
Administrator 2	I have the opportunity to just walk into my professors office— and it's not office hours or conference hours—I can go in with my questions.	My closest relationship on campus now is my study partner for P-Chem.	I call my family up and I talk to them and we work through those personal problems	The reason I chose to come here was due to the fact that my parents attended historically black universities and I have met other scientists or professionals that attended HBCUs and I was really impressed by their professionalism.	. . . I'm focused on what I'm doing and I'm going to do whatever is necessary to be successful in it.	In order for you to get through a program such as chemistry, or maybe math, computer science, or whatever, it takes team work . . . It's competitive in that even though you are studying together . . .you want to outdo the other.

them in times of need. After observing Stephen on the GSU campus, I found his statement regarding the level of interaction he maintained with faculty to be somewhat questionable. Although I believed that Stephen provided an open and honest response to the question, I found Stephen's level of interaction with faculty far more significant than he intimated in the interview. Stephen's relationships with his professors, especially Teacher 2 and Administrator 2, who had both served as his instructors at various times, were extremely close.

From my observations, it was my belief that Stephen had such numerous and sustained contacts with his professors that his concept of maintaining a "relationship" with these individuals became muddied. These interactions were so commonplace and appeared to be so natural for Stephen that attaching a moniker to them seemed somewhat odd. Stephen's relationship with his research advisor and mentor, Teacher 2, and the strong ties he maintained with Administrator 2 were significant in that they extended beyond engagements in the classroom. Stephen's relationships with these two African American academicians provide a needed source of support and are characterized by Julian Roebuck and Komanduri Murty (1993) as being many sided, sustained, and personal; they are important in their establishment of a strong orientation toward success. Stephen commented in the interview:

> *If I have problems outside of the classroom, I could go to Administrator 2 or any of the professors. They really instilled the confidence within me.*

Stephen made a number of comments about his professors and the respect and admiration he had for them. Several of his comments were not recorded in the interview data but occurred during our informal exchanges. Hence, I viewed Stephen's relationships with faculty as much more significant than would appear from the statements recorded in Table 7.1.

Friend 1 and Friend 2 also cited what they perceived to be significant interactions they had with faculty members beyond the classroom. According to Friend 2:

> *That's one of the things that I'm pleased with Grambling about. . . . . About the fact that you do have access to the professors. I've had professors at my apartment for socials and things like that.*

Friend 2 echoed the sentiments expressed by Friend 2. Thus, the perception advanced by these two students is that the relationships between students and faculty not only existed but also occurred in venues outside of the classroom context. Both students indicated that their interactions with faculty were ongoing and consistent.

Teachers 1 and 2 both expressed their opinion regarding the relationships they believed to exist between students and faculty; both perceived that there were significant interactions. What I found interesting was the relative significance the instructors placed on these relationships. The message conveyed in their dialogue concerning these relationships revealed what they thought to be strong, committed relationships that in many ways mirrored peer-to-peer as opposed to student-faculty relationships. The faculty member was often identified as the source of social as well as academic support. In addressing the question that asked the respondent to describe the student's on-campus network, Teacher 2 said:

> *It could be the faculty members of the department, especially my research mentor, or I should say my advisor. My research mentor is my advisor as well.*

Teacher 2 went on to provide the following comment at the conclusion of the interview. He desired to again address the relationship between faculty and students with his department (chemistry):

> *It's a small department. This is important in preparing our students and keeping track of them. That means a lot to a student who you never know exactly how their life will bend and fold. You don't know which way your journey will tend to bend itself. But you know there are people there who care. And that's one thing that I found important here at the university.*

The research of Roebuck and Murty (1993), again, revealed that African American faculty on HBCU campuses consider their students to be a source of pride and joy; students with a status they once occupied, as future African American professionals; as a more enlightened and privileged generation than their own; and as surrogate children. Administrator 1 confirmed this statement, particularly the identification of these students as surrogate children:

> *That's just a part of Grambling. That's just the way it is, the nurturing process. While you're dependent, you're also—no! While you're independent, you're also somewhat dependent, being away from home and whatever. Some faculty members will step in and try to help you, you know.*

Administrators 1 and 2 both perceived a significant amount of contact between students and faculty both on- and off-campus, resulting in what they termed "lasting relationships." Table 7.1 depicts Administrator 1's statement acknowledging the importance faculty placed on establishing and maintaining relationships with students. She also recognized the depth of these connections.

In Summary: Relationships with Faculty

Although Stephen did not perceive that he had significant personal interactions with faculty outside of the classroom, my observations of his interactions revealed that his perceptions were not exactly aligned with what I witnessed. Stephen maintained a number of key relationships with faculty members both within and outside of the classroom context. He very readily admitted that his relationships with faculty were an ongoing source of academic support, assisting him in a number of ways, including the identification of key summer internship opportunities.

Despite Stephen's claim that he did not maintain personal relationships with faculty, he did state that faculty members were accessible to him whenever he needed them—even beyond the time spent in classroom engagements. In relating

Stephen's comments to the guiding research question that sought to find out how his relationship with faculty translated into the institution's support of his giftedness, it appeared that Stephen perceived he was supported. This became manifest in the assurance and confidence he exhibited when responding to questions regarding his academic success and its connection to faculty support. For example, when discussing how the faculty provided valuable recommendations that assisted him in securing a summer internship, he stated:

> *Their [faculty members'] recommendation accommodated my personal willpower.*

PEER RELATIONSHIPS

Stephen reported that he had a number of friends on the GSU campus, although he said that he did not have a "true friend" on campus. My interpretation of his comment was that he did not have a "best" friend who attended the institution. Stephen said that his contacts with peers were primarily connected to his academic pursuits, namely, research projects or classroom assignments. When questioned about the relative importance of campus social relationships, Stephen asserted:

> *When it comes time for studying, it's always good to study in groups or something like that. If I didn't know something, I could always call on one of my classmates, you know, other students. They're real important.*

Stephen also maintained a close personal relationship with his cousin who attended GSU. He stated that he occasionally stopped by her apartment to "shoot the breeze." Through my numerous visits to the campus I was able to observe the relationship Stephen had developed with Friend 1. Stephen and Friend 1 were research partners and worked for Teacher 2 in his laboratory.

I found that the peer relationships described by Friend 1 and Friend 2 were parallel yet distinct in several ways. Looking at the statement in Table 7.1, I ascertained that the relationship Friend 1 was describing was not a relationship he maintained with his peers but a relationship he had developed with one of his instructors. Although he mentioned several peers, friends he spent time with in various academic and social contexts, it was the relationship he maintained with this particular faculty member that he embraced as the most important. This observation piqued my interest and subsequently led me to ask myself the following question: Could an instructor be viewed as the college student's best friend? Roebuck and Murty (1993) found that African American students in the HBCU environment perceived African American faculty as older brothers, sisters or surrogate parents as well as competent and helpful professors.

Friend 2 identified his relationship with an individual in his major as his closest peer relationship. He spoke briefly about two other students that he "hung out with" on occasion. He also spoke about his relationship with his girlfriend, who was also a student on the campus. When responding to the question of whether campus social relationships were important, Friend 2 said:

> My relationships are limited to my group of friends; I don't feel like I have to be the ambassador to the campus.

Friend 2's statement is supported in the literature: according to R. Davis (1986), African American college students' support network variables (African American student unity and African American male/female relationships) proved to be better predictors of African American student academic outcomes on Black as opposed to White campuses regarding student academic success. Friend 2 also reported that his relationships with his peers and with his girlfriend provided him with a "close knit, specific kind of support" that he found to be extremely valuable in his collegiate matriculation.

Teacher 2 identified the peer relationships he perceived an academically gifted African American male would engage in during his collegiate experience. He reported that these relationships would be centered on research and scholarly pursuits. He stated that the intense nature of the courses and the amount of time required to complete required research projects justified his hypothesis. When responding to the question about the on-campus social support network an academically gifted African American male would establish, Teacher 2 replied:

> It consists mainly of the people who are in the department, because I spend a great deal of time there. I guess it would be centered on the department.

Administrators 1 and 2 both perceived the academically gifted African American male as engaging in a number of peer relationships, and both highlighted the importance of these relationships in the student's overall success. Both administrators tended to emphasize, even overemphasize, the nature of these relationships as being constructed mainly around academic needs. When asked to describe the close campus social relationship she perceived an academically gifted African American male would establish, Administrator 2 immediately replied that the relationship would be established with a student partner within the department.

> We were freshman together and we studied general chemistry and organic chemistry together, so we've developed a relationship.

In Summary: Peer Relationships

The importance of peer relationships was discussed by each participant in the study. Despite the varying levels of significance placed on these relationships, each one of the participants in the study viewed them as playing an instrumental part in the undergraduate experience. Historically, researchers have talked about the importance of these relationships in the student's success. As early as the 1970s, researchers like William Sewell and Robert Hauser (1975) reported on the significance of peer relationships on student educational attainment.

My interest in Stephen's commentary on his peer relationships was to relate this information to the guiding research question: How do Stephen's relationships with his peers influence his perception of the institution's support of his giftedness? This question is essentially answered by the concluding sentence in the previous paragraph, which spoke to the importance of these relationships to educational attainment. Stephen is encouraged to attain his educational goals through his interactions with individuals who are not only supportive of him but also invested in his academic success.

Key peer relationships serve as a compass, providing Stephen with directions to his destination to achieve his educational goals. His academic successes led the institution to support his giftedness by providing him with valuable recommendations for internships, scholarships, and awards. According to Michael Hanks and Bruce Eckland (1976), peer relationships may expose students to a social network of other achievement-oriented peers, thereby generating and reinforcing higher aspirations and goals. Stephen was aware of the benefits he received from his peer relationships. More importantly, these relationships reinforced his academic achievement potential, which in turn led the institution to support his academic giftedness.

FAMILY INFLUENCE AND SUPPORT

The importance of familial support for the gifted student can not be understated. Familial support is critically essential for all students, but for the academically gifted collegian, this support plays an even more key role. Stephen remarked that he often consulted with his family but also reported that he was trying to decrease his level of dependence on them as he sought to make more independent decisions. Nevertheless, he enthusiastically talked about his relationships with his father, mother, and sister. When asked about the frequency of his consultations with his family on various matters, Stephen replied:

I would say at least 70 percent. I need to like try and become more independent.

Most of the references Stephen made to his family members concerned their support in assisting him with his college selection process. Both of Stephen's parents were alumni of GSU, and both had subsequently gone on to pursue graduate level education and received their master's degrees—they were very influential in his decision to attend the institution.

Friend 1 and Friend 2 identified an extended family member—an aunt—as their major sources of familial support, each one citing the respective aunt's status as a college graduate as providing him with the directions he needed to be successful in the collegiate environment. Whereas Friend 1 was also very appreciative of the support he received from his foster parents, he advanced the notion that they were not as knowledgeable about college because neither had attended. Friend 1 did state that his sister served as a source of support. She was completing doctoral studies at a nearby institution, and he consulted with her on a routine basis.

Teacher 1 and Teacher 2 both expressed their opinions concerning the support they perceived an academically gifted African American male would need and should receive from family. Both found familial support as necessary and for the student to be successful. Teacher 1 cited the influence of parents who were knowledgeable about the HBCU experience in general and the GSU experience in particular as being important. Teacher 1 cited parents who were aware of the campus culture and environment and the cadre of campus officials who were genuinely concerned about their child's achievement.

Teacher 2 also addressed the importance of the family in his interview. When questioned how often he perceived that an academically gifted African American male student would contact his family for advice on academic as well as nonacademic issues, Teacher 2 reported:

> *Often. . . . Anytime there's something that leads me to a question I really want, well, am not sure about, then I'll go to my parents for advice. And sometimes, I'll go to my parents before I even go to a faculty member because I want to feel out the question, to make sure that I'm looking in a proper way.*

Administrator 2 provided key insight on the importance she perceived to exist in the relationship between the academically gifted African American male and his family. When asked to identify the off-campus support network she perceived the student maintained, she asserted:

> *Off-campus support system would be . . . my mother and my father.*

Administrator 2 took an interest in my study, and we conversed on several occasions about a number of issues related to the study and its completion. During one of our conversations, she shared with me the overwhelming support she perceived that Stephen received from his family. She was also extremely complimentary of his family's strong commitment and tie to him and attributed a major part of his academic success to them.

In Summary: Family Influence and Support

This section has highlighted the importance of family support in the undergraduate experience of the academically gifted African American male undergraduate. The relationships Stephen maintained with his family members often provided him with the assistance necessary to achieve academic success. The purpose of this section was to show how familial influence and support impacted Stephen's perception of how the institution supported his giftedness.

Stephen's parents were active agents in his collegiate experience—from his initial selection of the institution in which he enrolled to his status as the highest academically ranked student in his department. In essence, it was the support and advice that Stephen received from his family that led to his academic achievement, which in turn prompted the institution to support not only his achievement but also his academic giftedness.

Prime examples of the support provided by Stephen's parents that resulted in the institution supporting his giftedness were the recommendations he received from Administrator 2, which assisted him in acquiring an important summer internship. Much of Administrator 2's support was initiated due to what she described as the very "strong family unit" from which Stephen emerged. Her recognition of the family's commitment to Stephen also prompted her to be supportive of him.

The support Stephen received from his family supplied him with the confidence to pursue his academic and professional goals. During the interview, Stephen said that his parents "paved the way for him and instilled in him the confidence that he could succeed." Due to their instilling this level of confidence in their son, Stephen's perception of the institution supporting his giftedness came to fruition in the form of assistantships, scholarships, awards, and recognition as the top student in his department.

An Interview with Stephen James—
Continued

This chapter is a continuation of chapter 7, in which Stephen James's responses as well as the responses provided by the friends, instructors, and administrators he interacted with on the Grambling State University (GSU) campus are highlighted. Please refer back to Table 7.1, which displays the six categories that emerged from this study; the names of the participants associated with the emergent categories are listed in the first column. Statements made by each participant are included in the corresponding cells.

The first three categories were discussed in chapter 7 (relationships with faculty, peer relationships, and family influence and support). This chapter will highlight the statements associated with the remaining three categories (factors influencing college selection, self-perception, and institutional environment). It is important to keep the guiding research question for this investigation in mind: What are the perceptions of an academically gifted African American male undergraduate student attending an HBCU, and what are the perceptions of an academically gifted African American male undergraduate student attending a TWI, concerning his relationship with the institution in the cultivation of his academic giftedness? Direct quotations from the respective interviews are used to provide depth to the respondents' expressed feelings.

FACTORS INFLUENCING COLLEGE SELECTION

Stephen readily identified the most significant influence on his selection of GSU—his parents. Stephen's parents were alumni of GSU and were strong advocates for his son to attend the institution. When responding to the question about the role his family played in the college selection process, Stephen stated:

They really left it up to me, but since both of them are alumni of Grambling, they kind of said, "Oh, you gotta go to Grambling," or something like that. I was always like hearing, you know, how Grambling was number one!

Stephen stated that his decision to attend Grambling was "an easy choice." He also identified an additional factor that influenced his college selection process—his desire to attend an institution that was not in close proximity to his hometown. Stephen stated that he desired to move away from South Louisiana and experience another part of the state.

Friend 1 identified the environment on campus as the major factor influencing his decision to attend the institution. Friend 1 stated that the individuals he met during a precollege visit sparked his interest in GSU, reporting that:

They really made it a comfortable setting for me, so I was just sold on Grambling from that point on.

Friend 1 also highlighted the benefits of being in classes with other individuals who looked like him. In responding to the question that asked Friend 1 what he saw when he entered his first class on the GSU campus, he said:

You know, it was really comfortable for me, you know. Because I came from a high school where it was like 60 percent White and 40 percent Black. And, you know, being that most of the Blacks weren't in the classes that I was in, and so, you know, it was like really comfortable to see, you know, all Black students in my classes.

Although Friend 1's experience of the GSU classroom environment occurred after his enrollment at the institution, it is still revealing in that it shows the level of comfort and satisfaction he derived from his selection of the institution. In discussing the move from a predominantly White to a historically Black collegiate context, William Harvey and Lea Williams (1996) found that certain features of Black campus life—a participatory ethos, an inclusive environment, an expectation of success, and the incorporation of a rich historical tradition—contributed to a successful transition.

Teacher 1 and Teacher 2 both reflected on the benefits of attending an HBCU as the primary reason for an academically gifted African American male selecting GSU. Teacher 1 asserted that Grambling had a history of providing assistance to students in preparation for their future careers. When asked what an academically gifted African American male would see when he walked through the doors of GSU on his first class day on campus, Teacher 1 replied:

Well, I saw what I expected to see. I expected to see a classroom filled with students that were much like me, you know, African American, and that sort of gave me the feeling of belonging.

Teacher 1's response provided valuable insight on what he perceived the student experienced relative to his choice as well as his initial contact with the institution. Teacher 1's use of the word "belonging" ties in directly with the inclusive environment that Harvey and Williams alluded to in their research.

Administrators 1 and 2 both cited the influence of parents who were alumni of the institution as major forces they perceived would impact an academically gifted African American male's selection of GSU. Both administrators also perceived that the numerous role models and professionals out in the community who were also graduates of the institution would strongly influence the student's selection process as well.

In Summary: Factors Influencing College Selection

A number of themes regarding factors influencing college selection were pervasive across the participants' responses to the interview questions. Recapitulated themes of influence included the HBCU tradition, parental alumni status, and reverence of noteworthy alumni graduates who were viewed as viable role models. The responses provided by participants incorporated one or a number of these themes.

The factors influencing Stephen's selection of GSU and the influence of this selection on his perception of how the institution had cultivated his giftedness served as an organizing framework for this section. Stephen's rationale for selecting GSU was due in part to his parents' past affiliation with the institution. His perception of the admiration and respect his parents had for the school, particularly from their vantage point as alumni, significantly impacted his college selection process.

Stephen also spoke of his parents' accomplishments: both had received advanced degrees and were thriving in their chosen career fields. Stephen's perceptions were influenced not only by the accomplishments of his parents but also by their recommendation of GSU as a viable collegiate option. The message conveyed to Stephen was that the institution would support his academic giftedness by providing him with an environment that was conducive to learning, an environment that would instill in him the confidence to achieve his goals. Additionally, his parents saw the GSU environment as a supportive enclave in which he would also have a rewarding social experience.

From the numerous conversations I had with Stephen throughout the course of this study, I perceived that he found just what he and his parents predicted. As Stephen reported at the conclusion of his interview:

> *I would just like to say that my academic experience at Grambling has been enriching.*

SELF-PERCEPTION

This category uncovered a litany of responses from study participants. The reported self-perceptions they shared ranged from "intelligent" and "confident" to "cool guy." In general, I found the comments associated with self perception to be generally positive, whether from the teachers and administrators or from the actual academically gifted African American males themselves. Stephen in particular exuded what I would describe as an air of confidence and a strong sense of pride in his achievements. He appeared to be very self-assured in articulating how he planned to achieve his academic and career goals. Table 7.1 depicts Stephen's statements in response to the question regarding his self-perception.

After reviewing Stephen's interview transcript, I made a number of interesting observations. One of the questions in the standardized open-ended interview asked participants to describe how they would respond if someone referred to them as *gifted*. A common rejoinder among participants was, "I'm not gifted; I just work hard," or "I question the definition of the term people use in describing my abilities as being gifted." Stephen was the only participant to respond and use the term *gifted* in his self description. He said,

> I think you could have many interpretations of that word—gifted. Yes, I think you could call me gifted.

Friend 1 and Friend 2 provided extremely positive reports regarding their self-perceptions. They also perceived that their friends viewed them very positively and held them in high regard. According to Friend 2,

> I think I probably am now starting to realize what it's like to get on with the rest of my life. When I was younger, I had this picture of myself, how I would turn out as an adult. But now I realize that, you know, that it doesn't really jive with reality. Now I see my life sort of laid out.

Friend 2 went on to say, "I think I'm doing great now!" Friend 2 was a student who transferred to GSU from a predominantly White institution. Perhaps it was his transition into the HBCU environment that prompted the statements quoted above and his subsequent image adjustment. According to Davis (1991), Black colleges regularly restore positive direction to transfers from White campuses with shattered confidence.

Teachers 1 and 2 both perceived that an academically gifted African American male would possess a positive self-perception. When questioned about the perception friends of the academically gifted African American male would have of them, Teacher 2 responded:

> I think they see me as a straightforward person, as an ambitious person, and a person who has come here with a purpose and who is trying to fulfill that purpose.

Administrators 1 and 2 perceived the self-perception of the academically gifted African American male to be one of determination and focus. They also perceived this individual's friends would possess these same characteristics. Administrator 1 provided this description of such gifted collegians:

> Probably a studious young man, serious about his work; one who will succeed.

All of the statements provided by respondents as they related to self perception were informative and greatly assisted me in conceptualizing the importance of individual self-concept. Research tends to depict the African American student on the HBCU campus as lagging behind his or her counterpart on the TWI campus in areas such as standardized test scores, campus facilities, and high school GPA. However, Patricia Gurin and Edgar Epps (1975) found that African American students at HBCUs possessed more positive self images, stronger racial pride, and higher aspirations that did those on White campuses.

In Summary: Self-Perception

Statements regarding self-perception were varied but all seemed to cluster together in a positive direction. The important consideration was Stephen's self-perception and its impact on the institution's support of his giftedness. The findings associated with this category were very closely tied to findings in the previous category, factors influencing college selection.

Stephen's confidence and drive were developed in part due to his parents' and the institution's belief in his abilities. Support from both entities bolstered Stephen's self-perception, leading to his academic success and the eventual support of his giftedness. Additionally, it is important to note that the institution played a significant role in supporting Stephen's giftedness. Part of the HBCU mission, whether explicit or implicit, is the uplifting of students regardless of their levels of academic preparedness. Although Stephen's status as a high-achieving student was prized, he would have received equal attention and support had he been academically unprepared.

Stephen perceived that GSU would be supportive of his academic successes, but also believed the institution would support him if he experienced periods of academic problems. Research by G. Kannerstein (1978) revealed that HBCUs emphasize reality, which in turn allows these institutions to educate students with superior preparation, students from the weakest educational backgrounds, and the majority of students who fall between these categories. Although Stephen was identified as a high-achieving student, just the assurance that he had the support of the institution provided him with the necessary confidence to know that his academic giftedness was supported.

INSTITUTIONAL ENVIRONMENT

The information provided concerning interview respondents' perceptions of the institutional environment was mixed. Respondents reported the institution as promoting an environment that extolled the benefits of collaboration. Many reported that they found a healthy mix of collaboration and competition, but even these individuals found a prevailing sentiment of cooperation and teamwork on campus. Stephen cited collaboration as a key element for success in his chosen field of study:

When it comes time for studying, it's always good to like study in groups or something like that. If I didn't know something, I could always, you know, call on one of my classmates—other students.

In addition to stressing the importance of collaboration, I found Stephen's comments regarding the advice he would provide an academically gifted African male who was thinking of attending GSU after high school graduation to be indicative of his feelings regarding the institutional environment. Stephen declared that

I would encourage him; I would definitely encourage him.

Stephen's statement seemed to emphasize not only the respect he had for GSU but also his level of comfort in recommending that another high-achieving student attend the institution. According to Ernest Pascarella (1980), much is to be learned from HBCUs in that they are able to develop supportive institutional climates for students while simultaneously maintaining academic standards and intellectual rigor.

Friend 1 and Friend 2 both reported that they found the institution to be collaborative—so much so that Friend 2 said he found it overly collaborative at times:

It's a good feeling to be in a partnership with the other students, and, you know, you have the collegiate type of atmosphere here, but it may be just a little bit overdone for me. Because what happens is, you have some students who kind of got into this place through the back door in the first place, and then, they just use that to kind of tread water. . . . I'm not sure that does them any good, and it drags down the high achievers because the professors always have to teach to the bottom of the class.

Friend 2's statement speaks to an ongoing problem that has been cited numerous times in the gifted literature: namely, our failure to provide differentiated instruction for our most able students. According to the United States Department of Education (1993), we have consistently failed to provide educational opportunities for students who perform at high levels. Additionally, the National Commission on Excellence in Education, although speaking to students in the K-12 sector, asserted:

Our goal must be to develop the talents of all to their fullest. Attaining that goal requires that we expect and assist all students to work to the limits of their capabilities. We should expect schools to have genuinely high standards rather than minimum ones, and parents to support and encourage their children to make the most of their talents and abilities.

I included most of Friend 2's comment to reveal the depth of his response regarding the institutional environment he perceived to exist on the GSU campus. I thought his statement was telling in that he found the environment to bend too far in the direction of collaboration, sometimes at the expense of academic excellence. Despite this brief diatribe, Friend 2 did go on to state that he had a great deal of administration and respect for the institution and was delighted to be enrolled there.

Teachers 1 and 2 perceived that an academically gifted African American male would find the institutional environment to consist of both collaborative and competitive elements. Each teacher stated that the competitive aspect of the institutional environment was generated primarily in classroom contexts. Competition was not said to be intense or negative but rather a natural part of the demands placed on the students by academic departments that demanded excellence. The collaborative component of the institutional context was viewed as a necessary part of the overall college matriculation process.

Administrators 1 and 2 provided comments that were closely aligned with the comments of Teachers 1 and 2. They too perceived that the environment would share collaborative and competitive aspects. Administrator 1 advanced an interesting dichotomy along these lines, stating that the environment was collaborative as far as classroom assignments and projects were concerned but competitive in the areas of internships and scholarships. Administrator 1 commented:

> *There's only so much space here. So, if you're not about the business, then sometimes you just might need to leave. So, it's competitive.*

The views expressed by the respondents related to their perceptions of the GSU environment provided a broad view of the campus community. Although each participant advanced the notion of a campus environment that promoted collaboration, a competitive undertone among students was also noted. The most striking discovery I made was that collaboration and competition worked together in a synergistic fashion in the HBCU context to produce a comfortable institutional environment for all of the respondents who were interviewed.

In Summary: Institutional Environment

Questions relating to the institutional environment category concluded the standardized open-ended interview with Stephen James and the other respondents at GSU. Stephen's perception of how the institutional environment impacted his perception of how the college supported his giftedness is reflected in his responses captured in Table 7.1. Stephen perceived the institutional environment as one of collaboration. He found his relationship with his peers as well as his instructors to be beneficial in his academic endeavors. When asked about the one thing he would change regarding his academic experience at GSU, Stephen replied: "I'm kind of content right now at this time. I don't think I would change too much, because like I say, I'm kind of complacent with things."

According to Ernest Pascarella (1980), if traditionally White institutions (TWIs) followed the lead of HBCUs in creating an educational environment that was more conducive to the success of African American students on campus, they could potentially contribute to the creation of a more supportive and validating climate for Black students when they are the minority culture on campus. Stephen's perception of a collaborative institutional environment shaped his view of the institution and led to his feeling of contentment. Because of the relationship he maintained with his peers and instructors, Stephen perceived the institution as being supportive of his academic giftedness, primarily by providing him with needed academic assistance and guidance to successfully matriculate at GSU.

Trey and Stephen: What I Learned from Their Experiences

The two cases presented in this study revealed a number of significant differences. The differences cited in the study enhanced my level of knowledge concerning the experiences and resulting perceptions of these two academically gifted African American males. These differences were noted regarding the relationships they maintained with their respective institutions in the cultivation of their academic giftedness.

One of the primary differences I found to exist was in the relationships Trey Williams and Stephen James maintained with faculty. Trey's relationships with faculty centered solely on academic issues. Relationships with faculty that extended beyond classroom interactions and engagements that included discussions on topics other than academics were virtually nonexistent, while Stephen maintained a number of relationships with faculty members both in and outside of the classroom context. Although Stephen reported his out-of-classroom interactions with faculty to be limited, subsequent interview and observational data revealed a problem with this report. His actual engagements with faculty ranged from casual interactions with his research advisor to planned formal consultations with the head of the chemistry department.

Relationships with faculty, although different in the two settings (HBCU and TWI), were extremely important across cases. It was the connections with faculty that these students were able to establish beyond the classroom that were proven to most significantly impact their academic success. Although both Trey and Stephen were experiencing academic success, this did not preclude their establishment and maintenance of key relationships with faculty. These relationships served to support these students not only academically but also in nonacademic pursuits.

Another key difference I noted after analyzing the interview data was associated with the category that addressed the influence and support provided by the family unit. Trey Williams's mother and brother served as a source of academic and emotional support, with his mother serving as his primary support source.

The counseling and guidance Trey's mother provided her son assisted him in achieving his academic goals. Her recommendations regarding his selection of TAMUC provided insight on her relative influence on his college decision-making process. Embedded in her recommendations were discussions related to issues such as class size and relationships with faculty.

Stephen James's family also played an integral role during his college matriculation. His parents' status as graduates of GSU was the key factor guiding his decision to attend the institution. Their recommendations that Stephen attend GSU were based on their experiences and the rich cultural tradition they perceived Stephen would find on the campus if he selected the institution. Thus, his parents' status as both advocates and graduates of Grambling greatly influenced Stephen's decision-making process.

This category revealed the various roles parents played in influencing and supporting their son's academic achievement. Issues such as class size and relationships with faculty were pervasive in the discussion Trey's family had with him in relation to his college selection process. Stephen's family members centered their discussion on more abstract issues such as cultural tradition and the institutional environment. Although issues such as class size and the importance of establishing relationships with faculty were probably issues of importance to Stephen's family as well, they were viewed as ancillary benefits that they believed their son would obtain if he selected an HBCU, namely, GSU, as his undergraduate institution.

The two cases also presented differences in the area of self-perception. Trey Williams's reported self-perception reflected a positive self-image. Yet when teachers and administrators at TAMUC were questioned, their responses tended to significantly vary from Trey's report. Some of the responses teachers and administrators provided reflected a deep sense of insecurity in academic ability. Trey's interview responses did not reflect this questioning and sense of reservation about his abilities. Stephen James presented positive statements regarding his self-perception. All of the individuals interviewed also presented these same positive views concerning self-perception. The only inferences made by faculty and administrators at GSU that could be construed as questioning the abilities of the academically gifted African American male were associated with the initial college experience (i.e., the first day of class or the submission of the first assignment), but did not imply that there existed an ongoing questioning of abilities as suggested by the faculty and administrators at TAMUC.

The final noteworthy difference between the two cases was observed in the interview data associated with institutional environment. Trey Williams found the institutional environment to be both collaborative and competitive. Trey's primary collaborations occurred with Friend 1, who served as his research partner. He expressed the view that the competitive side of the institution was found primarily in classroom engagements. His perception that White students received an unfair competitive advantage greatly impacted his view of the institutional environment. Teachers and administrators reported in their interview statements that they perceived the campus environment as balanced in its level of collaboration and competition; some stated that competition was nonexistent.

Stephen James found the institutional environment on the GSU campus to be collaborative in nature. His relationships with his peers were said to have greatly influenced his success at the institution. Although the teachers and administrators reported a mixture of collaboration and competition, they all expressed their view of the two coexisting in harmony on the campus. One of the participants identified the competitive element on campus as a "friendly type of competition."

This category revealed the importance of institutional environment regardless of campus demographic profile. I also discovered how the institutional environment molds and shapes the experiences and resulting perceptions of academically gifted students. My initial thoughts were that gifted students were either not affected or only minimally affected by the institutional environment due to their status as high achievers. Yet what I found was that although these students were gifted, they were greatly impacted by the context and culture on their respective campuses. From my own personal experiences, I was reminded of how important peers and collaboration and a supportive faculty and campus community were for students completing a rigorous program such as chemistry. Additionally, this category revealed the importance of promoting collaboration and minimizing competition in the higher education context—regardless of institutional racial composition.

GROUNDED THEORIES

Theories were developed regarding both Trey and Stephen subsequent to analyzing the case study data. Theory 1 categorized findings from Case 1 (Trey) and Theory 2 categorized the findings from Case 2 (Stephen).

> *Theory 1:* The research-oriented approach to education maintained by Texas A&M University—Commerce (TAMUC) supported Trey Williams's academic giftedness in the institutional setting but did not thoroughly support his academic giftedness outside of the institutional setting.
>
> *Theory 2:* The liberal arts approach to education maintained by Grambling State University (GSU) supported Stephen James's academic giftedness within and outside of the institutional setting.

Theory 1 was developed based on the collected findings from the data. The issues presented in Case 1 focused on Trey's relationship with the institution. The findings from the categories suggested that the institutional climate and the general approach to education maintained by TAMUC impacted Trey's perception of how the institution cultivated his academic giftedness. In essence, all of the categories were related to the institution's overall approach to education.

Data revealed that TAMUC, although a liberal arts institution, approached education from a research-oriented perspective. Trey's interactions with faculty were overwhelmingly one-dimensional, solely reflecting an adherence to matters of academic importance. There appeared to be a lack of rapport between student and faculty beyond the classroom. Thus the general wellness, the view of the student as a "whole person," as both academic and social, was split and the social side truncated. Processing students through course syllabi appeared to be the standard modus operandi.

According to Robert and Jon Solomon (1993), the most obvious source of neglect among undergraduate student populations often occurs when the university adheres to the idea of being a research enclave or attempts to make the conversion to such an enclave, that is, to become a research university. Although I am exercising some license and stretching this statement to apply to Trey's situation within his department and institution, the overall implication is essentially the same. Once beyond the classroom or the threshold of the laboratory, Trey's relationships with faculty seemed to evaporate into thin air. The emphasis and educational approach of the institution and its agents seemed to highlight research and scholarly activity without as much concern for the human factor, a factor that is indicative of the liberal arts model.

In responding to the question of whether he perceived the institution as being helpful during his transition process from high school to college, Trey asserted,

No, as far as the people are concerned, educators or academic advisors, I would say no. I'm the only one who was instrumental in doing all that. It was, like, get your money and they were gone on to the next person somewhere else.

This statement revealed Trey's perception regarding institutional support. Additionally, Trey commented on the competition and favoritism that he believed existed within his department as well as within the institution. In the informal conversational interview I conducted with him, he stated:

I'm just here to do the best I can because I know the people who are being favored, they're not making my way; I have to make my own, so I just have to do the best I can.

Statements such as these speak to the level of competition and also the level of support Trey perceived to exist for his academic achievement and ultimately his giftedness. According to Jacqueline Fleming (1984), African American students in White schools often report increasing dissatisfaction with academic life, negative attitudes toward teachers who, they feel, grade unfairly, limited return for time and effort invested in schoolwork, and no net improvement in their academic performance.

In addition to these findings, the educational mission of the institution was found to significantly influence Trey's perception of how the institution supported his giftedness. According to Ernest Boyer (1987), the mission of liberal arts and comprehensive colleges has been focused mainly on undergraduate teaching; yet, it is critical to note that many of these institutions embrace the research model approach. The adherence to the research model, with its emphasis on empirical and dispassionate inquiry, tends to move away from the liberal arts model, which embraces wellness and a concern for the whole student. The adoption of this model by TAMUC appears to have influenced Trey's perception concerning the institution's lack of support of his academic giftedness.

Addressing the needs of the gifted collegian, S. R. Friedlander and C. E. Watkins (1984) reported that these students cope with the same pressures that all college students face, such as independence, difficulty in assuming a sense of responsibility, increased competition and loneliness, and changing values and self-concept. For Trey Williams, these pressures appeared to be exacerbated by the research-oriented model adopted by TAMUC. From my observations, this model has led to something of a void in the number of meaningful relationships that students and faculty are able to establish and a dichotomous approach to academic and social issues. This model varies from the liberal arts model with its advancement of student learning, growth, and development as the central tenets in its approach.

Another key finding associated with Trey Williams's interview as it related to the institutional context had to do with his statement regarding his need for an environment that promoted creativity. Based on the research by Barbara Shade (1982) and Walter Allen (1986), African American students fare better in institutional contexts that provide opportunities for self-expression, creativity, and innovation rather than in settings that stress forms of teaching and learning that are overly structured and pedantic. Thus, Trey's statement, "I try to be creative; I like being spontaneous. I'm the type of person that I don't like people to know my next move," should be particularly meaningful to the institution in that it speaks to the level of importance he was attaching to his creative skills and abilities; information that is instructive of the type of institutional environment that is critical for the cultivation of academic giftedness.

The focus of the research institution is on scholarly pursuits through actively research-oriented engagements; hence, activity outside of this research-oriented focus tends to be subordinated to these efforts. Boyer, again, said that the undergraduate college, at its best, is an institution committed to knowledge, backed by wisdom—a place where students through creative teaching, are encouraged to become intellectually engaged. Trey cited the need for creativity in his academic pursuits, but perceived that this need was not being thoroughly supported.

As Allen (1986) asserted, the need for creativity has been identified as an important component in the African American student's academic experience. This component is especially important for the academically gifted student. Yet Trey found the institutional environment to be contrived: "preplanned" was the actual term he used. If the institution is to truly support Trey's academic giftedness, amendments must be made to the institutional environment in general and to classroom teaching and learning engagements in particular—amendments that may run counter to the research-oriented approach to education the institution has embraced.

Theory 2 is also based on research findings gleaned from interviews, observations, and written documents. Stephen's relationship with the institution proved to be supportive of his academic giftedness within and outside of the institutional setting. The primary means of supporting Stephen's giftedness was through the liberal arts approach the institution maintained toward education. According to Joan B. Hirt in her book *Where You Work Matters: Student Affairs Administrators at Different Types of Institutions* the mission of the liberal arts college focuses on "'personal education' that emphasizes 'critical thinking' and 'personal growth' and leads to 'professional success' and 'productive lives as global citizens' upon graduation" (p. 23). This approach to education appeared to become manifest in a number of areas on the GSU campus.

Why would an HBCU such as Grambling adhere to the principles set forth in the liberal arts approach to education? According to Charles Willie and Ronald Edmonds, on the conceptual level, Black colleges believe in a liberal arts education but also insist on the utility of this education; they embrace and do not fear its combination with career education. The very inception of the HBCU was based on egalitarian ideals, a commitment to serve the needs of a population that was denied access to the benefits of obtaining a college education. This ideal subsequently advanced the notion of meeting not only the academic needs of the student but also the social, emotional, and spiritual needs of the student as well—characteristics indicative of the liberal arts approach to education. Willie and Edmonds go on to note that "The HBCU wished to graduate seniors whose diplomas marked the completion of an undergraduate education, not simply the removal of educational handicaps."

The HBCU philosophy advanced by Willie and Edmonds essentially characterized the GSU campus community. I found Stephen's interactions with faculty inside and outside of the classroom setting to provide him with a continual source of support. My findings were based on observations and interview data I procured from Stephen and the numerous other respondents on campus. The institution's liberal arts approach, the relationship Stephen maintained with his peers, and the institutional environment that promoted collaboration provided an enclave that promoted success. Roebuck and Murty's (1993) research found HBCUs that provide an African American culture and ambiance that many students found essential to their social functioning and mental health. Grambling provided Stephen with these essential elements through its commitment to enhancing Stephen's collegiate experience from both an academic and a nonacademic perspective. According to S. J. Barthelemy (1984),

> The characteristics of the institution are not easy to discern, but we can point to the *esprit de corps* that is evident among students, the interactions among faculty, and between faculty and students outside the classroom, and above all, the philosophy and value orientation of the institution. (p. 16)

When asked to complete the statement, "Grambling is . . .", Stephen reported:

> *Grambling is a university, a great tradition, a great people, and it's a good place for an education and a true college experience. That's how I would define Grambling.*

This characterization of the institution encapsulated Stephen's overall perception of GSU and his positive image of the education he was receiving. An education based on a concern for developing and cultivating the whole student and on preparation for the student to function in society was what he perceived the institution was providing. When questioned about exposure and opportunities to interact with non-African Americans outside of the GSU campus, Stephen replied:

> *I can adapt to each culture and I think that's what makes an adult an adult—being able to communicate with others. I don't say that I'm-one dimensional because I chose to come here to Grambling . . . that I can only communicate with my own kind.*

Although GSU's student population was primarily African American, Stephen perceived that the institution provided him with the support necessary for him to function beyond the HBCU context. W. M. Hemmons (1982), in a comparative study of African American student attitudes on a Black campus and those on a predominantly White campus, found that twice as many African American students on Black campuses as on White campuses felt that their school (their HBCU) prepared them for membership in the American mainstream.

Another major area in which the liberal arts model was promoted on the GSU campus was through the numerous interactions Stephen had with faculty. The relationships he maintained with faculty provided him with the support systems necessary to achieve academic success. These relationships also protected Stephen's confidence and belief in his abilities. In discussing the impact that relationships with faculty had on the achievement potential of African American students, Benjamin E. Mays, (1971) the late president of Morehouse College, posited: "It wasn't affluence. . . . it was a few able, dedicated teachers who widened the Negro's horizon and made him believe that he could do big and worthwhile things" (p. 173).

The founding mission of the HBCU embraces the tenets set forth in the liberal arts tradition, namely, the education of the whole student. According to Kannerstein (1978),

> The Black college has a dual mission. It is about human excellence, the superior education and training of tender minds, nourishment of the creative imagination, and reverence for learning; it is also about the development of moral character and the production of better men and women for a more humane, decent, and open world. (p. 55)

Through a commitment to this mission and an attendant belief in the ideals advanced by the liberal arts approach to education, GSU provided support for Stephen's academic giftedness within and outside of the classroom environment. GSU's adherence to this approach has also served to shape Stephen's perceptions regarding the institution's commitment to his educational success. When asked to state his perceptions regarding the school's role in the cultivation of his giftedness, Stephen said:

I can truly say that Grambling has molded me to become more mature. In high school I was more naïve and I just wanted to get through, but when I came to Grambling, it really opened my eyes to industry and the real world.

W. E. B. Du Bois (1961) stated that the Black college "must maintain the standards of popular education, it must seek the social regeneration of the Negro, and it must help in the solution of problems of race contact and cooperation" (p. 87). Although Du Bois's ideas were expressed many years ago, this tripartite charge continues to characterize the mission of the HBCU today. Fortunately, students like Stephen James are the beneficiaries.

RECOMMENDATIONS AND CONCLUSIONS

This study served as an empirical investigation of two different institutional environments and of the way each environment affected an African American male's perception of how the institution cultivated his academic giftedness. The original research question was answered; the perceptions of both case study participants were uncovered and subsequently addressed. The study raised important questions for individuals working in fields such as gifted and talented and postsecondary retention. A number of findings presented widespread implications for individuals interested in identifying salient psychosocial issues impacting the gifted postsecondary student.

Important questions raised by this study included the following: Did the institution's approach to educating students affect the student's perception of the cultivation of his giftedness? Did the homogeneity of the institution affect the student's perception of the cultivation of his giftedness? To answer first question, the data revealed significant differences in the approach the two institutions appeared to take in their educational missions. Although both institutions were classified as four-year liberal arts institutions, TAMUC did not seem to fit within the parameters of this classification. The campus environment at TAMUC closely resembled the environment of a typical research institution. The liberal arts model advances the notion of the whole student, with an emphasis on the social as well as the academic.

Trey's interactions with faculty were limited, primarily centering on research and engagements within the confines of the classroom. Stephen James experienced a campus environment that fostered collaboration, an environment in which instructors took an active role in their students' lives. A more holistic approach to student education appeared to characterize the GSU campus context. Much is to be said for the liberal arts model in relation to the benefits students accrue from their engagements with peers, faculty, and administrators.

According to Gurin and Epps (1975), the liberal arts curricular emphasis significantly enhanced the prestige, academic ability levels, and nontraditional career choice of Black males at the end of their freshman year. GSU's true emphasis on the tenets of the liberal arts model provided Stephen with the institutional support necessary for the cultivation of his academic giftedness. Although GSU and TAMUC were similar in size, GSU's commitment to addressing the needs of the whole student was apparent during my many campus observations. Kannerstein (1978) found that the dedication of Black colleges is an expression of the belief that they can truly serve *their* people and preserve *their* culture while they offer an education and a unique experience to people of all backgrounds.

The second question highlighted the differences in racial composition on the two campuses and the effect of these differences on the student's perception of the institution's cultivation of his giftedness. Inasmuch as racial composition was noted, primarily due to the two different types of institutional contexts selected for this study, it did not overly influence the primary case study participants' campus experiences. When Trey Williams was asked to respond to a question concerning his collegiate experiences if TAMUC had been a predominantly Black institution, he said, "You can't live in a Utopian type of world. You have to have diversity." He also commented, "If I had to choose going to a college all over again, Black or White, I'd really choose the one that's Black and White."

Trey's statements reveal that racial composition was not perceived as being of great significance in his overall collegiate experience. His interview responses revealed that other factors, such as relationships with faculty, family influence and support, and relationships with peers, took precedence over issues such as the campus racial demographic profile. My recommendation to the field and to those who work with academically gifted African American male students is to focus on these factors and perhaps the other categories uncovered in this study to determine the relative impact they have on the students' perceptions of how the institution cultivates their giftedness.

Stephen James also provided a number of responses indicating that the campus racial composition was not an important factor in his perception regarding the institution's support of his giftedness. When asked if being an African American mattered on the GSU campus, Stephen stated, "No, it doesn't, because I truly believe in the campus motto—'Everybody is somebody.' So, just because I'm Black, I can't say that I would be treated differently." The fact that Stephen was in an institution with other African American students appeared to become manifest solely in his responses related to campus racial composition. Still another statement Stephen made during the interview, which lends credence to this assertion, asked him to identify the factor(s) that most significantly contributed to his academic achievement. Stephen's reply was, "My ambition to learn, my devotion to studying."

Institutional racial composition appeared to play a minor role in the views these two students expressed regarding their perception of how the institution had cultivated their academic giftedness. Again, these findings indicate the importance of observing factors beyond the commonly held notions concerning the impact of racial composition on the collegiate experience of the African American student—particularly the gifted student. Therefore, my recommendation to the field is to focus on alternative issues that appear to exert a greater impact on the academically gifted African American male's perception of institutional support of his giftedness. Perhaps this population could be better served by focusing on issues stemming from the categories listed above, categories such as relationships with faculty, peer relationships, and institutional environment. While race is an important consideration in the cultivation of academic giftedness for these students, it is not of overarching importance.

Retrospection and Contemplation:
An Interview with Trey Williams
10 Years Later

As I was pulling together the final chapters of this book, I decided to see if I could locate Trey Williams. A few phone calls, Facebook connections, and general inquiries later, I was able to track him down. When I asked him about his past experiences and present position, he told me that he completed his undergraduate studies in chemistry in 1997 and went on to graduate school, completing a doctorate of pharmacy degree in 2002. Since completing both his undergraduate and his graduate (professional) studies, he has been employed as a clinical pharmacist by a major food store chain. We agreed to meet not only to catch up but also to complete a short interview—an interview that would highlight Trey's perspectives as a gifted African American male some 10 years after the initial interview.

1. Does your giftedness play a role in your professional life? If so how?

Trey: I would not necessarily categorize it as giftedness. . . . I work hard, I had excellent teachers, a mother, which all helped to captivate my mind and lead me in a certain direction in life. So just based on those things I would not say it was about giftedness. But to answer the question directly, yes, yes I am very detailed and in my profession and that's what it is all about: detail. If you miss the detail you pretty much miss the whole boat.

2. If someone described you as gifted, how would you respond?

Trey: Well again. . . . Early on I was steered in the direction of mathematics and usually mathematics and science go hand-in-hand.
Bonner: So, if someone described you as gifted. . . . you would say?
Trey: No I am not gifted: everyone has a gift. . . . whatever that gift is, I just have an inclination. We are all born with gifts, it is just I had people to captivate my mind.

3. Who comprises your professional support network?

Trey: My professional support network is first and foremost my mom. Even though she is in an unrelated discipline, she is still part of my support system. Also my staff that I manage, they are part of my immediate professional network. I think my immediate staff is the closest to my professional network that I can speak about at this point in time.

4. Who comprises your social support network?

Trey: It is kind of funny, my mom wears many hats when it comes to my life—professional and social. She is a major part of my social network. But my girlfriend also is a big part of my social network as well. Besides them I have some colleagues that I keep contact with from time to time, but on a constant basis, I would say my mother and girlfriend comprise my social support network.

5. Does mentoring play a role in your professional life, and if so how?

Trey: To group this question with the previous question I answered, my brother also plays a role in my social support network—I forgot about him. But to answer this question, mentoring, well. . . . I have not formally mentored anyone yet but it is coming on the horizon. I will become a "preceptor," which is a type of mentorship program where professional students go on different rotations to gain insight on various work experiences. But informally I have a couple of people, related to me as well as not related to me, who just graduated from high school that I mentor. They look up to me because they see someone they know, not just someone they saw or heard on TV; they see someone who is out here making a difference. They really know me and I guess that inspires them to say, "I want to follow in his footsteps." That gives me a good feeling to know that, so definitely on an informal basis I am doing some type of mentoring—just nothing formal yet.

Bonner: Okay. . . . now let me just flip it around. What about you being mentored? Does mentoring play a role in your professional life?

Trey: Well, I wasn't mentored by anyone other than my mom. When I was three years old, that was when the mentoring came about. Every single day there was some type of mathematics or mathematics training that she drilled me on. . . . It could have been counting money or other things. She drilled and drilled and my interest grew. But I wasn't mentored in the formal ways you see now, you know, like the Boys and Girls Club or Big Brothers of America (I forget the correct title for it), but growing up in my small town they did not have those types of opportunities for us. So I had to rely on the one person who could mentor me, and of course that was my mother.

6.   Have you had an opportunity to mentor a gifted African American student?

Trey: Again, on an informal basis, yes. I have a cousin that is going into the same discipline I was in. He is graduating from high school next year and he is doing really well. I try to make time for my cousin; it helps because he relates to me. Another relative who graduated last year is also interested in my discipline; I take real pride in that. It is really powerful for me to know that someone close to you is doing good things, rather than having to only see people on TV who are doing good things. I really hope that I can be part of the drive they have for this discipline.

7.   If you have changed since your undergraduate days, what has changed the most?

Trey: From a professional point of view, I think I am more detailed. My attention to detail is more focused then when I first began. Frankly, in my discipline, I am demanded to be focused on details to get the job done or else I am in trouble. I can't complain about how things are going in my life. But the attention to detail is the most important thing that has changed about me.

8.   Did your undergraduate academic experience affect your professional success? If so, how?

Trey: Yes it did! My undergraduate degree program did not have that many African Americans at the time. I don't know how it is now, but at that particular time there were not that many. I was cool with it, but I was made to feel quite aware of it. I had a professor who told me that I was not going to make it due to the fact of my race. But that did not affect me; I already had a drive for school. It [his achievement] would have been the same even if my professor did not tell me that. But that experience was something to note. I did get my undergraduate degree in chemistry
Bonner: This was a high school teacher or professor?
Trey: Professor! So again it was something to note, and it was not surprising. This was not surprising to me; I come from a small town and racial barriers are still there so I was not shocked that this happened to me. But again it is something to note and raise an eyebrow at. It interesting that someone in academia would hint towards something like that. But that's the world!

9.   Did your undergraduate social experience affect your professional success? If so, how?

Trey: Yes! I had some classmates that made the experience more enjoyable; we had a great time. They were a good group of classmates; there were actually three, two were twins and one was not. I felt that they made class lots more fun because we had fun with it. We cracked jokes and laughed; our discipline was like cut and dry so having those classmates helped.

10. Did the type of institution you attended play a role in your professional success? And by the type of institution you selected, I mean attending a predominantly White institution versus a predominately Black institution.

Trey: I really didn't think of comparing those two at all really, for my undergrad or even for the professional school I went to. As a matter of fact, it is kind of ironic because I was going to go as an undergrad to the university where I got my professional degree, but I took a tour. It was such a huge university and the classes were very large. My mom was like, "You need to apply to a university where they have more hands-on and more one-on-one attention." Then we chose a smaller university. We didn't narrow it down based on if it was a White- or predominately Black-serving institution. Now, I would say that with my professional degree, I never did again think of anything like that. I just overheard that my chosen school was the best university to go to.

I took a gamble and I don't gamble, but I took a chance and chose to apply to only that one professional school. If they didn't accept me, then that was it. I don't know why I didn't leave myself an alternative. So that was the school I wanted. Only when I got into the program did I start hearing about other universities that were predominately African American universities. And I was told, directly, that they were at the bottom of the barrel. Folks said that they [predominantly Black institutions] didn't have their act together. I didn't know that was what some people thought until I got admitted into the professional program I was in and, um, that is unfortunate, but those were some of the things that people said at the time. I don't know how it is now.

11. What advice would you give another gifted African American male to insure his academic success as an undergraduate student?

Trey: Well, know what you came here for—to get a degree—and do not party all the time and just go wild. Be specific in what you are doing to achieve your undergraduate degree, because it is so easy to slip, especially when you don't have any oversight. It is not like when you're in high school or grade school when your parents say do your homework, get this done, get that done; when you get to college you are in charge of yourself. You have to do it all, because nobody else is going to tell you.

Some of the professors don't care—as a matter of fact, I was told by a professor that I get paid the same if you are here or not. So I learned that it is always on you. You have to have that type of drive; no matter what you are there for, you have to go for it. I am not saying that you shouldn't have fun because, yeah, it's a different experience and there is nothing wrong with having fun, but you are there to graduate.

12.   In retrospect, what is the most significant barrier to the success of gifted African American students, both male and female? So if you have to look back at your experiences and identify some barriers, what are the most significant?

Trey: Let's see. Applying to me personally, specifically it is my skin color. I didn't really experience that [skin color as a barrier] until I got into my professional program to obtain my professional degree, but definitely it's skin color. That is the most significant barrier I can think of. It is quite unfortunate, but again you have to learn to be there and stick with it and not give up and realize that you should not get wrapped up in it. And I realized that I was there to obtain the degree that I wanted to obtain. So definitely it's skin color and my race.

Bonner: Would you say that this [skin color] is a barrier for African American females as well?

Trey: Well, yes, I do. Not saying that the experience is going to be overwhelming, but it is still a factor. I don't care what anybody says. It is the new millennium and if you think otherwise you are kidding yourself. It [skin color and race] is always going to be a barrier, I guess. From the time you're born to the time you are dead. It is going to be one of the barriers with every situation, but the main thing is your persistence and your determination in achieving the goals that you want to achieve. If you can do those things, you'll succeed and move past those barriers. You don't want to have that barrier dictate or determine your fate.

The gender difference is another barrier, you know, men versus women. I feel that it still plays a role, but how much I don't know as opposed to skin color, which I know does play a role. It is kind of funny that you mentioned that [gender], because in my undergrad years, I had a high school classmate that was African American and she was one of two who went to the same university I attended. She wanted a job, so we created this scheme to call the company and ask if there were any positions available, and she was told that there were no positions available. Not even 10 minutes later she called back and sounded like a White girl, and all of a sudden there were positions available. That was the race card, and honestly we knew what the outcome would be. We just wanted to call and confirm it. And again it wasn't surprising, but gender, yeah, I think there is still some trouble.

13.   What environment would you create for a gifted African American undergraduate student that would be more helpful than the situation you faced as an undergraduate?

Trey: I don't know if I would create an environment that is all that different from mine. One of the main factors of college is how well rounded you are, both in social and academic circles. College is not about academics only, and again it is not about social only. It's a mixture of the two, and people who give out scholarships look at that. And the same thing applies just in general, especially in the lives of African Americans. You have to be well rounded. You can't just be in a utopian environment and that's it. Now, I don't think I had this rough time growing up.

I know my parents didn't want me to be exposed to things, but, you know, when the time came when I was older I was able to handle situations. Certain racial experiences. I am sure that there are some African Americans who went through more situations than I have, but definitely everything in life is a stage. And I would tell people that things aren't always how you want them to be, but basically that is the price you pay for advancement. I don't know if I would change the environment that I went through, because again I didn't go through a laundry list of racial issues myself. . . .

14. What would you do to help improve the conditions for another African American male who is coming through—if you could improve the conditions of the environment you previously mentioned?

Trey: I would talk to the individual and let them know this is what you are going to have to do if you are here. On the way you may face an issue that may simply be there just to teach you how to handle life. You have to handle life and not go off the deep end. I have seen things in life happen, and I always wonder how people will respond, and all people have to do sometimes is say the wrong word or do the wrong thing and things spiral down. I was always taught to keep a level head, regardless. It is important to never let your emotions get to you, so definitely I would tell them something like that. I think I would say something to that effect and get the person to become aware of things that could happen, not saying that they will, but they are certainly a possibility.

15. If you had a sizable amount of money to give support to African American students, what stipulations would you place on these funds in an effort to help these students succeed?

Trey: Definitely their academics, because that is why they are there. Yes, academics are important but social-wise, I would be worried about them getting in trouble. I am talking about anything in regards to the law, so none of that could be part of their experiences. I don't want that; I have never been in trouble like that and I made it, so I know the person can make it without getting into trouble. I see that people who are African American or other minority races have more excuses, they sometimes say things like "trouble always finds me," but you know basically if you don't hang around people who are troublemakers then you won't get into trouble. I think more so that people have excuses more than they have reasons. They should maintain a proper grade point average. I'm not just looking more towards people who get cum laude grades or magna cum laude grades, but towards people who care about social issues. I want them to be active in the community; that is definitely a plus. It wouldn't be a final deciding factor, because I wasn't very active in my community when I was an undergrad, but now it's an important factor.

16.   If you could structure the ideal academic environment for academically gift-
       ed African American males, what would you include and what would that
       environment look like?

Trey: As far as giftedness, or can it be anything?

Bonner: It can be anything. This is your world and you can make an ideal
environment for gifted African American males to be successful; what do you
think should be included in this environment?

Trey: I think that the parents play the utmost vital role. The parents will instruct
the kids and not let the kids raise themselves. I know it's hard when the parents
don't raise them and you have someone who is not qualified raising them, but definitely that. The source of your success is often the parents, mom and dad.

It can also be who you hang out with even after you receive instructions from
your parents to not hang out with people who are troublemakers; who are known
to get into trouble, and again, it's always guilt by association. Even though you
are not the one who is a part of it, that type of person or troublemaker will hold
you down, because if you are there it means you are doing it [some nefarious act]
too. It is one of those things that can make you or break you if that's who you are
associating yourself with. Along with that come extracurricular activities. I mean
everything comes with a price. I don't drink alcohol and I don't do recreational
drugs and I never have. . . . not even one time. I'm more like a disciplinarian; I'm
strict like that because that was instilled in me. I know people drink and do recreational drugs, but that's their prerogative, but it's not for me. I think those would
be the main things.

I would also tell them to make sure they are on top of their academics. I'm
not a reader. Of course again, my mom didn't have me read for enjoyment;
she didn't stress that. It was more about the math, but certainly I was exposed
to things. . . . I would have these males to read for enjoyment if that was their
thing.

I think a lot of times people go and graduate from high school and then college and they have a dream of what they want to be and how much money they
want to make, but then they never really view what they need to do to get to that
point. And not to discredit any degree, but you can't really have a "rinky dink"
type of degree and expect to make all this money. You just can't do it! You have to
set yourself up in a discipline that warrants the type of luxury you want. You can't
just sit there and get those different types of degrees and expect to be making all
this money. I think that especially these days with the economy so bad, people are
having a hard time finding a job, and a lot of times the jobs they find are not in
the fields that their degrees are in. So if you set yourself up in the right field, you
shouldn't have that problem.

I'm thinking that this [finding a stable profession] is why my mom forced me to
focus on math and science because it is key to becoming financially successful—if
that is what you determine success to be. Though the chemistry classes and the
biology classes are hard, you can do it and then you can expect the type of financial

success that you want. I would definitely steer those individuals towards that, because that is what I went through and I have no complaints.

17.   If you could name the most important academic or personal issues that are key to the success of gifted African American males, what would they be?

Trey: Okay, determination and persistence. That's key. Again it goes back to who you surround yourself with; that is very vital. Having the thought of what you came here for and not wavering from that is important. If you knew that, I think that would be very, very crucial to your success. Otherwise you run around lost and wondering. So in general, knowing what you want to do and knowing how you want to do it and having a plan is critical to determine your success.

18.   What advice would give another gifted African American male who is interested in pursuing a professional degree?

Trey: Be influenced by your own mind and don't let anybody else determine your fate. If you have a plan of action and you know what you want to do, don't let anyone else tell you otherwise, whether it is someone on the professional or social side. That happened to me, but I wouldn't let that person deter me. If I had listened to that particular individual, I wouldn't have this professional degree that I have now. It is certainly hurtful and very dissatisfying, but don't let anyone control you like that. There are a lot of people who don't want you to make it, to be quite frank, and it's not only Caucasians but it's African Americans too.

19.   What is the most pressing issue that gifted African American males face in the professional world?

Trey: A lot of times people just don't want you to attain your goals. and that is when your own self-persistence and determination comes into play. I think that happens regardless of race. So, the pressing issue is the people who stand in the way of your success.

20.   So what are the most significant detractors of professional success of African American gifted males, if you had to name the top three?

Trey: One being who you surround yourself with, your social network—it could be bad. The next is an unsupportive faculty. The third one is really your own self. You can defeat your own self; you don't have to have anyone help you do that.

21.   What are your future personal and professional goals—in five years?

Trey: Hopefully, I will still be in the discipline that I'm in. Maybe someday I might transition into a different career like becoming a mortician. . . . I wouldn't mind becoming more of an expert in a certain discipline like in medicine or pharmacy—I have always had an interest in oncology or psychiatry.

22.   What are your future personal and professional goals—in 15 years?

Trey: Hopefully, I will be living! Hopefully, most of my goals by then will be a reality, and mostly I will be just enjoying life. There are a lot of things that I did not get to do socially when I was growing up and when I was in college, and it's kind of like I am doing it now as I get older. Now that I have the financial means to do it, I keep going back and saying, "Now I can do this, now I can do this." So now I am doing this retro thing and I would like to continue that, because I think I missed out on a whole lot. So I plan to just enjoy life the best way that I can and do things that I like to do.

23.   When you interviewed 10 years ago, I was blank and now I'm blank. Fill in those blanks.

Trey: Ten years ago, I was *dependent* in so many ways and now I'm *more independent*, not saying that I'm totally independent, but I'm independent in so many ways such as my professional and social life. I know I'm still dependent on my mom, and that will still continue. I will never be completely independent from her. Even with advice in my professional degree and even when I get sick, it's not like I even went to school to become a pharmacist. I mean, I tell people what to do when they are sick and what meds to take and I'm still calling home and asking my mom what is good to take for my ailments. Somehow for me, it's different, so I still call home to my mom what I need to do. So, yeah, I was dependent then and I am more independent now.

24.   Is there anything that I didn't ask that I need to ask, or anything you'd like to say, or closing comments?

Trey: Well, definitely. While I never really had anyone just interview me like you did. When you first came to me I thought, "This is great!" It gave me a really good feeling that someone really wanted to know my thoughts. Things happen for a reason; whether they are good or bad, they happen for a reason.

I went through a lot of things along the way, so now good things are on my path. I have no animosity towards any individual in my past; it's important to stay positive and that is what I want to give to other African Americans who are trying to achieve their goals. Things might not always be peachy, but it all depends on how well you are able to handle things. Also, don't let get pride get in your way, because sometimes you could be your worst enemy—just you alone and how you think about certain things and how you think about yourself and how you go about handling things in certain situations makes a difference. It's all about your attitude. And it's also about what you determine success to be.

Bonner: We're basically done; I just want to end by getting a bit more insight from you. This is a really loosely coupled question, and it's not structured to get you to respond in terms of your political affiliation or beliefs. There is much to be said about the gifted African American male who is running for president. What are your thoughts about Barack Obama becoming president of the United States?

Trey: Have mercy! Thank God! I thought I would never see a day like this, and certainly my parents did not think they would see this day come either. It gave me a sense of joy and accomplishment. It's not like we're related by blood, but to see that [the election of Obama as president] is like seeing someone who is related to me assume that type of position. and it gives me a sense of joy and also gives people who are younger than me a sense that anything can be accomplished. Him becoming president is more than him being Black. . . . It sends a tidal wave of "I can do it" or in his words "Yes, we can" across the country, and that is in itself good. I am so happy for him and I am so happy for African Americans!

11

Retrospection and Contemplation: An Interview with Stephen James 10 Years Later

Finding Stephen James did not require much extra effort on my part, as he had contacted me several months prior to my decision to conduct an interview with him. While sitting in my office here at the university one afternoon, the phone rang and to my surprise on the other end of the line was Stephen. He stated that he had been "surfing the Net" and thought about me and the study he engaged in with me and simply "wondered what I was doing." After catching up on 10 years of elapsed time, Stephen told me that he completed his undergraduate studies in chemistry in 1997 and went on to graduate school, completing a master's degree in materials science and engineering in 2000. Since completing both his undergraduate and his graduate studies, he has worked in semiconductor packaging, developing microelectronic devices. He has been employed for the last five years as a packaging engineer with a major firm. We agreed to meet at his home to conduct the interview regarding his perspectives as a gifted African American male some 10 years after the initial interview I conducted with him as an undergraduate.

1. Does your giftedness play a role in your professional life? And if so, how?

Stephen: Okay, define giftedness.
Bonner: I'm going to let you do that.
Stephen: Okay.
Bonner: This interview is being conducted with you some 10 years later, so, does your giftedness play a role in your current professional life, and if so, how?
Stephen: I would say yes. First, it starts off how I was raised. I mean just having qualities to get the job done and having that drive; I mean that's from a personal level. Having that will to develop good study habits. . . . You know I took that mindset with me from day one. And, you know, I used it in elementary, high school, grammar, and even my day-to-day activities now.

Bonner: This next question was asked of you 10 years ago. How would you answer it now?

2.   If someone described you as gifted, how would you respond?

Stephen: Well, you know, I'm not the type to, you know, "toot my own horn" or anything like that; I try to handle everything with the greatest humility. I mean, I would handle it [being described as gifted] in a gracious fashion. Yeah, that's what I would pretty much do right now.
   Bonner: So if someone described you as gifted, your response would be . . .?
   Stephen: I have, to say, yeah, I would basically say, yeah. . . .

3.   Who comprises your professional support network?

Stephen: Well, you know, everything I do is based on God's grace. That's number one. But, I mean, I always have strong family support, so I mean, that connection with family always dictates my actions from that standpoint. Professionally, you know, I now have Danielle [pseudonym for his fiancée] in my life, so she is a strong support system. And, you know, I get along pretty well with folks at work, so I mean we have some sense of synergy.
   Bonner: So now when you say that you have some sense of synergy, what do you mean?
   Stephen: Well, I'm the type of person who goes straight to the source, so I have a pretty good relationship with my direct supervisor. You know that [relationship] is really important and we go to lunch all the time; so by going to the source, that kind of affords you different opportunities in terms of building relationships. Having that relationship opens the door; that has kind of like always been my mindset—always go to the source. But then I need to also have a strong relationship with my peers. So I don't exclude anyone. I'm the type of person that could talk to the CEO of the company as well as to someone who is at the bottom of the barrel in the company with the same degree of confidence. That is how I would characterize myself and my support network.

4.   Who comprises your social support network?

Stephen: Well, I could probably answer that with the last question, so I mean definitely my mom and dad. They have always been in my life. Danielle, my fiancée, would also be included in this network. She's very encouraging and ambitious. And, then my children, even though they don't know that they provide inspiration by just having them in my life, they are important to me. You know, they just give me that extra something—you know when I'm tired. I just pick up and start moving because I know I have to set an example for them.

5.   Does mentoring play a role in your professional life? And if so, how?

Stephen: Yes, it does. I had one, actually the senior technical member of staff over at AB [his current employer/ technology-based firm]. He has basically been my mentor since I've started, in terms of showing me the ropes. I appreciate him, and I try to express my gratitude. So I mean I have always had mentors in my life, all the way through from parents. Dr. Hubbard [an undergraduate professor] has definitely been there for me since I graduated from Grambling. He definitely still helps me out today. So I mean I have always had, I have always been blessed to have folks that, you know, that have been integral in my life to push me along the way. So you know I definitely appreciate them. . . .

Bonner: Something you just said has prompted a follow-up question that I will pose to you later.

Stephen: Oh, okay.

6.   Have you had an opportunity to mentor a gifted African American student?

Stephen: Not to the degree I would like to, but you know from time to time I might get a call from some students at Grambling seeking some advice. But not to the extent I should, and I think it's very important that I should give back, and I am going to make a stronger effort to do that. But I mean to answer the question, as of now, definitely not the way I should. I could use some improvement in this area and take this on as a personal challenge—to do more mentoring.

7.   If you have changed since your undergraduate days, what has changed the most about you?

Stephen: I could tell you my confidence—I could say that. I think I have become more assertive, just since leaving Grambling and going to obtain my master's degree. That experience just gave me the utmost confidence and has given me more confidence in terms of speaking, in terms of doing, because it has given me confidence in terms of what I have to say. So in terms of confidence, assertiveness, yes. . . . but also improved ambition, because one thing that I found coming from an HBCU [historically Black college or university] structure and going to, you know, a school like Georgia Tech, it can be intimidating. Because you know from Grambling State for instance. . . . picture this scenario. I will never forget I was in this class at Georgia Tech; I was sitting in the center of the room and to the left of me were students from Johns Hopkins, from MIT, and Stanford. And here in the center of the room, here I am from Grambling and I held my own! So I mean just from that experience, you know, showed me that I am ready for this. That is the confidence I am talking about. Not arrogance, but confidence.

8.   Did your undergraduate academic experience affect your professional success? If so, how?

Stephen: A hundred percent. No doubt about it. One thing that I love about my undergraduate education that I actually speak about very often is that I was able to get an opportunity for supplemental education. So besides getting the theoretical knowledge and the textbook, I was afforded the opportunity to have an internship. So that [his internship experience] enabled me to understand industry and apply what I was learning from the textbook. From the beginning you have individualized attention; I got it [individual attention] at Grambling, and it enabled me to understand more than technique and fundamentals. I think that's what got me by in grad school and even at work. That's one of my competitive edges, having had that individualized attention and really adhering to fundamentals. I think that is what really, you know, put me ahead. You know, I am a strong proponent of the HBCU because of that; I see the benefits of it in terms of, you know, in terms of having the competitive edge.

9. Did your undergraduate social experience impact your professional success, and if so, how?

Stephen: My social experience?

Bonner: Yes, you have talked about your academic experience, so what about the social experiences that impacted your professional success?

Stephen: Yes, okay.

Bonner: Did anything about the social experience of being at a HBCU . . . was there anything about this experience that has influenced your professional life in any way?

Stephen: It does, but I would say not so strongly, you know. Actually, you know, I think my situation was a little bit different because, you know, I had the twins; so a lot of my social activities were basically limited because I was going home to be with them. But, in terms of social experiences, you know for the most part they do have some advantages; but for me, based on my own situation it [social experience] wasn't my strongest influence at the time, so to speak.

10. Did the type of institution you attended as an undergraduate, HBCU, play a role in your professional success? And if so, how?

Bonner: You addressed much of what I was getting at with this question earlier. . . . do you want to expand a bit more?

Stephen: Right. You know, well, it's like I credit the HBCU education for my success today. You know there are no bones about that. I can't stress enough just having the small class sizes and being able to talk to my department head at that time, Dr. Walton, being able to go into her office and speak about anything, you know, that was invaluable. And, you know one thing that I really appreciate is having the opportunity for the supplemental education, you know, like the internship. You know, from NASA, from Dell Labs. . . . these experiences really propelled me, my graduating from Grambling to finishing graduate school. Grambling really gave me a chance at some real diverse educational perspectives. I had the pharmaceutical experience, the aeronautical experience, you know, with NASA and the semiconductor field in which I am employed today. They [Grambling State University] really opened lots of doors in terms of exposure. Meeting different folks and basically giving me the confidence to know that I could operate in the professional world coming from an HBCU compared to the some of the folks that went to CalTech or Berkeley—you know, I've met them [students] from everywhere and you know, I held my own; that makes me proud that I wasn't losing anything by going to school there. So, you know, some folks could always fall into stereotypes or believe that you get an inferior education at an HBCU, but I would like to be a testament to the fact that that's not true. Of course, that [education] depends on the person and that person's study habits and your zeal and ambition in life.

11.   What advice would you give another gifted African American male to ensure his academic success as an undergraduate student?

Stephen: Right. Don't cut any corners, because doing that will come back to haunt you. It definitely will. That would be the most important advice. I guess in my case I was interested in the material, so one thing I did was to develop a passion. So, I think if you are serious about it, you develop that passion and it'll come easy to you. But just have a strong conscience and do the right thing. Don't cut any corners. Be as diligent as you can and be as hungry and ambitious as you can, and, you know, that passion develops.

12.   In retrospect, what is the most significant barrier to the success of gifted African American students, both male and female?

Stephen: Well, I mean it's the harsh reality of just being Black. I mean, you know you are always going to have the stereotype that because you are Black in a majority atmosphere, being in a White corporate world, that you are "less than." But it all goes back to believing in yourself and having the confidence in yourself and knowing that you could do it. And, you know, going back to my experience of being at a predominately Black school and having opportunities to go to a White environment and seeing that I could perform was important. Well, these are just the harsh realities of life, but hey, you know, that's how it goes.

Bonner: I want to tag on that question. Question 12. You mentioned barriers being in predominately White settings or majority settings; were there any barriers or did you experience any barriers in the HBCU setting?

Stephen: Oh, yeah, major barriers. One is the resources; there are definitely some shortcomings. You compare a Georgia Tech to Grambling. . . . I think our academic budget must've been in the thousands of dollars, I mean . . . You know Tech could be in the millions, but I mean the resources are unbelievable; there are big disparities, you know. So one thing that is a barrier is the resources. . . . But I think that you could overcome the barriers by the instruction you get, instruction that adheres to the fundamentals. I think if you have the fundamentals, you could do anything. Also, some of the techniques, analytical techniques, for instance, that you know students in predominately White institutions might have, we sometimes don't have—another harsh reality of going to an HBCU; that [deficiency in access to analytical tools] probably won't change.

13. What environment would you create for a gifted African American under-graduate student that would be more helpful than the situation that you faced as an undergraduate? What would you do to help improve the conditions for another African American male who is coming through?

Stephen: I would tell them to just place yourself in nurturing environments. That's what I always did—especially when I used to play sports. I always liked to play with folks that were older than me. So it's the same thing in academics, uh, try to associate with folks that are at your level or above, so that you are able to get better. One thing with me with me, when I set my goals, always aim them high. I am always reaching! They are almost not attainable—so I say that to say that I am always reaching, because not once would I settle for stagnancy. I mean I guess one thing, just continue to place yourself in a nurturing environment where you are always progressive. You can imagine at an HBCU that there are many distrac-tions—you know, from women or the extracurricular activities. So you just have to remain on the road to success, but the temptation is quite strong.

14. If you had a sizable amount of money to give to a university to support gifted African American students, what stipulations would you place on these funds in an effort to help these students succeed?

Stephen: I would be frank. For instance, to have this opportunity the whole point is I would be real frank and mandate that the student maintain a minimum GPA. What that does is keep the student on the right path. I would probably add that students are required to do some research to supplement what's going on in the textbooks. That way knowledge is not just being obtained, but applying hands-on principles to the students learning is taking place. . . . Probably request their involvement in some types of societies; that way some leadership qualities could be learned also. I think those would be the main three.

15. If you could structure the ideal higher education environment for academi-cally gifted African American male college students, what would it include? That is, if you could construct the ideal collegiate environment, what would it look like?

Stephen: I think it would be one of balance. Academics are important, but one thing I support is that you have to deal with people. So I think the social aspect is also important. So I guess to answer the question, an ideal or utopian environment would be made of a strong academic foundation and would really have a strong component in the social activities, something that caters to many people to help establish relationships because that is important in the workforce. I am trying to think of something more concrete, but . . . balance is important. The type of environment that promotes balance between academics and that social world.

16.   What are the five most important academic and issues that should be addressed as it pertains to the future success of gifted African American male students in higher education? The question reads, what are the five most important academic and personal issues? . . . , so if you want to combine both of those as it pertains to the success of academically gifted African American males that's okay.

Stephen: Okay, so I guess for personal issues—have a strong conscience. That would be one. That again goes back to our saying before, dealing with people, so that is why this skill is definitely needed. . . . Oh, okay, what is the first part of the question again?

Bonner: [repeats the question]

Stephen: So making sure that first of all, the personnel at the institution are qualified to teach the classes. One thing can be having the university hire more specialty professors for particular subjects that help promote a particular subject.

Bonner: Okay, you mentioned some of the issues when you were talking about leadership, but if you had to articulate these as the necessary things that they [gifted African American male students] should have to help them be successful . . .

Stephen: So one is money, whether it comes from a grant or some other source. That enables students to focus more on academics as opposed to getting a job. That would be one. If possible, you can see that a particular student has a strong propensity to learn. That professor takes that student under his wing and tries to get the most out of that student.

Bonner: So far you said strong conscience, money, qualified faculty, and a willingness by faculty to assist students who have a strong propensity for learning. So essentially you have four.

Stephen: And, um, let's go back to leadership.

Bonner: When you say leadership, you mean opportunities?

Stephen: Yes. Yes. Opportunities to put that student in an environment for leadership. I was a chemistry major; so you know a group like NSBE [the National Society of Black Engineers] enabled me to do important leadership stuff.

17.   What advice would you give another gifted African American who is interested in pursuing a graduate or professional degree?

Stephen: I would just . . . I would give them my personal experience. When I got my master's I felt like superman. I felt that I could answer any question and it gave me the utmost confidence. The advice I would give is to better yourself and make yourself more well rounded, and this will definitely make you more marketable. And, more advice I would give that student is to be prepared in regards to getting your own money for school. That is one thing that really helped me out—getting my own money when I went to Tech. So being able and having diligence to solicit on campus, in the industry, or on Web sites for money that is out there. This really gives you more autonomy to have your own money and do research on the schools you are more interested in, as well as the schools with professors who are doing research in areas you are interested in. . . . The whole thing is to get out. You don't want to be hung up in school for a significant amount of time. Be meticulous as you can, up front about your goals in order to guarantee your success. Just be sure to finish and do well. You need to also be sure to make graduate school an enjoyable experience.

18. What is the most pressing issue that gifted African American males face in the professional (work) world?

Stephen: Well, um, the most pressing issue is, and I don't know if I have experienced this too much, but in some ways the most pressing issue is to prove yourself. . . . I don't have a problem with that because you know, um, like I said, I am confident in what I do, but sometimes as a minority you may have to prove yourself more than someone who maybe is majority. That is just the harsh reality so that so, uh, that would be my answer to that question.

Bonner: What are the most important contributors to the professional success of African American gifted males, if you had to name the top three?

Stephen: Being prepared. Going the extra mile. What I mean by going the extra mile is always trying to have a competitive edge on someone else; that means like doing any supplemental reading that you do to put you ahead of where you need to be, which feeds into the first one. And let's see one more, can you repeat the question again?

Bonner: [repeats the question.]

Stephen: Okay, well, not to sound like a broken record, but sometimes I am in the pits, and it takes God and my spiritual faith to get me out of it. I have come a long way and that is due to my belief in God. I mean there are no small words to say regarding that. . . .

19. What are the significant detractors from the professional success of African American gifted males, if you had to name the top three things?

Stephen: Um, in my case. I don't know if mean this more like in a generic sense but, uh, but not being prepared. In some ways you might not be prepared, and that is the harsh reality of the structure of the system [undergraduate school]. Another detractor for me is not getting a break—you know, sometimes that happens. Whether this person may look better on paper, you know, doesn't always mean that person can't do a good job. Another detractor, especially for gifted African American male students could be . . . Well, I guess what I want to say is if you exude confidence you tend to get more work put on you. So a detractor could be that you get overworked—that happens to me a lot of times. You may exude confidence and that gives the impression that you can handle things, so that could be a detriment also.

Bonner: So no good deed goes unpunished?
Stephen: Yes, you are right.

20.   What are your five-year personal goals?

Stephen: Five-year personal goals. Number one is marriage. I think I found the right one, so that is number one. I have always wanted to seek improvement, so get a better financial plan is another goal. I am also hoping to grow closer to my spiritual faith, because that dictates the endeavors that I pursue. I want to continue to be the best example of having patience for my twins; they are from a different generation than I grew up in, and that patience is going to be of the utmost importance to get them through. Another personal goal is that I want to give back; I mean, I have had a lot of help along the way and I think I can offer help. You know give back in any way I can. I need to do better in that regard.
Bonner: Okay, okay. What about your professional goals?
Stephen: You know, being in the engineering field, I want to be promoted. We have different technical ladders, so in the next five years I want to be promoted and become a member of the technical staff. That is a strong personal goal. Next I want to be considered an expert in what I do, you know, in terms of the materials that I work with in my specific job. In terms of professional, I would like to get more involved in terms of the technical side and expose myself to other things within the industry. You know like what you are doing now; you are outside of the A&M circle [speaking about my, Bonner's, research agenda, which takes me outside of my university setting]. I want to try to continue to progress in my technical arena.
Bonner: Okay, we're almost there; I want to push you a little bit more.

21.   What are your 15-year personal goals?

Stephen: Okay, my 15-year personal goals?
Bonner: Yes, I am talking about your 15-year personal goals.
Stephen: Well, as far as my personal goals, I would expect those five-year goals to be in full motion, at least I hope. I expect to be an expert in what I do and be the person who is sought out for my expertise. I will probably have some more children and hope to be better in terms of giving back. I really want to establish a better relationship with Grambling, because Grambling has done a lot for me. I want to serve as a mentor and be in a position to be able to do that in 15 years. I guess that's it.
Bonner: And anything professionally in 15 years?
Stephen: Not be superficial, but I hope to be making some pesos! And I also hope to be a senior technical staff member at that point. This will help me command some of the hopes I have for better pay and higher authority in the company in terms of being an expert. With everything I have worked for . . . I hope I will be put in a place for a position of excellence. I hope to be at the pinnacle of my career or at least almost there.

22.   When you interviewed me 10 years ago I was blank but now I'm blank.

Stephen: I was definitely less confident and, um, I think my answers were not as, quite as thought provoking, and, um, and now it's maybe a little bit more on the flip side. I have definitely matured; it's a maturation process and my prior experiences have allowed me to mature. Now, I am better able to answer these questions and I am in sync at a higher level. It goes back to the confidence I now have, and that's who I am today.

23.   Is there anything that I did not ask that you would like to add?

Stephen: Um, let me think about that one. Yeah, when I look back in retrospect at the whole study you are doing, it was captivating to me, because you basically had two students from the same level competing in two different environments. To see that both of us turned out to be successful is a pretty good thing coming from these two different backgrounds.

Bonner: So here is one follow-up comment and question. So what I am seeing is a theme that has been emerging across the interview data I have been collecting. Not just from you two guys who participated in this study, but also from those who are currently participating in a grant project I am completing and other studies I have conducted. Namely, what I am seeing is that when you mention giftedness, invariably African American respondents say things like "It's a gift from God" or "I have these talents and gifts and I am smart because the Lord has endowed me." There is always a spiritual element that seems to be culturally specific—why did you make this connection between spirituality and giftedness?

Stephen: It certainly defines the point of our people. I mean, you know when we see the documentaries on television about the slaves, they were singing those spiritual hymns. That has become the foundation of our people, who have always been strong spiritual-based people. We've always had an appreciation of Jesus and I believe it's our upbringing. That's what makes Blacks special as a people. With God, it gives you confidence in yourself that you are not doing it alone. That [spirituality/God] is what we have to hold on to when there's nothing else. and when you look at it, not to give any prejudice, we have come pretty far and that's just the reality. I mean separate but equal, but there's never really been a separate but equal. Looking at it [racial oppression] from a strong spiritual faith, that enables us to be constantly in a minority environment, but able to perform. White folks don't understand that—you're definitely right. It's definitely culturally based, and I am not shocked to hear that some of the others are commenting on that.

Bonner: Last follow-up. This was on my mind driving over here. This is a very loosely coupled question and it is not written down, but I just want to know, and it is not to get you to respond in terms of your political proclivities, but I think there is much to be said about the gifted African American male who is running for president. What is your thought about, not necessarily about Obama becoming president, but just the image of an African American male in that capacity? What do you think that would do for our notions on how we view high-achieving, gifted African Americans?

Stephen: For years and years, we have thought that the Black man was ignorant. Obama is very articulate. It [his nomination] really exemplifies the preeminence of Blacks and the view of many folks. You know I love him. Folks like Obama or a gifted Black student are viewed as a threat and a lot of folks can't figure out why. On the surface, a lot of folks feel that if you are Black you don't know anything, and to see Obama constantly spending time campaigning and debating is great. I am really looking forward to the debate with McCain—he [Obama] will dominate and I love it. I think it's exactly what we need, and I am rallying around his theme of change; I am looking forward to big things. He's Black, but he's capable. He is a good example of a person who just happens to be Black, and let's hope more folks see that towards the time of the election. Let me tell you, I am shocked. I thought I would never live, and I am 32, to see the day that this would happen. I didn't live during any of the segregation periods, but I have lived in the South and I have experienced a lot of prejudice. I am just shocked to see Obama reach this point, because anything now is possible in America.

Afterword

For more than a dozen years, I have devoted my personal and professional life to desegregating gifted education for Black and, more recently, other culturally different, males and females. This goal has not been easy to attain, and challenges remain. Too often, as Bonner notes, Black students, and more specifically Black males, are deemed inferior and, accordingly, incapable not only of achieving at high levels, but of being gifted and motivated and academically inclined. Sadly, some five decades after Brown vs. the Board of Education (1954), Black students are still fighting not only for equality but for equity, in school settings. Nowhere is the fight more vigorous than in gifted education and special education.

All areas of education are raging with controversy and debate. However, like myself and too few other scholars, Bonner has chosen to take the road less traveled by focusing on gifted education rather than special education. And like myself, Bonner has confronted the obnoxious question that he shares in his book: "You're interested in studying whom?—the academically gifted African American male—you know the greater academic community doesn't believe this being exists!"

Contrary to popular opinion and misperception, this being *does* indeed exist! But so many educators at all levels refuse to acknowledge and accept this reality. No group, as I have written elsewhere, has a monopoly on gifts and talents, despite issues of underrepresentation of Black students and overrepresentation of White students in gifted education! What are we witnessing regarding representation issues is human-made; those who make definitions, theories, instruments, policies, and procedures often fail to do so with cultural and racial differences in mind and with an eye toward justice and equity. This colorblind or cultureblind—and genderblind—approach definitely impacts who is viewed and identified as gifted. And, too often, Black males lose.

Thus, it was a pleasure, a joy, to see that Bonner focused on the most demonized and disenfranchised students in school settings—Black males. What is even more heartening is that the two males he studied—Steve and Trey—are gifted! Seldom have we heard from or listened to Black males, no less Black males who are gifted. What a joy and a treasure. How refreshing!

The overriding question this book seeks to answer is: What are the perceptions of academically gifted African American males attending historically Black colleges or universities (HBCUs) and academically gifted African American males attending traditionally White institutions (TWIs) concerning their relationships with their respective institutions in cultivating their academic giftedness? More pointedly, are there identifiable factors influencing the success of the academically gifted African American male collegian, and if so, are these factors specific to the type of institution attended?

Bonner identifies several experiences that are common between Trey and Steve, and some ways in which their experiences are different. The juxtaposition of the experiences and realities of these two gifted Black males is enlightening. On the one hand, their different experiences can be attributed to who they are as individuals, and as gifted Black males, and to how they were reared and educated in P-12 settings. On the other hand, it would be foolish, unwise, and unprofessional to trivialize or deny that the context of higher education matters—being at an HBCU or a TWI seems to matter to these young men . . . which has also been the focus of previous research.

We all are a product of our culture. And who are and what we value and desire does not diminish when we enter higher education. The decision as to which college or university to attend is always riddled with questions and uncertainty. Add to that the question or dilemma of whether to attend a predominantly Black or White institution. . . . What a decision!! Frankly, White students are rarely asked to make this choice. All types of questions plague us, especially if the college or university is not close to home, if our support base is too far away or not within immediate physical reach.

Bonner has given readers much to think about regarding how to improve the educational experiences of gifted Black males. This discussion is important and must continue. Black males are, indeed, the proverbial diamonds in the rough. They are brilliant, they have much to offer, but they also need refining. Bonner's book is one important, vital step in that direction.

Donna Y. Ford, PhD
Professor, Vanderbilt University

African American Giftedness: Our Nation's Deferred Dream

Fred A. Bonner II

Bowling Green State University

What happens to a dream deferred?

> Does it dry up
> like a raisin in the sun?
> Or fester like a sore—
> And then run?
> Does it stink like rotten meat?
> Or crust and sugar over—
> like a syrupy sweet?
> Maybe it just sags like a heavy load
> Or does it explode?

—Hughes, 1951

Traditionally, African Americans have faced widespread underrepresentation in our nation's gifted and talented programs. Black students, particularly males, are three times as likely to be in a class for the educable mentally retarded as are White students, but only one half as likely to be in a class for the gifted or talented (Carnegie Corporation, 1984/1985; College Board, 1985). Data of this nature should send an alarming message to educators, administrators, parents, and students. Why do we continually fail to recognize gifted and talented African American students?

Attempts to address the issue of African American giftedness have, in the past, led to a blame game. Parents attribute the problem of underidentification to the schools, the schools attribute the problem to the gifted coordinators, and the gifted

Fred A. Bonner II, "African American Giftedness: Our Nation's Deferred Dream," *Journal of Black Studies* 30, No. 5 (May 2000): 643–663. Reprinted with permission of Sage Publications, Inc.

coordinators attribute the problem to the various testing agencies. The end result is typically a deluge of dialogue without any requisite action. This problem can only be addressed when classroom teachers and gifted coordinators draw their attention away from Black children as a group and focus on the individual child (Rhodes, 1992).

In a review of the literature on gifted African Americans, Ford (1994) found that only 2 percent of the articles and scholarly publications focused attention on gifted minority learners in general, and even fewer focused specifically on African American students (the largest U.S. minority population). To understand gifted African Americans, more resources should be channeled into initiatives that focus attention on understanding the unique academic, social, and cultural needs of these students.

This article addresses the issues that have perpetuated the underrepresentation of African Americans in gifted and talented programs. These issues include inadequate definitions, standardized testing, nomination procedures, learning style preferences, family and peer influences, screening and identification, and gifted underachievers. The article concludes with a discussion on alternative theories of giftedness and the implementation of multicultural education in teacher preparatory programs.

PROBLEMS WITH DEFINING GIFTEDNESS

The definition of giftedness followed in most states is in many instances the primary cause of the underidentification of African American students. All writers of definitions should be required to show a logical relationship between their definition on one hand and recommended identification and programming practices on the other (Renzulli, 1986). Official definitions of giftedness have surfaced in 1972, 1978, and 1993. The Marland (1972) definition, adopted in federal legislation in P.L. 93–380 (Special Projects Act), set forth by the U.S. Office of Education states,

> Gifted and talented children are those identified by professionally qualified persons who by virtue of outstanding abilities are capable of high performance. These are children who require differentiated educational programs and/or services beyond those normally provided by the regular school program to realize their contribution to self and society. Children capable of high performance include those with demonstrated achievement and/or potential ability in any of the following areas, singly or in combination: (1) general intellectual ability, (2) specific academic aptitude, (3) creative or productive thinking, (4) leadership ability, (5) visual and performing arts, (6) psychomotor ability. (p. 64)

Although the Office of Education recognized the broad range of abilities gifted individuals display, a number of problems continued to exist. Renzulli (1986) noted three distinct problems with the 1972 definition: First, the definition failed to include nonintellective (motivational) factors; second, the definition failed to address the nonparallel nature of the six categories—creativity and leader-ship do not exist apart from a performance area in which they can be applied; and third, the definition treated each category as if it were a mutually exclusive entity.

The 1978 definition, according to Ford (1994), offered encouragement primarily in its inclusion of the "potentially" gifted. It appeared to recognize a need to serve those students who have, for various reasons, yet to manifest their gifts—that is, students who might otherwise go unrecognized. The most recent federal definition of the gifted (U.S. Department of Education, 1993) offers even greater promise, including increased attention to equity in terms of identifying gifted African Americans and other minority children:

> Children and youth with outstanding talent perform or show the potential for performing at remarkably high levels of accomplishment when compared with others of their age, experience, or environment. These children and youth exhibit high performance capacity in intellectual, creative, and/or artistic areas, and unusual leadership capacity, or excel in specific academic fields. They require services or activities not ordinarily provided by the schools. Outstanding talents are present in children and youth from all cultural groups, across all economic strata, and in all areas of human endeavor. (p. 2)

This definition expands the boundaries to include students who would ordinarily go unidentified. An important issue this definition addresses is the measurement of performance and potential with those who share comparable experiential and environmental backgrounds. According to Renzulli (1986), the way one views giftedness will be a primary factor in constructing a plan for identifying certain youngsters and providing services that are relevant to the characteristics that brought them to our attention in the first place.

STANDARDIZED TESTING

Standardized testing has been the primary modus operandi in the identification of gifted students. Hilliard (1976) noted that there seem to be two fundamental questions that are asked by assessors (or tests) and that symbolize two fundamentally different approaches to the assessment of human behavior:

1. Do you know what I know?
2. What is it that you know?

The first approach is what most standardized tests measure. The language, culture, and experiences of the individuals who construct these tests become the prevailing benchmarks of success. The tests then become a measure of which students have a better grasp of White, middle-class culture—not what knowledge and information they have acquired. According to Hilliard (1976), by definition, standardized assessment is convergent and therefore is unable to deal with divergent or novel thinking, expression, or problem solving. Sternberg and Davidson (1986) have suggested that exceptional intelligence is best measured by tasks that are "nonentrenched" in the sense of requiring information processing of kinds outside people's ordinary experience. These are two very distinct but parallel statements recapitulating the same theme: The sole reliance on traditional assessment measures such as the standardized test places African American students at a great disadvantage. Concurrently, the lowering of standards or the addition of points to standardized tests is not appropriate; nor are programs designed to raise minority IQ scores to the cutoff point, because both methods overlook the inadequacies of standardized tests (Frasier, 1989b).

It is important to note that standardized tests have some usefulness as assessment instruments, but they should never be used as the sole indicator of multifaceted concepts such as giftedness. Hilliard (1976) noted that assessment must be more than testing. This does not mean that standardized tests must be eliminated. It does mean that standardized tests must be developed so that real differences are not obliterated and real similarities are not overlooked.

TEACHER NOMINATIONS OF GIFTED AFRICAN AMERICAN STUDENTS

The task of identifying potentially gifted and talented students often begins with nominations from classroom teachers. Although gifted and talented coordinators are trained in recognizing signs of giftedness, traditional classroom teachers do not usually receive such training (Rhodes, 1992). Without proper training, teachers make judgments based on their own preconceived ideas of what characteristics a gifted student should exhibit. Unfortunately, this mode of identification has proven to be very ineffective and has exacerbated the problem of underidentification of African American students.

Teacher nominations of gifted students are often based on the subjective parameters of White, middle-class society. Students who are out of "cultural sync" with their teachers will go unidentified, regardless of their intellectual abilities. For African American students, initiation into the ranks of gifted and talented typically begins with a realignment of their cultural behavior to fit the mold of what teachers deem acceptable conduct. Often, the realignment process means totally relinquishing the cultural nuances that would identify the students as members of a racial group. This guilt by association implies that Black students must demonstrate to teachers that the negative stereotypes generally associated with Black students' behavior do not pertain to them. This imposed denial and refutation of one's cultural heritage and racial identity are directly related to Black self-hatred, lowered self-esteem, and heightened anxiety, and possibly to lower academic achievement, as well (Irvine, 1990).

Research by Brophy and Everston (1981) revealed that when Black students behave in ways different from or contrary to Black cultural norms, teachers treat them as individuals. Behaviors that represent a deviation from what teachers view as the norm are summarily branded as inappropriate. Gouldner (1978) found that teachers in the all-Black school in her study thought a good class had children who learned to sit quietly at their desks, raise their hands before talking, wait patiently for the bell to ring before leaving their seats, stand in line with their partners in an orderly way, and when in school repress any expression of anger, frustration, or exuberance. (p. 29)

Feshbach (1969) conducted a study of pupil behaviors that student teachers preferred: they preferred behaviors indicating rigidity, conformity, orderliness, dependence, passivity, and acquiescence rather than behaviors indicating flexibility, nonconformity, untidiness, independence, activity, and assertiveness. Yet these latter characteristics are said to describe gifted children (Hilliard, 1976).

Teachers must be properly trained if they are to serve as conduits to gifted and talented programs. Proper training should include not only specific gifted and talented identification measures but information on multiculturalism and diverse learning styles as well. Torrance (1973) contends that if educators are really interested in identifying gifted and talented students in minority groups, they will direct their searches to those characteristics that are valued by the particular minority groups. Without proper training, teachers will continue to have misperceptions about minority students, and underidentification will continue. This lack of training decreases twofold the probability that gifted African American students will be identified and placed (Ford, 1994).

LEARNING STYLE PREFERENCES

To determine the most effective instructional methods and instructional tools to be used in the classroom, it is important to have some understanding of student learning styles. Understanding how gifted minority students learn is an important variable of effective teaching; however, student learning styles have gained meager attention from educators (Dunn & Dunn, 1992).

A confusing array of definitions describe *learning style*, a term often used interchangeably with *cognitive style* or *learning ability* (Haensly, Reynolds, & Nash, 1986). McCarthy (1990) defined learning styles as approaches to cognitive, affective, and psychological factors that function as relatively stable indicators of how one concentrates on, perceives, interacts with, and responds to the learning environment. Torrance and Reynolds (1978) have indicated that individuals exhibit different styles of learning and processing information, not only through their preferences but also through the efficiency with which they use one or the other style and through knowing when to employ primarily one style or the other.

The learning environment for gifted African American students often presents challenges stemming from the incongruity of school culture and individualized learning styles. African American students rely on their perception of the teacher and the affective aspects of the environment to determine their involvement with learning (Shade, 1982). Hilliard (1976) posited that schools approach curriculum and instruction from an analytical rather than a relational cognitive style. Black students are assumed to be relational—that is, predisposed to learning that

is characterized by freedom of movement, variation, creativity, divergent thinking approaches, inductive reasoning, and a focus on people. Schools, on the other
hand, emphasize an analytical style, or learning characterized by rules and restriction of movement, standardization, conformity, convergent thinking approaches,
deductive reasoning, and a focus on things.

Peters (1990) noted that when Black lower-class children go to school at age
four or five, they discover that the behavioral rules have now changed. Although
there are attractive things to explore, there is also a new emphasis on sitting still.
Play and interaction with others are encouraged only during specific times of day.
Music is heard only at music time. Physical activity, body movement, and expression, not being associated with cognitive learning, are relegated to activity or play
periods or physical education class. Black lower-class children are often lost, punished, or put down in the process.

Similar to Hilliard's findings is the research of Shade (1982), which suggested
these differences in social cognition: Blacks' recognition patterns focus on affective
rather than physical characteristics, and Black children prefer a variety of stimuli
in the learning environment and a variety of teaching methods and materials. As
for perceptual style, Shade made observations similar to the research of Witkin and
Moore (1975). Both found that Blacks tended to have a field-dependent rather than
a field-independent cognitive style. Table 1 highlights these two cognitive styles.
Field-dependent individuals have a more global and interrelated approach to visual
information and are thus unable to distinguish the necessary parts for problem
solving. The opposite approach, field independence, is characteristic of people who
are able to isolate the necessary parts from distracting elements to solve problems.

For many gifted African American students, this "line item" incongruousness of
teaching and learning styles, coupled with a foreign classroom environment, presents a formidable problem. Assessment of the learning style preferences of gifted
African American learners and the use of a multifaceted approach to instruction

Table 1   Field-Dependent and Field-Independent Teaching Strategies

Field-Dependent	Field-Independent
1. Focuses on needs, feelings, and interests of students	1. Focuses on task
2. Acts as a consultant or supervisor in the classroom	2. Fosters modeling and imitation
3. Uses an informal approach and elicits	3. Uses a formal, lecture-oriented approach class discussion
4. Uses personal rewards	4. Uses impersonal rewards
5. Encourages group achievement	5. Encourages individual achievement
6. Narrates and humanizes concepts	6. Emphasizes facts and principles
7. Identifies with class	7. Remains emotionally detached

could greatly enhance the classroom environment. The treatment of cultural differences does not imply a superiority or inferiority relationship between Eurocentric (analytical) and Afrocentric (relational) styles. Unfortunately, most teachers use one method of instruction—analytical—and ignore relational methods. Hence, they fail to capitalize on the strengths of Black and other children's learning modalities, making a direct contribution to the students' school failure (Irvine, 1990). Research on learning styles of gifted minority students is therefore important because it can lead educators to recognize that the minority gifted, a unique source of talent, have preferences to learn in uniquely different ways (Ewing & Yong, 1992).

FAMILY AND PEER INFLUENCES ON GIFTED AFRICAN AMERICAN STUDENTS

Gifted African American children face many dilemmas in and out of the classroom environment. Perhaps the most formidable dilemmas are encountered within family and peer interactions. To gain acceptance by family and peers, gifted students will often mask their abilities to fit in with the group. Unlike White students, most Black students must simultaneously manipulate two cultures—one at home and the other at school—that may be quite diverse (Ford, 1992).

In the school setting, students are expected to achieve and perform at levels commensurate with their gifted and talented designation. At home, students are expected to act in a manner that conforms to their environment and social climate. One widely held supposition is that many Black children hide their academic abilities by becoming class clowns, dropping out, and suppressing effort (Comer, 1988), to avoid being perceived as "acting White," being raceless, or otherwise not reflecting Black culture (Fordham, 1988). The possibility that Black students may sabotage any chance they have of succeeding in school is a disturbing prospect in urban and gifted education (Ford, 1992).

Although the possibility that African American students would sabotage their chances at success in gifted and talented education programs is unconscionable and hard for many educators to understand, it nevertheless occurs at an alarming rate. Literature highlighting the postsecondary psychosocial problems many African American students experience provides a term that can be applied in gifted and talented education as well. The term is *survival conflict*, a reaction to surpassing the accomplishments of family and/or peers (Whitten, 1992). It can manifest itself in one or more emotional responses, including guilt, ambivalence, anxiety, and depression. These feelings are frequently subconscious and can be debilitating if not recognized and worked through, resulting in various forms of self-sabotage, procrastination, decreased productivity, and devaluation of one's self-concept, accomplishments, and ambitions.

Many families are clearly supportive of their members' accomplishments; some families are more ambivalent due to jealousy, competitiveness, or a fear of being abandoned or belittled by the achiever. These families induce survival conflict, directly or indirectly, in students who otherwise may or may not be subject to these reactions (Whitten, 1992). Survival conflict is similar to fear of success (Horner, 1972) in that an individual anticipates negative consequences from competitive striving. The most disquieting issue concerning this phenomenon is that family and peers view students with strong intellectual abilities as "sell-outs" or "pawns of White society." It is unfortunate that success and intellectual ability are not traits these individuals view as indigenous to African Americans.

GIFTED AFRICAN AMERICAN UNDERACHIEVERS

Student underachievement is a problem faced by students across all racial, cultural, and socioeconomic boundaries. This problem is especially detrimental to gifted and talented African American students. Whitmore (1986) suggests,

> Lack of motivation to excel is usually a result of a mismatch between the student's motivational characteristics and opportunities provided in the classroom. Students are typically highly motivated when (1) the social climate of the classroom is nurturant, (2) the curriculum content is relevant to the students' personal interests and is challenging, and (3) the instructional process is appropriate to the students' natural learning style. (p. 423)

It would not be a chance occurrence if African American students lacked a "goodness of fit" with all three factors. Ford (1992) suggests that a combination of psychological, social, and cultural forces contributes to the problem of underachievement. Still others suggest that the identification of gifted students through intelligence tests early in their school careers is a barrier for many African American students. This is due to the manifestation of underachievement behaviors by many African American students at the first-, second-, and third-grade levels—typically, the time of testing for inclusion in gifted and talented programs. Poor performance on intelligence tests, coupled with entrenching the defining characteristics of gifted students in psychometry, means that a vast majority of African American students go unidentified as gifted, as underachieving, or as both.

Sternberg and Davidson (1986) contend that tests only work for some of the people some of the time—not for all of the people all of the time—and that some of the assumptions we make in our use of tests are, at best, correct only for a segment of the tested population and, at worst, correct for none at all. Hilliard (1976) notes that to be successful on standardized tests, students' language, vocabulary, general experience pool, and basic approach to the solution of problems must coincide with the narrow experiences of the person or persons who framed the questions.

A reliance on the old adage, intelligence is "what intelligence tests measure" (Weinberg, 1989), is no longer valid if underidentification of diverse learners is to be eradicated. The vast numbers and proportions of our most productive people are not those who score at the 95th percentile or above on standardized tests of intelligence; nor were they necessarily straight A students who discovered early how to play the lesson-learning game (Renzulli, 1981). The sacrosanct intelligence tests must make way for a myriad of alternative modes of assessment and models that will expand the definition of giftedness. Alternatives focus on unbiased, nontraditional, multidimensional, and multimodal assessment strategies, using culturally sensitive instruments and broadened definitions and following theories of giftedness espoused by theorists such as Howard Gardner, Joseph Renzulli, Robert Sternberg, as well as other researchers and practitioners (Ford, 1994).

The idea of expanding the boundaries to include a broader range of students in gifted and talented programs should not be viewed as a prelude to destruction, ushered in by a decline in standards. A happy medium can be achieved if rigid nomination and identification procedures for gifted students are modified to provide a more globalized view of this term; a view that does not promote underidentification of any student group.

SCREENING AND IDENTIFICATION

Creating a more inclusive gifted and talented program clearly should address the theoretical underpinnings of the identification and nomination process. Sternberg and Davidson (1986) state that if we are to optimize our use of giftedness as a national resource, we will have to take into account the multiplicity of forms in which it can be found.

According to most studies, five factors contribute to the disproportionate number of minority students identified as gifted. These include (a) the criteria used to determine eligibility, (b) the screening process, (c) problems in the student referral process, (d) lack of understanding of cultural and ethnic diversity, and (e) the lack of in-service training (Kofsky, 1992). Factor A has been addressed in the previous discussion on standardized testing. Factors D and E will be addressed in a subsequent section, "Teachers and Multicultural Education." However, Factors B and C have not been addressed and are instrumental issues when considering the underidentification of gifted African American students.

The screening and identification process that many schools employ has proven ineffectual and even contrary to the aim of increasing African American student participation in gifted programs. For example, Parke (1989) found that the procedures and instruments used to refer potentially gifted elementary students are neither effective nor efficient in identifying students from culturally different backgrounds, students with handicapping conditions, young children, and girls.

Teacher checklists and rating scales, in combination with standardized test scores, are the primary screening measures schools employ in the identification and referral of students for gifted and talented programs. According to some educators, the problem of identifying minority gifted students is more a problem of how you integrate the information from a set of multiple criteria into the traditional screening and identification process (Baldwin, 1980; Eby, 1983; Frasier, 1989a; Renzulli, 1981).

Unfortunately, the lack of teacher training and user-friendly assessment instruments has increased the ambiguity in the screening process. Many assessment instruments are poorly worded, are esoteric, or lack validity in describing the student population under consideration. Research conducted by Pegnato and Birch (1959) proved that teachers were able to identify only 45 percent of the gifted children in their junior high classes—a figure that drops to 10 percent for kindergarten teachers (Jacobs, 1971). Without proper training, teachers will continue to refer only those students who fit their preconceived ideas of how a gifted student behaves; this misconception immediately rules out many students who, by the current definition, show gifted potential (Rhodes, 1992).

ALTERNATIVE THEORIES IN THE IDENTIFICATION PROCESS

The work of Lewis Terman, which included the introduction of the Stanford Binet Intelligence Test, has caused many to view intelligence from a unitary point of view. The ideal gifted student, in theory, is identified by the attainment of high IQ scores. What many fail to realize is that there is no "one size fits all" intelligence or achievement test (Ford, 1994). Giftedness is defined, shaped, and adjudged in a societal milieu and is not something merely inside a person's head. Tests used to identify the gifted tend to oversimplify because they try to find inside a person something that is outside that person as well (Sternberg & Davidson, 1986).

Theories and definitions used to identify gifted learners are no longer acceptable if they choose to disregard the intimate liaisons that exist between culture and individual behavior. A number of theorists are recognizing the importance of the unique characteristics displayed by diverse gifted learners. Renzulli's (1986) three-ring conception of giftedness attempts to describe the term from a broad view. Giftedness is identified as three interlocking clusters (rings). These rings consist of above average (although not necessarily superior) ability, task commitment, and creativity. It is important to point out that no single cluster makes giftedness. Rather, it is the interaction among the three clusters that research has shown to be the necessary ingredient for creative-productive accomplishment.

Gardner's (1983) theory of multiple intelligences has offered educators a comprehensive framework within which fundamentally different solutions can be devised and implemented. The seven intelligences Gardner has identified are linguistic, logical-mathematical, spatial, musical, bodily-kinesthetic, interpersonal, and intrapersonal. Gardner and Hatch (1989) are convinced that these seven intelligences are highly independent and that nearly all children and adults show distinctive profiles of strength and weakness in the different kinds of intelligence. Gardner believes that the development of high-level competence requires innate capacity, motivation, and opportunity. Environment, cultural context, and language may influence all of these important factors.

Sternberg's (1985) triarchic theory of intelligence is composed of three sub-theories that serve as the governing bases for understanding extraordinary intelligence:

> The first subtheory relates intelligence to the internal world of the individual, specifying the mental mechanisms that lead to more and less intelligent behavior. The second subtheory specifies those points along the continuum of one's experience with tasks or situations that most critically involve the use of intelligence. The third subtheory relates intelligence to the external world of the individual, specifying three classes of acts—environmental adaptation, selection, and shaping—that characterize intelligent behavior in the everyday world. (p. 223)

What each theorist advances is a more globalized view of giftedness, one in which a unitary standard such as intelligence tests is not the sole means of assessment. Another important advance, perhaps the most important, is theorists' recognition of social and cultural influences in the expression of gifted behavior. Renzulli (1986) contends that at the very least, attributes of intelligent behavior must be considered within the context of cultural and situational factors. Gardner (cited in Maker, Nielson, & Rogers, 1994) has implied that culture, language, and environment do not determine whether an individual will be gifted: instead, they influence the specific ways in which giftedness is expressed. Sternberg and Davidson (1986) state that exceptional intelligence cannot be fully understood outside a sociocultural context, and it may in fact differ for a given individual from one culture to the next. What do these statements and theoretical reconceptualizations offer the gifted and talented African American student? Hope.

TEACHERS AND MULTICULTURAL EDUCATION

The curriculum of the schools and the instructional materials we use to help impart knowledge, skills, information, and experiences are powerful forces that control the kind of education our children receive (Arnez, 1993). Therefore, the message schools should convey is one of democracy and the inclusion of all students. One means of accomplishing this goal has been multicultural education and programming.

The resurgence of multicultural education is testimony to the impact of changing demographics and changing student needs (Billings, 1994). However, there is confusion over what is meant by multicultural education (Sleeter & Grant, 1988). Gollnick and Chinn (1990) contend that multicultural education is the educational strategy in which students' cultural backgrounds are viewed as positive and essential in developing classroom instruction and school environments. It is designed to support and extend the concepts of culture, cultural pluralism, and equality into the formal school setting. Still others, such as the American Association of Colleges for Teacher Education (AACTE) state,

> Multicultural education is education that values cultural pluralism. Multicultural education affirms that schools should be oriented toward the cultural enrichment of all children and youth through programs rooted to the preservation and extension of cultural diversity as a fact of life in American society. (Hunter, 1974, cited in Arnez, 1993, p. 510)

Why is multicultural education important to gifted African American students? These students, like their minority peers in nongifted programs, experience the same forms of racism and discrimination at the hands of classroom teachers. According to Lightfoot (1978), teachers, like all of us, use the dimensions of class, race, sex, and ethnicity to bring order to their perception of the classroom environment. Rather than gaining a more in-depth and holistic understanding of children with the passage of time, teachers tend to develop increasingly stereotyped perceptions, and children become hardened caricatures of an initial discriminatory vision.

A prime example of the problems associated with teacher perceptions of minority students and the need for multicultural education was uncovered in an often cited study conducted by Rubovits and Maehr (1973). Using 66 designated teachers (White female undergraduates) in a simulated teaching group of four students—two Blacks and two Whites—these teachers were told that one of each race was gifted. The end result of the study was a significant difference in the praise and criticism given to the students based on their ethnicity. The White students were given significantly more praise and encouragement, whereas the Black students were often criticized and ignored. The researchers called these results "a disturbing instance of White racism" (p. 56). They also stated that, perhaps, these teachers experienced dissonance about these gifted Black males because they did not confirm their expectations of Black children as nonachievers.

Studies of this nature reveal the pressing need for multicultural education. Issues such as our nation's declining pool of minority teachers and the simultaneously increasing pool of minority students are also legitimate reasons to implement these educational programs. A recent survey of 10 southern states revealed that between 1980–1981 and 1983–1984, the number of Black teachers declined by 5,000 or 6.4 percent. At the same time, the total number of teachers in these 10 southern states increased by 3,300 (Rodman, 1985). This is an alarming prospect if we couple this information with the prediction that by the end of the decade, students of color will represent close to 40 percent of total school enrollment nationwide (Hodgkinson, 1988).

Multicultural education can no longer be viewed as ancillary to teacher preparation programs. All teachers must be exposed to issues dealing with multiculturalism and diversity in the classroom environment. A dangerous precedent is set when schools assume that minority teachers should be exempt from training programs dealing with these topics, solely because they are minorities. It is incorrect to assume that all White teachers are ineffective instructors of minority children. It is also incorrect to assume that all minority teachers are effective instructors of minority children (Irvine, 1990). Yet it is correct to assume that teachers who are out of cultural sync with their students can benefit from multicultural education.

There are avenues that can be explored to help expand the knowledge base as we prepare teachers to educate African American learners (Billings, 1994). Some of the suggestions are

(1) Prospective teachers need to systematically study the long history of African-American education; (2) There is a need for clearer and more plentiful explanations of African-American culture as a vehicle for better understanding African-American learners; (3) There is a need for more and better scholarly investigations of the pedagogy of those teachers who are successful with African-American learners; and (4) There is a need to develop a more extensive network for advocacy on behalf of African-American learners. (Billings, 1994, pp. 140–142)

By tearing down many of the cultural barriers through multicultural education, we will give gifted African American students fewer obstacles to circumvent as they seek a chance at success. With the elimination of bias from the teaching process and the emergence of proactive teachers who seek to best meet the needs of individual students, the classroom can become a stimulating experience for most students, regardless of their cultural background and experiences (Gollnick & Chinn, 1990).

CONCLUSION

Renzulli (1986) speaks of our nation's fascination with the gifted from its earliest recorded history. Although our fascination has not waned, our willingness to dub an individual worthy of this lofty title is often determined by a unitary display of unbridled wisdom—scoring high on an intelligence test. For African Americans, this rite of passage has consistently disregarded issues that are important contributors to their matriculation in gifted and talented programs. Some individuals assert that if the definition for gifted is expanded, the quality of students in these programs will decline. Still others agree that de-emphasizing the intelligence test will trivialize the identification process. What are we to do? If we address this issue in retrospect, are we willing to test a Martin Luther King? Would an IQ of 120 be enough to label a Josephine Baker? Do we need to give a No. 2 lead pencil to a Jesse Owens? Are three hours enough to test a Booker T. Washington? The dreams of gifted African American students can no longer be deferred simply because of cultural differences or the unfilled ovals in an examination booklet.

REFERENCES

Arnez, N. (1993). Equity and access in instruction. *Journal of Black Studies, 23*(4), 500–514.

Baldwin, A. (1980, April). *The Baldwin Identification Matrix, its development and use in programs for the gifted child.* Paper presented at the Council for Exceptional Children, Philadelphia.

Billings, G. L. (1994). Who will teach our children: Preparing teachers to successfully teach African-American students. In E. R. Hollins, J. E. King, & W. C. Hayman (Eds.), *Teaching diverse populations: Formulating a knowledge base* (pp. 129–158). Albany: State University of New York Press.

Brophy, J., & Everston, C. M. (1981). *Student characteristics and teaching.* New York: Longman.

Carnegie Corporation of New York. (1984/1985). Renegotiating society's contract with the public schools. *Carnegie Quarterly, 29/30*(1–4), 6–11.

College Board. (1985). *Equality and excellence: The educational status of Black Americans.* New York: Author.

Comer, J. (1988). Educating poor minority children. *Scientific American, 259*(5), 42–48.

Dunn, R., & Dunn, K. (1992). *Teaching elementary students through their individual learning styles.* Boston: Allyn & Bacon.

Eby, J. W. (1983). Gifted behavior: A nonelitist approach. *Educational Leadership, 41*(8), 30–36.

Ewing, N. J., & Yong, F. L. (1992). A comparative study of the learning style preferences among gifted African-American, Mexican American, and American-born Chinese middle grade students. *Roeper Review, 14*(3), 120–123.

Feshbach, N. D. (1969). Student teacher preferences for elementary pupils varying in personality characteristics. *Journal of Educational Psychology, 60*, 126–132.

Ford, D. Y. (1992). Determinants of underachievement as perceived by gifted, above-average, and average Black students. *Roeper Review, 14*(3), 130–136.

Ford, D. Y. (1994). *The recruitment and retention of African-American students in gifted education programs: Implications and recommendations* (RBDM 9406). Storrs: National Research Center on the Gifted and Talented, University of Connecticut.

Fordham, S. (1988). Racelessness as a strategy in Black students' school success: Pragmatic strategy or pyrectic victory? *Harvard Educational Review, 58*(1), 54–84.

Frasier, M. M. (1989a). Identification of gifted Black students: Developing new perspectives. In C. J. Maker (Ed.), *Critical issues in gifted education: Vol. 2. Defensible programs for cultural and ethnic minorities* (pp. 213–215). Austin, TX: ProEd.

Frasier, M. M. (1989b). Poor and minority students can be gifted, too! *Educational Leadership, 50*(7), 16–18.

Gardner, H. (1983). *Frames of mind: The theory of multiple intelligences.* New York: Basic Books.

Gardner, H., & Hatch, T. (1989). Multiple intelligences go to school: Educational implications of the theory of multiple intelligences. *Educational Researcher, 18*(8), 4–9.

Gollnick, D. M., & Chinn, P. C. (1990). *Multiculturalism education in a pluralistic society* (3rd ed.). Columbus, OH: Merrill.

Gouldner, H. (1978). *Teachers' pets, troublemakers, and nobodies: Black children in elementary school.* Westport, CT: Greenwood Press.

Haensly, P., Reynolds, C. R., & Nash, W. R. (1986). Giftedness: Coalescence, context, conflict, and commitment. In R. J. Sternberg & J. E. Davidson (Eds.), *Conceptions of giftedness* (pp. 128–148). New York: Cambridge University Press.

Hallahan, D. P., & Kauffman, J. M. (1991). *Exceptional children: Introduction to special education.* Boston: Allyn & Bacon.

Hilliard, A. G. (1976). *Alternatives to IQ testing: An approach to the identification of gifted "minority" children* (Report No. PS 009 639). Sacramento: California Department of Education, Special Education Division. (ERIC Document Reproduction Service No. ED 147 009)

Hodgkinson, H. (1990). The right schools for the right kids. In J. J. Irvine (Ed.), *Black students and school failure* (p. 55). New York: Greenwood Press.

Horner, M. (1972). Toward an understanding of achievement-related conflicts in women. *Journal of Social Issues, 28,* 157–176.

Hughes, L. (1951). A dream deferred. In X. J. Kennedy (Ed.), *Literature: An introduction to fiction, poetry, and drama.* Boston: Little, Brown.

Hunter, W. A. (1974). Antecedents to development of and emphasis on multicultural education. In W. A. Hunter (Ed.), *Multicultural education through competency-based teacher education* (pp. 11–31). Washington, DC: American Association of Colleges for Teacher Education.

Irvine, J. J. (1990). *Black students and school failure.* New York: Greenwood Press.

Jacobs, J. (1971). Effectiveness of teacher and parent identification of gifted children as a function of school level. *Psychology in the Schools, 8,* 140–142.

Kofsky, G. E. (1992). *Increasing the number of minority elementary students found eligible for placement in gifted programs by enhancing the quality of screening instruments and in service training provided to school staff* (Report No. EC 301 312). Fort Lauderdale-Davie, FL: Nova University. (ERIC Document Reproduction Service No. ED 346 697)

Lightfoot, S. L. (1978). Worlds apart: Relationships between families and schools. In J. J. Irvine (Ed.), *Black students and school failure.* New York: Greenwood Press.

Maker, C. J., Nielson, A. B., & Rogers, J. A. (1994, Fall). Multiple intelligences: Giftedness, diversity, and problem-solving: Multiple intelligences and diversity in educational settings. *Teaching Exceptional Children, 27*(1), 4–19.

Marland, S. (1972). *Education of the gifted and talented: Report to the Congress of the United States by the U.S. Commissioner of Education.* Washington, DC: Government Printing Office.

McCarthy, B. (1990). Using the 4MAT system to bring learning styles to schools. *Educational Leadership, 48,* 31–37.

Parke, B. N. (1989). Educating the gifted and talented: An agenda for the future. *Educational Leadership, 49*(7), 5.

Pegnato, C. W., & Birch, J. W. (1959). Locating gifted children in junior high school: A comparison of methods. *Exceptional Children, 25,* 300–304.

Peters, M. F. (1990). "Making it" Black family style: Building on the strengths of the Black family. In N. Stinnett, J. DeFrain, K. King, P. Knaub, & G. Rowe (Eds.), *Family strengths three: Roots of well-being* (pp. 73–91). Lincoln: University of Nebraska Press.

Renzulli, J. S. (1981, May). The revolving door model: A new way of identifying the gifted. *Phi Delta Kappan,* 648–649.

Renzulli, J. S. (1986). The three-ring conception of giftedness: A developmental model for creative productivity. In R. J. Sternberg & J. E. Davidson (Eds.), *Conceptions of giftedness* (pp. 53–92). New York: Cambridge University Press.

Rhodes, L. (1992). Focusing attention on the individual in identification of gifted Black students. *Roeper Review, 14*(3), 108–110.

Rodman, B. (1985, November 20). Teaching's "endangered species." *Education Week 5*(1), 11–12.

Rubovits, P C., & Maehr, M. (1973). Pygmalion Black and White. *Journal of Personality and Social Psychology 25,* 210–218.

Shade, B. J. (1982). Afro-American cognitive style: A variable in school success? *Review of Educational Research, 52,* 219–244.

Sleeter, C. E., & Grant, C. A. (1988). *Making choices for multicultural education: Five approaches to race, class, and gender.* Columbus, OH: Merrill.

Sternberg, R. J. (1985). *Beyond IQ: A triarchic theory of human intelligence.* New York: Cambridge University Press.

Sternberg, R. J., & Davidson, J. (1986). *Conceptions of giftedness.* New York: Cambridge University Press.

Torrance, E. P. (1973, September). *Emergent concepts concerning culturally different gifted children.* Paper prepared for the Work Conference on the Culturally Different Gifted Child, Rougemont, NC.

Torrance, E. P., & Reynolds, C. R. (1978). Images of the future of gifted adolescents: Effects of alienation and specialized cerebral functioning. In J. C. Gowan, J. Khatena, & E. P. Torrance (Eds.), *Educating the ablest.* Itaska, IL: Peacock. (Reprinted from *Gifted Child Quarterly, 22,* 40–54)

U.S. Department of Education. (1993). *National excellence: A case for developing America's talent.* Washington, DC: Office of Educational Research and Improvement, U.S. Department of Education.

Weinberg, R. (1989). Intelligence and IQ: Landmark issues and great debates. *American Psychologist, 44,* 98–104.

Whitmore, J. R. (1986). Understanding a lack of motivation to excel. In D. Hallahan & J. Kauffman (Eds.), *Exceptional children: Introduction to special education.* Boston: Allyn & Bacon.

Whitten, L. (1992). Survival conflict and survival guilt in African-American college students. In M. Lang & C. A. Ford (Eds.), *Strategies for retaining minority students in higher education* (pp. 64–74). Springfield, IL: Charles C Thomas.

Witkin, H. A., & Moore, C. A. (1975). *Field-dependent and field-independent cognitive styles and their educational implications.* Princeton, NJ: Educational Testing Service.

Fred A. Bonner II, EdD, is assistant professor of higher education and student affairs at Bowling Green State University. His current research in the area of postsecondary education focuses on academically gifted African American males, historically Black colleges and universities, and diversity initiatives within student affairs.

Transitions in the Development of Giftedness

Fred A. Bonner II

The history of education in the United States is replete with stories highlighting movements intended to facilitate the education of our unlearned masses. From the initial establishment of postsecondary education to the requisite implementation of secondary schooling, ours has been a complex journey toward discovery.

One of the more noted junctures in the evolution of our educational system has been the creation of specific school types designed to meet the learning needs of children. The creation of these school types is predicated upon correlations between the students' levels of developmental readiness and the schools' provision of learning contexts to meet them. The evolution of the middle school concept provides a particularly relevant example of this process. According to Alexander and George (as cited in Chance, 1998),

> The concept of a bridging school is not enough, however, because children of middle school age have their unique characteristics and needs which cannot be subordinated to the impact of the elementary school or to the demands of the high school. An effective middle school must not only build upon the program of earlier childhood and anticipate the program of secondary education to follow, but it must be directly concerned with the here-and-now problems and interests of students. Furthermore, the middle school should not be envisioned as a passive link in the chain of education below the college and university, but rather as a dynamic force in improving education. (p. 2)

It was the establishment of the middle school that served as a means to address a number of issues (e.g., curriculum relevance, environment, developmental readiness, self-esteem, teaching practices) students were experiencing with school

Fred A. Bonner II, "Transitions in the Development of Giftedness," *Gifted Child Today* 28, Issue 2 (Spring 2005): 19–25. Reprinted with permission of Prufrock Press Inc. (http://www.prufrock.com).

transition processes. Add these to the complexities associated with this transition-ing experience (the myriad issues impacting gifted students), and many individuals, particularly teachers, are left perplexed. Yet, these two areas of focus (i.e., middle school education and gifted education) should be complementary. As Chance (1998) asserted, "Gifted education and middle school education share many of the same constructs and ideas. Not only should they not be in conflict, but gifted educa-tion within the middle school setting should be a perfect fit" (p. 138).

METHOD

The purpose of this investigation was to assess the factors that lead to success in transitions of giftedness among a middle school student cohort. As part of the Yale University (PACE Center) Transitions in the Development of Giftedness evalua-tion plan, qualitative data were collected via a semistructured interview protocol. The qualitative interview protocols were structured in a manner in which the initial questions were more generic in nature, "to get people talking and to help people feel comfortable" (Krueger & Casey, 2000, p. 44). These data allowed the re-search investigators to add to the "thick description" (Geertz, 1973) of the various contexts in which the Transitions project was implemented.

A total of 63 sixth-grade students enrolled in a middle school in Connecti-cut were interviewed. The school included grades 6–8, with a total enrollment of approximately 915 students with a racial and ethnic breakdown of 18 percent African American, 3 percent Asian, 11 percent Hispanic, and 67 percent White. Roughly 37 percent of the students received free or reduced-price lunch.

Audio-taped interviews of the students yielded 338 pages of transcript. Tran-script data were indexed in order to make the analysis process more manageable for interpretation. According to Coffey, Holbrook, and Atkinson (1999), indexing allows components of data to be aggregated in ways that are relevant to a specific theme, topic, or hypothesis.

Index codes were assigned to various paragraphs and sections of the data that proved to be salient. Through the process of analytic induction, a number of themes were uncovered. The process of analytic induction is a means to derive explana-tory hypotheses that apply to all the data available on a particular phenomena or problem (Bloor, Frankland, Thomas, & Robson, 1999). The themes that emerged from the data and the analytic induction process included localizing the locus of control and deconstructing the definition of giftedness.

FINDINGS

Interview data collected across the 63 student respondents were aggregated and will be discussed in the following sections. Six of the key questions included in the interview protocol are used to facilitate discussion.

What Are the Three Most Important
Factors Contributing to Success?

Several factors were identified across interview data as being the most important contributors to the respondents' success: self-confidence, intelligence, and determination. The students invariably cited the interconnectedness among these factors as facilitating their success. Self-confidence was viewed as playing a vital role in not only their academic experiences but also their nonacademic encounters. Students employed self-confidence in the classroom in order to be successful in completing assignments, mastering course content, and developing new skills. Outside of the classroom, students used self-confidence to engage in a range of extracurricular pursuits such as music and sports. The following are quotes from several of the respondents:

> You will have to have like faith in yourself and you have to believe that you can do it to be able to be successful.
> If you can't believe in yourself, then you probably will not be able to achieve it.
> You have to believe in yourself to do something. . . .
> Everyone needs self-confidence when it comes to taking a test or answering questions because, if you do not think you can succeed, you probably won't.
> Always believing in yourself, that you can do many things and not always bringing yourself down and saying, "I am not good at this," instead of saying that, you should say that I can do this and probably just try.

Several students equated self-confidence with having a sense of respect for self. As one student asserted, "Because you have self-confidence in yourself, you respect yourself."

Intelligence and determination also served as important factors in success. Students viewed intelligence as a core variable in their academic pursuits. Often cited in combination with determination, intelligence was viewed as a necessary factor to assist them in negotiating the educational terrain. According to one respondent, "When you are doing jobs, when you are working toward success, you need to be able to learn and reason." Another student commented, "You know, if you make a mistake in school, you need intelligence to realize that you made that mistake and figure out what you can do to avoid doing that again and to reason with others."

Determination was perceived to be a necessary condition to attain success by several respondents:

> If you are not determined to do anything at all, then you a re not going to do anything at all. It is like a ladder to success. If you are 100 percent determined, you can give 100 percent.
> If you are determined, it drives you to do more. . . .
> A lot of things in your life can happen if you are determined.

What are the three least important factors contributing to success?

Students were quite outspoken in their responses to the question that required them to identify the factors they perceived to be the least important contributors to their success. Overwhelmingly, three factors were cited: luck, money, and physical attractiveness.

Luck was often cited as being transitory and fleeting, a factor that was arbitrarily experienced by individuals through no predetermined or orderly set of patterns or circumstances. Myriad responses regarding luck were cited across interview data:

> I guess luck is really not important; it is only like a belief.
> Because if you set yourself out to do a good job . . . you don't really need luck to guide you. . . .
> Luck really only happens a few times, so you can't really depend on that.
> It is not a success factor and you are not giving anything to get it or accomplish it.

Money was viewed as a plausible means of achieving some form of life satisfaction, but not as a critical component in achieving success. According to several of the responses provided in the interview data,

> We do not always need money to be successful. . . . For example, passing classes: You do not need money to succeed and get good grades.
> Money does not always buy you happiness; but, if you are working hard and trying your best, then you will probably be happier than if you were just passing off all the time and you just had money.
> Because if you are working and can achieve your goals, like sentimental goals, you do not need money for that.

Physical attractiveness was also seen as a factor of diminished importance when identifying necessary and sufficient components to ensure success. Much like the views expressed concerning the arbitrary and capricious realizations of luck, many respondents commented on the random and subjective qualities associated with physical attractiveness. Some of the comments taken from interview data include:

> It really does not matter how you look.
> People don't get good grades because they are good looking.
> I see guys who are successful, but no offense, they don't particularly look that great. Their appearance is not appealing. They do great. They are millionaires. I don't see why physical attractiveness has anything to do with success.
> It really does not matter how you look; what matters is how you work.

Again, much was shared through the commentary provided by the respondents regarding the factors they viewed as least likely contributors to their success. Most of the factors selected were external factors, factors that had no true connections to the respondents' motivation and drive. Although the frequency of responses for these three factors was significantly greater than the other factors identified as possible contributors, connections and risk taking were also factors that warrant mentioning. Respondents provided these statements in reference to these factors:

> If you have connections, you do not know your real true potential because you are always leaning on someone else.

I only go for goals that I feel I will be successful at, not something that I can obtain by chance and if I blow that chance then I have to start all over again to achieve another goal.

What Factors Did You Use to Be Successful?

Factors identified most frequently across the interview transcripts among respondents regarding their attainment of past successes were self-confidence, learning from mistakes, intelligence, determination, and creativity.

Self-confidence, much like the discussion in the previous section highlighting the three most important factors used for success, was viewed as a primary ingredient in these students' academic experiences. Many also spoke of their use of self-confidence in extracurricular events or activities outside of the school setting.

Oftentimes, expressed concomitantly was their discussion of learning from mistakes. Just as these students used their self-confidence to engage in various academic and nonacademic pursuits, they were also quite aware of when they needed to step back and evaluate the outcomes of these pursuits; if they proved to be unfavorable, it was important to learn from these experiences. The following statements in relation to self-confidence and learning from mistakes were provided:

> The homework, I did not understand it, and then my mom sat with me. She gave me this long talk and got my self-confidence up, and then I was able to get it.
>
> Last year, I won the spelling bee for my school and I had to study and have a lot of self-confidence.
>
> I feel if you have self-confidence, you can give comfort to yourself or other friends. . . .
>
> If you want to be successful in dance, if you do something wrong one time in your routine, the next time you would not do that thing.
>
> Because if you make mistakes in any of your classes, then you go back and see what's wrong, why you did it, or how you correct it.

Intelligence, determination, and creativity were also cited as factors the respondents used to accomplish academic and nonacademic goals. Again, much like the discussion included above highlighting the most important factors these students perceived necessary for success, intelligence and determination received virtually the same number of responses, with creativity not far behind. A number of salient quotes related to these three factors include:

> I have to go with intelligence, because in elementary school I had a reputation of being the, well, the smartest kid in the class and people looked up to me when they could not figure out something and I usually helped them.
>
> I used intelligence to use what I knew and what I was trying to figure out.
>
> I used determination. I believed in myself to try to get the answers right and to know that, if I got one wrong, I would not make a big deal and I just got it, worked my hardest to try to figure out what was right and wrong.
>
> Like I had to use my determination to study harder. . . .
>
> There was a test and I needed to study harder and use this determination.

I use my creativity to write my books and my stories and whatever I am doing. I can think about it and, whenever I have a story to write in school and when-ever I feel like writing at home, I just think and write things down.

What Factors Did You Not Use to Be Successful?

There were two predominate factors cited by students that they could have employed to be successful in a particular situation, but did not for various reasons: self-confidence and learning from mistakes. Ironically, these factors had been cited earlier as being critically important to success. Just as respondents saw the benefits of using self-confidence and learning from mistakes to achieve noted success, they also saw how they missed many opportunities by not employing these very same factors at critical personal junctures:

> When I get home and have to study, I don't like to just give up if I don't get it right. And for self-confidence, if I get something wrong, I would like think it over and then I fix it up. . . .
> If we said something wrong the first time, you go back and understand why I did it that way and so next time you would not do it like that.
> One time I twisted my ankle really bad and I thought I could still play. So, I got up and then I started running and then I twisted it even more. . . . I had to go on crutches for a week.

What Success Factors Would You Add to or Remove from the List?

A number of success factors were added to and removed from the list. Factors added to the list were varied, including responsibility, generosity, imagination, happiness, and making friends. Factors removed from the list were typically taken from the existing list provided to the respondents during the interview. The factors most frequently cited to be excised were money, physical attractiveness, and connections.

A cursory glance at the factors added to and deleted from the list reveals an important pattern: these factors mirror the choices respondents made regarding the most and least important contributors to success. The factors that were added to the list seem to be derived from some individualized, internal, self-constructed notion of success—happiness, imagination, generosity. On the other hand, the factors the respondents slated for deletion from the list—money, physical attractiveness, and luck—appear to be more collective, external, and socially constructed in nature.

CONCLUSIONS/INTERPRETATIONS

Two emergent themes were identified through the data analysis process. Both themes, localizing the locus of control and deconstructing the definition of giftedness, are discussed in the following section.

Localizing the Locus of Control

Perhaps one of the most salient themes that emerged across the transcript data involved the respondents' connections to locus of control. According to Rotter (1966), the locus of control is how an individual interprets outcomes based on his or her perception of internal versus external factors. This research evaluation affirms the notion that gifted students tend to possess positive levels of self-perception and tend to have an internal locus of control (Yong, 1994). In addition, the research is resolute in identifying the intrinsic motivational tendencies of gifted and talented students (Skollingsberg, 2003).

Interview data revealed that students consistently selected self-confidence, determination, intelligence, and learning from mistakes as the most important factors as having contributed to their success. According to Yong (1994), students with an internal locus of control are better able to recognize their special abilities and have the motivation to strive for higher goals. By using the factors previously listed, each of which emanates from an internal core, students were able to experience success within and outside various educational contexts.

The factors students perceived to be least likely to contribute to success were luck, money, and physical attractiveness. These factors differ from the factors chosen as necessary for success in that they are extrinsic motivators and elicit an external locus of control. In addition, these factors were cited most frequently for needed deletion from the list of factors contributing to success. Factors falling beyond the control of the respondents—factors they perceived to be out of their sphere of influence (e.g., luck, money, and physical attractiveness)—were not seen as being important contributors or as essential elements in their perceived opportunities for success.

Deconstructing the Definition of Giftedness

A question included in the interview protocol required students to define giftedness and subsequently to define success. Although definitions ranged in length and complexity, students provided quite similar commentary. In providing definitions for giftedness, most responses recapitulated the same terms and statements that identified giftedness as a "special gift," a "gift from God," or possessing "something that not everyone else has." A review of the literature reveals that the definitions these students constructed were not new, but were instead reminiscent of traditional definitions of giftedness.

Although the field of gifted education has evolved in terms of how giftedness is identified and operationalized in various contexts, these students still adhered to a more mainstream definition of giftedness. Renzulli (1986) has referred to this giftedness as schoolhouse giftedness, "the kind most easily measured by IQ or other cognitive ability tests" (p. 57). Many responses were even reminiscent of the age-old controversy surrounding the "g" factor conceptualizations of intelligence; namely, that giftedness is "that certain something that is genetic, 'a gift'" (p. 23).

When asked to define the term *success* or to explain what it meant to be success-ful, responses typically centered on the realization of some predetermined goal or the acquisition of capital (i.e., material wealth or status). Counter to the views expressed by the students regarding giftedness as a quality that was inborn or be-stowed upon a select few individuals, success was viewed as a phenomenon that could be experienced by anyone who was willing to work toward a goal. Factors such as ambition, determination, self-confidence, and wisdom were often cited as prerequisites for achieving success. Hence, giftedness was viewed as being more static and absolute and was inversely related to success, which was viewed as being more fluid and uncertain.

RECOMMENDATIONS

Because this research investigation included only a small number of partici-pants, it is difficult to provide an exhaustive list of recommendations. However, it is certainly possible for the reader to take information gleaned from this article and the ensuing recommendations (programmatic and research) and use it in similar educational contexts.

Programmatic Recommendations

- The developmental needs of gifted students within and outside of the educa-tional context must be considered. Endemic to the experiences of gifted chil-dren in schools is the fallacy that they will somehow "make it on their own." Casey (2000) posited, "A serious developmental penalty may be imposed when gifted children are deemed to need less and are given less, an all too common occurrence" (p. 229). Emotional and affective needs, as well as the career aspi-rations of these students, must be met. The literature suggests mentoring as but one way to deal with these issues.
- The middle school curriculum should be assessed to determine if gifted students are being appropriately challenged. According to Tomlinson (1994), "Gifted middle school learners are at a special risk in the absence of appropriately chal-lenging instruction. . . . To delay presentation of complex and demanding ideas and to defer development of habits of scholarship for highly able learners until high school may result in diminished potential to develop their capacities as producers of knowledge" (p. 179). Proper assessment of the relevance of the middle school curriculum for this age cohort will enhance the chances for suc-cess in the transition of their giftedness.
- Careful consideration of the major issues that impact gifted minority students must be considered. A host of issues, although prevalent to some degree among nonminority students, impacts the educational experiences of gifted minor-ity students. Teacher nominations, standardized testing, peer group influences, environmental influences, self-efficacy and self-esteem, and family support

(Bonner, 2000) must be considered in developing programs aimed at assisting students in the transition of their giftedness. An important consideration must be how giftedness is realized and operationalized within cultural contexts: "Our most intelligent individuals might come out much less intelligent in another culture, and some of our less intelligent individuals might come out more intelligent" (Sternberg & Davidson, 1986, p. 235).

- Evaluation procedures for gifted students must be tied to their interests and motivations. Data uncovered in this investigation reveal the primacy of factors associated with an internal locus of control. Therefore, homework assignments and tests should be constructed in a manner that recognizes and supports their motivations. According to Sternberg (1982), exceptional intelligence is best measured by tasks that are "nonentrenched," meaning they do not require individuals to process information outside of their ordinary experiences. For gifted students, the incongruence between their areas of expertise and the evaluation procedures selected to assess these areas is often problematic. To ensure students' successful transition of their giftedness, a closer alignment of evaluation processes and areas of interest and expertise must be maintained.

Classroom Action Research Recommendations

- Teachers may conduct informal assessments to determine how middle school students conceptualize the term *gifted* and how they see it fitting into their daily lived experiences in both academic and nonacademic contexts. These assessments should be tracked along ethnic/racial and gender dimensions.
- Teachers may explore both themes uncovered in this evaluation: (a) localizing the locus of control and (b) deconstructing the definition of giftedness. They should develop questions that elicit feedback regarding students' perceived locus of control, giftedness, and levels of success.
- Teachers may conduct focus groups with respondents to acquire critical information that is unique to this form of investigation. Focus groups would be primarily used in this context to explore the range of ideas, understand differences in perspective, capture meaningful language, and understand factors of influence (Krueger & Casey, 2000).
- Teachers may investigate ways to integrate the best practices in middle school education with the best practices in gifted education operationalized through content, instruction, and delivery systems (Chance, 1998).

REFERENCES

Bloor, M., Frankland, J., Thomas, M., & Robson, K. (1999). *Focus groups in social research.* Thousand Oaks, CA: Sage.

Bonner, F. A., II. (2000). African American giftedness: Our nation's deferred dream. *Journal of Black Studies, 30,* 643–664.

Casey, K. (2000). Mentors' contributions to gifted adolescents' affective, social, and vocational development. *Roeper Review, 22,* 227–230.

Chance, P. L. (1998). Meeting in the middle: Gifted education and middle schools working together. *Roeper Review, 21,* 133–139.

Coffey, A., Holbrook, B., & Atkinson, P. (1999). Qualitative data analysis: Technologies and representations. *Sociological Research Online, 1*(1). Retrieved January 11, 2005, from http://www.socresonline.org.uk/1/1/4.html

Geertz, C. (1973). *The interpretation of cultures.* New York: Basic Books.

Krueger, R. A., & Casey, M. A. (2000). *Focus groups* (3rd ed.). Thousand Oaks, CA: Sage.

Renzulli, J. S. (1986). The three-ring conception of giftedness: A developmental model for creative productivity. In R. J. Sternberg & J. E. Davidson (Eds.), *Conceptions of giftedness* (pp. 332–357). New York: Cambridge University Press.

Rotter, J. (1966). Generalized expectancies for internal versus external control of reinforcement. *Psychological Monographs, 80*(1). (Whole No. 609).

Skollingsberg, G. E. (2003). A comparison of intrinsic and extrinsic classroom motivational orientation of gifted and learning-disabled students. *Roeper Review, 26,* 53.

Sternberg, R. J. (1982). Lies we live by: Misapplication of tests in identifying the gifted. *Gifted Child Quarterly, 26,* 157–161.

Sternberg, R. J., & Davidson, J. (Eds.). (1986). *Conceptions of giftedness.* New York: Cambridge University Press.

Tomlinson, C. A. (1994). Gifted learners: The boomerang kids of middle school? *Roeper Review, 16,* 177–181.

Yong, F. L. (1994). Self-concepts, locus of control, and Machiavellianism of ethnically diverse middle school students who are gifted. *Roeper Review, 11,* 192–195.

Copyright of *Gifted Child Today* Magazine is the property of Prufrock Press and its content may not be copied or emailed to multiple sites or posted to a listserv without the copyright holder's express written permission. However, users may print, download, or email articles for individual use.

Never Too Young to Lead: Gifted African American Males in Elementary School

Fred A. Bonner II
and Michael Jennings

Just within the past two decades, we have witnessed the proliferation of a variety of literature, both academic (Fashola, 2005; Ferguson, 2000; Hopkins, 1997; Polite & Davis, 1999; Taylor & Phillips, 2006; Watson & Smitherman, 1996) and popular (Hrabowski, Maton, & Greif, 1998; Kunjufu, 1985, 1989, 2005; Porter, 1998; Wynn, 1992), regarding the underachievement and underrepresentation of African American males in U.S. schools (Holzman, 2006). According to the literature, African American males have been disproportionately placed in special education classrooms (Harry & Anderson, 1994; Kearns, Ford, & Linney 2005; Watkins & Kurtz, 2001) and underrepresented in gifted and talented programs (Bonner, 2000; Ford, 1995; Ford, Grantham, & Bailey, 1999). Despite the efforts at broadening the definition to include multifaceted categories and criteria in the identification of giftedness, we continue to see widespread underrepresentation of African American students in gifted and talented programs, by as much as 50 percent nationally (Donovan & Cross, 2002). In this article, we discuss the promise offered by one of the ability areas cited in the federal definition of giftedness—*leadership ability*—as a potential means of addressing the problem of underrepresentation. We focus not only on key mentoring initiatives but also on promising national programs. The article concludes with practical recommendations for practitioners.

DEFINING GIFTEDNESS

The terms *gifted* and *giftedness* have both undergone significant changes over the years in their functional and symbolic definitions. According to Matthews (2004),

Fred A. Bonner II and Michael Jennings, "Never Too Young to Lead," *Gifted Child Today* 30, Issue 2 (Spring 2007): 31–36. Reprinted with permission of Prufrock Press Inc. (http://www. prufrock.com).

Beginning with its origins in the early history of psychology, giftedness was defined primarily in terms of intellectual ability. By the 1950s, however, spurred by factors that included the multifaceted model of intelligence developed by Guilford and the elaboration by DeHann and Kough of 10 categories of gifts and talents, a variety of efforts began leading toward a broader conceptualization of giftedness. (p. 77)

Perhaps the most significant attempts at broadening the conceptualization of these terms came by Congressional mandate and the subsequent efforts of Commissioner of Education Sydney Marland's attempt in 1972 to publish the first formal definition of giftedness. According to the United States Department of Education's (1993) *National Excellence: A Case for Developing America's Talent* report, giftedness includes the following:

> Children and youth with outstanding talent perform or show the potential for performing at remarkably high levels of accomplishment when compared with others of their age, experience, or environment. These children and youth exhibit high performance capacity in intellectual, creative, and/or artistic areas, and unusual leadership capacity, or excel in specific academic fields. They require services or activities not ordinarily provided by the school. Outstanding talents are present in children and youth from all cultural groups, across all economic strata, and in all areas of human endeavor. (p. 19)

When considering the amount of variation found to exist in state definitions (National Association for Gifted Children [NAGC], 2005), it becomes readily apparent that some states embrace more traditional definitions of giftedness—those focusing on academic ability and intelligence,—whereas others use a more multifaceted and fluid approach in this process. Although there is great variability across these states' definitions, many have been consistent in employing leadership capacity or leadership potential as an area of importance. Significant in these definitions is Matthews' (2004) observation that "Leadership has been retained in the federal definition of giftedness across major revisions, since its inclusion in the Marland Report (1972) definitions more than 30 years ago" (p. 77).

Gifted African American Males: The Elementary School Context

The story of the African American male in gifted and talented programs is one of widespread underrepresentation. Ford, Harris, Tyson, and Frazier Trotman (2002) offer some plausible explanations for this phenomenon—lack of teacher referral, low performance on standardized norm-referenced test scores, and student and family choice. According to Grantham and Ford (2003), these barriers are but a few in the list of many that have impeded the progress of gifted African American males, but they appear to be the most pernicious.

Other potential barriers for African American males that are particular to the elementary school context are included in Bonner's (2001) article. Due to the potential for underachievement among African American students in first, second, and third grade, a time in which most identification processes for gifted and talented programs are implemented, these students often go unidentified. The outcome of this conundrum is typical in what Donovan and Cross (2002) reported, namely, that the representation of racial and ethnic groups in gifted and talented programs favors some groups more than others. The study found that gifted and talented programs were composed of

- 7.64% Asian/Pacific Islander students,
- 72.59% White students,
- 8.44% African American students (of which 3.65% are African American males),
- 10.41% Hispanic/Latino students, and
- 0.93% American Indian/Alaskan American students

For the African American male, the elementary context is a time in which capitalizing on gifts and talents is critical, especially if these gifts are going to be harnessed and channeled in positive and rewarding directions. Unfortunately, much like the information reported by Donovan and Cross (2002), unless we tackle the issue of underidentification and underrepresentation early on, we will continue to see inequities. Perhaps one way of addressing these inequities is to focus on areas in which giftedness is promoted and valued among African American populations. From W.E.B. Du Bois's (1903/2003) notion of the "Talented Tenth" to some of the contemporary initiatives enacted by civic, Greek-letter, and religious organizations, leadership or leadership capacity as it is codified in the federal definition of giftedness promises to be an excellent starting point.

Scholars have discussed several possible reasons for the underrepresentation of African American males in gifted and talented programs. One primary reason that has emerged relates to the definitions used in defining giftedness. Research by Ford (1994) and Bonner (2001) found that existing definitions of giftedness have not taken into account the unique attributes, learning styles, and cultural backgrounds of African American male students. One of the primary components of these definitions of giftedness is an emphasis on the characteristic of leadership (Matthews, 2004). This emphasis on leadership as a requisite for defining giftedness raises concerns regarding how leadership potential is perceived and defined vis-à-vis African American male students. The implications of these perceptions are of particular importance for African American males in elementary school because the study of leadership ability in young children has possible implications for leadership development in older children (Parker & Begnaud, 2003).

Walters and Smith's study (as cited in Kershaw, 2001) found that the role of leadership in the African American community has been a contested issue since at least the turn of the last century. Although there are numerous discussions in academic literature about African American leadership, most of this literature is focused on the development of political and community leaders at the national level (Kershaw, 2001). There has been little discussion in mainstream academic literature regarding the development of leadership qualities among African American student cohorts, particularly at the elementary education level.

Developing leadership qualities is of paramount importance to enhancing access to gifted and talented programs for African American males. This is especially significant given the fact that leadership ability has consistently been recognized as an important component of how giftedness is defined (Matthews, 2004). Despite this recognition, leadership remains the most underinvestigated aspect of the several domains that define giftedness (Matthews, 2004). One of the reasons that leadership has not been more thoroughly investigated in relation to giftedness may be due to the difficulty of defining the characteristics of leadership. Although it is beyond the scope of this article to examine the various definitions of leadership, it should be noted that such definitions are numerous (Edmunds & Yewchuk, 1996; Simonton, 1995), complex (Bass & Stogdill, 1990), and highly contested (Matthews, 2004). Notwithstanding these complexities, it is possible to draw connections between the identification and development of leadership potential and the identification and development of gifted and talented African American male students.

In a recent examination of the existing literature on leadership and its connection to gifted and talented youth, Matthews (2004) identifies several specific studies as particularly compelling. One study in particular was completed by Roach et al. (1999). According to Matthews, this is "The only study addressing the long-term development of youth leadership and its relationship with adult leadership" (p. 94). Roach et al. note that theories of adult leadership tend to focus on individual abilities, whereas theories of youth leadership are primarily situational in orientation and focus on *self-knowledge*. This emphasis on self-knowledge stands in contrast to the emphasis on charisma that permeates theories of adult leadership (Matthews, 2004).

Although there is a lack of academic literature focusing on leadership as a component of giftedness, an even greater scarcity of literature specifically focuses on leadership among African American gifted student cohorts. A body of literature related to self-knowledge could potentially inform the development of leadership models for African American boys. This literature fits readily into the areas of mentoring and rites of passage programming (henceforth referred to as RITES). Many of these initiatives, especially RITES programs, are designed specifically for young, African American males; however, they largely have been overlooked by researchers in the field of gifted and talented education.

ENCOURAGING LEADERSHIP POTENTIAL

Mentoring has been frequently discussed as an appropriate intervention for aiding African American boys who are struggling with academic achievement (Hrabowski et al., 1998; Price, 2002; Struchen & Porta, 1997). Organizations such as the Boy Scouts of America (http://www.scout-ing.org); 100 Black Men of America, Inc. (http://100blackmen.org); and Concerned Black Men (http://www. cbmnational.org) have traditionally offered group mentoring for young men throughout the country. More specifically, African American fraternal organizations, such as the Most Worshipful Prince Hall Masons (2004), Alpha Phi Alpha Fraternity, Inc. (Wesley, 1981), and Kappa Alpha Psi Fraternity, Inc. (Crump, 1991) have offered mentoring programs targeting African American males. Although these programs have existed for many years throughout the United States, they have generally operated in isolation from each other, as well as from schools. In addition, there has not been a sustained and unified attempt at achieving key mentoring goals among these groups.

RITES programs in particular have been found to be highly effective in promoting successful achievement among African American boys (Alford, 2003; Hare & Hare, 1985; Harvey & Hill, 2004; Hill, 1992). Generally speaking, RITES programs have discouraged labeling students as gifted. Instead, Hill (1999) points out that RITES programs are based on African-centered principles that strive to eliminate distinctions such as "gifted," "average," or "impaired." Grantham (2004) discusses the role of mentoring and its potential to increase the representation of African American males in programs for the gifted and talented, and highlights the importance of personal motivation and racial identity development as important factors for practitioners to understand in their attempts to recruit and retain African American male students who are gifted and talented.

This concept of racial identity development corresponds with the focus on the development of self-knowledge that is endemic in many RITES programs. RITES programs offer a unique opportunity for African American males to develop the leadership skills necessary to garner academic success in school-based gifted and talented programs and to subsequently make a successful transition into adulthood. Alford (2003) describes RITES ritualistic acts as "symbolic and meaningful events that mark transitional periods for individuals as specified stages of life occur" (p. 3).

Alford (2003) uses the work of Warfield-Coppock (1990) to further characterize RITES as bringing "stability, ease of transition, and continuity to life, as well as groundedness, balance, and order" (p. 6). Warfield-Coppock (1992) explains that the primary goal of RITES programs is "instilling a strong, positive sense of self and achievement in African-American youth" (p. 472). Successful RITES programs for African American youth across the country revealed that most of these programs had improvement of self-concept as one of the major indicators for success of the program and that self-knowledge was a crucial attribute for African American youth making the transition to adulthood. For those who are tasked with designing curricula or implementing effective programming to encourage the leadership potential among gifted African American males, both features should be taken into consideration during key planning stages.

Other examples of programs that show promise for enhancing the leadership potential among African American males in general and gifted African American males in particular include the Young Leaders' Academy (YLA) in Baton Rouge, LA. YLA "exists to nurture the development of leadership abilities of young African American males, empowering them to improve the quality of their lives and assist them in becoming productive citizens" (Young Leaders Academy of Baton Rouge, n.d., p. 1). Still another program is the African American Male Achievers Network (A-MAN), a California state-approved mentoring initiative with the expressed purpose of "increasing the number of African American and other minority students who are excited about and who enter the fields of science and technology" (A-MAN, n.d., p. 2). Whether the focus on African American male leadership potential is on specific academic fields or more general academic and social endeavors, programs can be found at local, state, regional, and national levels—from the state-focused Gentleman on the Move program in Georgia to the nationally focused Youth to Leaders Institute sponsored by the Tavis Smiley Foundation.

CONCLUSION

By targeting both mentoring and rites of passage programming initiatives, leadership potential can be cultivated as early as elementary school. To offer administrators, faculty, and parents' viable information on how to effectively meet the needs of these students, we offer the following recommendations.

1. *Involve civic, clergy-based, community, and historically Black Greek letter or-ganizations in the planning process when designing curriculum emphasizing leadership ability.* These groups have a longstanding history of cultivating and providing leadership experiences for African American males. To capture important cultural nuances and idiosyncrasies, it is important to get input from those individuals who are indigenous to these communities.
2. *Infuse "authentic" experiences into leadership ability curriculum or training opportunities.* It is critical to avoid a purely academic approach to leadership, one in which students only learn lessons in leadership processes through temporal exercises. Even at the elementary school level, leadership oppor-tunities can be structured in classroom or schoolwide interactions that are meaningful.
3. *Create a more seamless connection between youth leadership behavior and adult leadership performance* (Roach et al., 1999). Students, especially at the elemen-tary level, are not afforded the opportunity to see how current leadership training will manifest itself later in leadership opportunities. Using adults in leadership capacities might be more of a stretch for this population (although this practice is not discouraged), but junior high school or high school leaders might be more reasonable models.
4. *Refrain from treating African American males as a monolithic group.* The development of programs emphasizing leadership ability for African Ameri-can gifted males must take into account the range of background experiences these students bring to the educational setting. Some students will have had many opportunities to be exposed to leadership and decision making in home

or community settings; others will have not been exposed to such opportunities and will flounder when first presented with these opportunities.

5. *Establish clear criteria in how leadership ability is to be used in the evaluation of giftedness.* The literature affirms the confusion and lack of specificity related to defining this particular form of giftedness. Thus, it is important for administrators, teachers, and personnel responsible for identifying gifted African American males to not only establish effective programs to enhance these abilities, but to also recognize them as viable identification constructs.

Leadership ability is a key area highlighted in the federal definition of giftedness. This particular area provides a great deal of opportunity to promote the gifts and talents of African American males, primarily due to its longstanding tradition within the African American community. It is never too early to begin recognizing giftedness, particularly as it is manifested through leadership potential among African American males. Thus, in order to improve the chances for optimal development, both short and long range for these learners, identification at any early age is not only encouraged, but required (Callahan, 2001; Guralnick & Bennett, 1987).

For practitioners who seek to tap into the leadership potential of gifted African American male cohorts, efforts should be aimed at using existing community agents and structures as a means to "jump start" their efforts. This approach will add a much-needed level of authenticity, genuineness, and legitimacy to the work they are attempting to engage in with these communities. Also, by using the indigenous agents and systems within these communities, practitioners are afforded the opportunity to cut across each of the recommendations cited above.

REFERENCES

Alford, K. (2003). Cultural themes in rites of passage: Voices of young African American males. *Journal of African American Studies, 7,* 3–26.

African-American Male Achievers Network, Inc. (A-MAN). (n.d.). Science and technology education for minority youth. Retrieved November 21, 2006, from http://www.aman.org/Default.htm.

Bass, B. M., & Stogdill, R. M. (1990). *Bass and Stogdill's handbook of leadership: Theory, research, and managerial applications* (3rd ed.). New York: Free Press.

Bonner, F. A., II. (2000). African American giftedness. *Journal of Black Studies, 30,* 643–664.

Bonner, F. A., II. (2001). Making room for the study of gifted African American males. *Black Issues in Higher Education, 18*(6), 80.

Callahan, C. M. (2001). Beyond the gifted stereotype. *Educational Leadership, 59*(3), 42–46.

Crump, W. L. (1991). *The story of Kappa Alpha Psi: A history of the beginning and development of a college Greek letter organization, 1911–1991.* Philadelphia: Kappa Alpha Psi Fraternity.

Donovan, M. S., & Cross, C. T. (2002). *Minority students in special and gifted education.* Washington, DC: National Academy Press.

Du Bois, W.E.B. (2003). *The souls of Black folk: 100th anniversary edition*. New York: Signet. (Original work published 1903)

Edmunds, A. L., & Yewchuk, C. R. (1996). Indicators of leadership in gifted grade twelve students. *Journal of Secondary Gifted Education, 7*, 345–355.

Fashola, O. (2005). *Educating African American males: Voices from the field*. Thousand Oaks, CA: Corwin Press.

Ferguson, A. (2000). *Bad boys: Public schools in the making of Black masculinity*. Ann Arbor: University of Michigan Press.

Ford, D. Y. (1994). *The recruitment and retention of African American students in gifted education programs: Implications and recommendations* (RBDM 9406). Storrs: National Research Center on the Gifted and Talented, University of Connecticut.

Ford, D. Y. (1995). Desegregating gifted education: A need unmet. *Journal of Negro Education, 64*, 52–62.

Ford, D. Y., Grantham, T. C., & Bailey, D. F. (1999). Identifying giftedness among African American males: Recommendations for effective recruitment and retention. In V. C. Polite & J. E. Davis (Eds.), *African American males in school and society* (pp. 51–67). New York: Teachers College Press.

Ford, D. Y., Harris, J. J., III, Tyson, C. A., & Frazier Trotman, M. (2002). Beyond deficit thinking: Providing access for gifted African American students. *Roeper Review, 24*, 52–58.

Grantham, T. (2004). Multicultural mentoring to increase Black male representation in gifted programs. *Gifted Child Quarterly, 48*, 232–245.

Grantham, T. C., & Ford, D. Y. (2003). Beyond self-concept and self-esteem for African American students: Improving racial identity improves achievement. *High School Journal, 87*, 18–29.

Guralnick, M. J., & Bennett, F. C. (1987). Early intervention for at-risk and handicapped children: Current and future perspectives. In M. J. Guralnick & F. C. Bennett (Eds.), *The effectiveness of early intervention for at-risk and handicapped children* (pp. 365–382). New York: Academic Press.

Hare, N., & Hare, J. (1985). *Bringing the Black boy to manhood: The passage*. San Francisco: Black Think Tank.

Harry, B., & Anderson, M. (1994). The disproportionate placement of African American males in special education programs: A critique of the process. *Journal of Negro Education, 63*, 602–620.

Harvey, A., & Hill, R. (2004). Africentric youth and family rites of passage program: Promoting resilience among at-risk African American youths. *Social Work, 49*, 65–74.

Hill, P. (1992). *Coming of age: African American male rites-of-passage*. Chicago: African American Images.

Hill, P. (1999, Fall). Harvesting new generations: Afrocentric rites of passage. *The Drum*. Retrieved October 1, 2006, from http://www.ritesofpassage.org/df99-articles/harvest.htm.

Holzman, M. (2006). *Public education and Black male students: The 2006 state report card*. Cambridge, MA: Schott Foundation for Public Education.

Hopkins, R. (1997). *Educating Black males: Critical lessons in schooling, community, and power*. Albany: State University of New York Press.

Hrabowski, F. A., III, Maton, K. I., & Greif, G. L. (1998). *Beating the odds: Raising academically successful African American males*. Oxford, England: Oxford University Press.

Kearns, T., Ford, L., & Linney, J. A. (2005). African American student representation in special education programs. *Journal of Negro Education, 74*, 297–310.

Kershaw, T. (2001). African American national leadership: A model for complementarity. *Western Journal of Black Studies, 25,* 211–219.

Kunjufu, J. (1985). *Countering the conspiracy to destroy Black boys.* Chicago: African American Images.

Kunjufu, J. (1989). *Critical issues in educating African American youth.* Chicago: African American Images.

Kunjufu, J. (2005). *Hip hop street curriculum.* Chicago: African American Images.

Marland, S., Jr. (1972). *Education of the gifted and talented, Volume I: Report to the Congress of the United States by the U.S. Commissioner of Education.* Washington, DC: United States Government Printing Office.

Matthews, M. S. (2004). Leadership education for gifted and talented youth: A review of the literature. *Journal for the Education of the Gifted, 28,* 77–113.

Most Worshipful Prince Hall Grand Lodge Free and Accepted Masons. (2004). History . . . and where is the beginning? Retrieved November 21, 2006, from http://www.prince hall-pa.org/GrandLodge/glhist.htm.

National Association for Gifted Children. (2005). State of the states 2004–2005. Retrieved July 10, 2006, from http://www.nagc.org/CMS400Min/index. aspx?id=532.

Parker, J., & Begnaud, L. (2003). *Developing creative leadership.* Portsmouth, NH: Teacher Ideas Press.

Polite, V., & Davis, J. (1999). *African American males in school and society: Practices and policies for effective education.* New York: Teachers College Press.

Porter, M. (1998). *Kill them before they grow: The misdiagnosis of African American boys in America's classrooms.* Chicago: African American Images.

Price, H. (2002). *Achievement matters: Getting your child the best education possible.* New York: Kensington Publishing.

Roach, A. A., Wyman, L. T., Brookes, H., Chavez, C., Heath, S. B., & Valdes, G. (1999). Leadership giftedness: Models revisited. *Gifted Child Quarterly, 43,* 13–23.

Simonton, D. K. (1995). Personality and intellectual predictors of leadership. In D. H. Saklofske & M. Zeidner (Eds.), *International handbook of personality and intelligence* (pp. 739–757). New York: Plenum Press.

Struchen, W., & Porta, M. (1997). From role-modeling to mentoring for African American youth: Ingredients for successful relationships. *Preventing School Failure, 41,* 119–123.

Taylor, G., & Phillips, T. (2006). *Improving the quality of education for African-American males: A study of America's urban schools.* Lewiston, NY: Edwin Mellen Press.

U.S. Department of Education, Office of Educational Research and Improvement. (1993). *National excellence: A case for developing America's talent.* Washington, DC: U.S. Government Printing Office.

Warfield-Coppock, N. (1990). *Afrocentric theory and applications, Vol. I: Adolescent rites of passage.* Washington, DC: Baobab Associates.

Warfield-Coppock, N. (1992). The rites of passage movement: A resurgence of African centered practices for socializing African American youth. *Journal of Negro Education, 61,* 471–482.

Watkins, A., & Kurtz, D. (2001). Using solution-focused intervention to address African American male over-representation in special education: A case study. *Children and Schools, 23,* 223–235.

Watson, C., & Smitherman, G. (1996). *Educating African American males: Detroit's Malcolm X academy solution.* Chicago: Third World Press.

Wesley, C. H. (1981). *The history of Alpha Phi Alpha, a development in college life.* Chicago: Foundation Publishers.

Wynn, M. (1992). *Empowering African American males to succeed: A ten step approach for parents and teachers.* Marietta, GA: Rising Sun Publishing.

Young Leaders' Academy of Baton Rouge, Inc. (n.d.). Vision and mission. Retrieved November 21, 2006, from http://www.youngleaders.org/mission.htm.

Copyright of *Gifted Child Today* is the property of Prufrock Press and its content may not be copied or emailed to multiple sites or posted to a listserv without the copyright holder's express written permission. However, users may print, download, or email articles for individual use.

Definition, Identification, Identity, and Culture: A Unique Alchemy Impacting the Success of Gifted African American Millennial Males in School

Fred A. Bonner II, EdD
Chance W. Lewis, PhD
Lisa Bowman-Perrott, PhD
Valerie Hill-Jackson, EdD
Marlon James, PhD

National efforts aimed at enhancing American schooling have led to numerous initiatives, movements, and policies aimed at addressing questions related to improving the *who, what, when, where,* and *how* of educational attainment. Despite these efforts, one group in particular continues to fall beyond the veil of benefits accrued by those who have been the beneficiaries of this enhanced focus on educational enhancement. Namely, extant research (Fashola, 2005; Ferguson, 2000; Kunjufu, 1985, 1989, 2005; Lee, 2005; Milner, 2007; Pitre, Lewis, & Hilton-Pitre, 2007; Polite & Davis, 1999; Taylor & Phillips, 2006; White & Cones, 1999) reveals that one population in particular, that of African American males, continues to suffer from underachievement and underrepresentation in our nation's schools. In part, this conundrum of underachievement can be attributed to the overinclusion of African American males in special education (Arnold & Lassmann, 2003; Fine, 2002; Kearns, Ford, & Linney, 2005; Shealey & Lue, 2006; Skiba, Poloni-Staudinger, Gallini, Simmons, Feggins-Azziz, 2006; Watkins & Kurtz, 2001) and their underrepresentation and lack of inclusion in gifted and talented programs (Bonner, 2000; Bonner, 2001; Bonner & Jennings, 2007; Ford, Grantham, & Bailey, 1999; Ford, Harris, Tyson, & Frasier-Trotman, 2002; Grantham, 2004; Grantham & Ford, 2003; Morris, 2002; Shaunessy, Karnes, & Cobb, 2004). However, another set of critical issues further problematizes the state of African American male giftedness: the deleterious effects of definitions gone awry, identity development issues, and generational challenges experienced by this cohort all serve as contributing factors. When these key component issues are not addressed in classroom

Fred A Bonner II, Lewis, C., Bowman-Perrott, L., Hill-Jackson, V. & James, M., "Definition, Identification, Identity and Culture: A Unique Alchemy Impacting the Success of Gifted African American Millennial Males in School," *Journal for the Education of the Gifted,* expected Fall 2009, Volume 33, Issue 1. Reprinted with permission.

engagements or through extant policy, they combine in ways that often lead to the stagnation of achievement for gifted learners of color in general and gifted African American male learners in particular. Hence, the overarching emphasis of this article is on the underrepresentation of African American males in gifted and talented programs, and the article offers a number of key recommendations to practitioners and researchers who seek viable strategies to address these issues. Beyond the main focus on underrepresentation, contributing topics for discussion include: (a) definitions of giftedness; (b) identity development, (c) student Millennial culture, and (d) gifted African American Millennial males in school contexts. Additionally, data collected from a recent study of a large Midwestern school district will be presented in an authentic case study format to further highlight the topics under investigation.

UNDERIDENTIFICATION AND UNDERACHIEVEMENT

Underidentification and underachievement represent common themes found across the literature (Bonner, 2001; Ford, Grantham & Bailey, 1999; Ford, 1995) on gifted African American males. Each topic alone could serve as fodder for an article-length dialogue concerning the lack of representation of this cohort in gifted programs. Ford, Moore, and Milner (2005) assert that for more than seven decades, African American students have been underidentified in gifted education. Additionally, Ford (1995) has ranked what she has identified as the three primary factors associated with the underidentification of gifted African American students, namely, (1) lack of teacher referral, (2) poor test performance, and (3) student choice. Ford's research implies that all too often it is the magnitude of these issues singly or in combination that lead to the absence of African American males from gifted programs.

Much like Ford's ranking of primary factors, this study identified teacher referrals as perhaps the most noted reason for the underidentification of African American males for gifted programming. What was noted is that teacher referrals were many times riddled with subjective tendencies and preconceived notions of who the student was and what the teacher perceived that the student brought to the classroom setting (Bonner, 2001; Grantham, 2004). A research investigation conducted by Elhoweris, Matua, Alsheikh, and Holloway (2005) investigated the effects of student ethnicity on teacher decision making regarding the inclusion of students in gifted education programs. These researchers stated:

> The results of this study indicated that the student's ethnicity does make a difference in teachers' referral decisions. . . . The results of this investigation—that some students are referred to a gifted and talented program whereas others are not—may add to the reasons why children from linguistically and culturally diverse backgrounds are enrolled in gifted and talented programs in disproportionately low

numbers. . . . in addition to the modification of teacher education programs, the referral process to gifted and talented programs must be monitored for any evidence of potential bias. (p. 30)

As evidenced by this study, teacher nominations to gifted education often overlook students from diverse cultural backgrounds. For African American males, encountering teachers (primarily White) who not only attempt to understand their unique cultural styles but who are also able to discern and identify their giftedness within these cultural frames is rare (Landsman & Lewis, 2006). Cultural incongruities between African American males and White teachers often represent not just gaps but wide gulfs. According to Howard (2006), "The assumption of rightness, as related to the achievement gap, often leads teachers to assume that the problem of school failure lies in the students and their families and not in the structure or function of schooling" (p. 119). It was Grantham (2004) who deftly portrayed through Rocky, in a case study of a high-achieving African American male, the complexities associated with being a gifted African American male in a predominantly White context. According to Grantham, research focusing specifically on teachers who serve as advocates for African American males is critical to more fully understand the strategies that can be implemented in an effort to retain Black males in gifted programs.

Just as underidentification is connected to an array of factors found deleterious to the progression of African American males in gifted education, so too is underachievement—the two accompany each other. While Ford (1995) identified the three factors cited above as associated with underidentification, often it is the combination of these factors, along with several others, that leads to underachievement. Whether it is the lack of a multicultural curriculum (Milner & Ford, 2005) reflective of the interests and motivations of African American males or classroom contexts that do not emphasize African American learning modalities and Afrocentric worldviews (Okara, 2007), underachievement will continue to serve as a formidable issue for this group. In their article, "Leaving Black Males Behind: Debunking the Myths of Meritocratic Education," Hughes and Bonner (2006) lament the fact that current research has tended to focus on what schools have reported as the failure and underachievement among African American male populations but has not chosen to focus on how schools have contributed to this dilemma of underachievement. They state, "Current research would have many of us believe that Black males are pathological and failing miserably in our nation's schools, when in actuality our nation's schools seem to be the purveyors of pathology and are miserably failing Black males" (p. 77). For gifted African American male cohorts, stemming the tide of underachievement should involve a multifaceted approach—with the first step consisting of educators and education policymakers moving themselves beyond deficit thinking.

Perhaps one of the most frequent debilitating issues associated with underachievement among gifted African American male groups is the deficit model approach used by many who have influence over key educational decisions that subsequently impact this group. An a priori list of maladies, pathologies, and shortcomings is often constructed to define this group—a list that is at best composed of stereotypical constructions and at worst grossly false attributions. Ford, Harris, Tyson, and Frazier-Trotman (2002) assert that this approach exerts a profound influence, evidenced by the seven major symptoms of deficit thinking they identified:

1. Traditional IQ-based definitions, philosophies, and theories of giftedness;
2. Identification practices and policies that have a disproportionately negative impact on Black students (e.g., a reliance on teacher referral for initial screening);
3. A lack of training aimed at helping educators in the area of gifted education;
4. A lack of training aimed at helping teachers understand and interpret standardized test results;
5. Inadequate training of teachers and other school personnel in multicultural education;
6. Inadequate efforts to communicate with Black families and communities about gifted education; and
7. Black students' decisions to avoid gifted education programs. (p. 14)

As previously stated, the problem of underachievement requires a multifaceted approach. The symptoms outlined here provide a coherent and structured framework with which to begin untangling this problem; however, just as Ford, Harris, Tyson, and Frazier-Trotman (2002) state, this list is by no means exhaustive. An authentic assessment of the policies, processes, procedures, and players in gifted education decision making at the local level is required; or, as these researchers assert, the ultimate challenge is to develop operating paradigms that consider culture and context and use these to enhance possibilities for diverse student populations.

DEFINING GIFTEDNESS

A good point of departure for a discussion about giftedness among African American populations, particularly among male cohorts, should begin with a definition of the term. This assertion is made primarily due to the strong influence of definitions on education policy and process decisions that are based on this codification. Essentially, who gets included in the discussions and who is left on the periphery is inextricably linked to how this term is defined. One of the earliest definitions of giftedness, recognized as the first federal definition of the term, was offered by then Commissioner of Education Sydney Marland (1972):

> Gifted and talented children are those identified by professionally qualified persons, who by virtue of outstanding abilities are capable of high performance. These are

children who require differentiated educational programs and/or services beyond those normally provided by the regular school program in order to realize their contribution to self and society. Children capable of high performance include those with demonstrated achievement and/or potential ability in any of the following areas singly or in combination: (1) General Intellectual Ability; (2) Specific Academic Aptitude; (3) Creative or Productive Thinking; (4) Leadership Ability; (5) Visual and Performing Arts; and (6) Psychomotor Ability (This was dropped from the definition. It was thought that students with great athletic talent were being discovered.). (p. 1)

Subsequent to its introduction, several versions of the Marland definition have been developed. Perhaps what has been one of the more vigorous contemporary discussions on defining giftedness was prompted by the United States Department of Education (USDOE, 1993) definition:

Children and youth with outstanding talent perform or show the potential for performing at remarkably high levels of accomplishment when compared with other of their age, experience, or environment. These children and youth exhibit high performance capacity in intellectual, creative, and/or artistic areas, and unusual leadership capacity, or excel in specific academic fields. They require services or activities not ordinarily provided by the school. Outstanding talents are present in children and youth from all cultural groups, across all economic strata, and in all areas of human endeavor. (p. 19)

When compared to Marland (1972), the USDOE definition (1993) offers what many have referred to as a renewed sense of hope and promise, particularly for African American children. The inclusion of the statement that "Outstanding talents are present in children and youth from *all* [emphasis added] cultural groups" alone portends a quantum progression in those whom educators and education policymakers include in discussions about giftedness. Much like Sternberg's (1985) statement made more than a decade ago, "What constitutes an exceptionally intelligent act may differ from one person to another. Thus, the vehicles by which one might wish to measure intelligence (test contents, modes of presentation, formats for test items, etc.) will probably need to differ across sociocultural groups" (p. 224). For African American males, a definition that honors the nuances and unique cultural perspectives they bring to the education context is critical. According to Ford, Howard, Harris, and Tyson (2000), the more educators attempt to understand the complexities associated with student cultural background, the more gifted students of color will achieve in the classroom.

IDENTITY AND IDENTITY DEVELOPMENT

The literature is far from extensive, but it does represent a number of studies that have focused on African American (Black) racial and cultural identity development (Hughes & Bonner, 2006; Majors & Billson, 1992). Yet, when a sieve is applied and the descriptor *gifted* is added as a library database search term, the number of scholarly articles and publications is drastically reduced. According to Rowley and Moore (2002),

> The role of race in the lives of gifted African American students is an understudied phenomenon. The discourse in the literature regarding the influence of racial identity on academic achievement has been relatively narrow, often ignoring such important conceptual issues as the fact that racial identity is dynamic across situations; that race is not important to all African Americans; that the individual's assessment of what is African American is most important; and that racial identity cannot be understood without examining the social context. (p. 1)

Understanding the implications of racial identity development among gifted African American males is critically important as we look to enhance how these students interface with schools and gifted education programming. As we look at some of the historical models of racial identity development, perhaps the more noted models have been found in Asante's (1988) book, *Afrocentricity*, and Cross's (1991) *Negro to Black Conversion*. Both of these cultural identity typologies provide insight on how to engage with gifted African American males; however, it is the theory of William E. Cross, Jr., who first introduced it as a means to frame the racial identity development process found to occur among African American populations in 1971, that has held the most promise. Cross (1971) referred to the four stages, or themes as they are sometimes referred to in his model, "preencounter, encounter, immersion, and internalization"; "each describes 'self-concept' issues concerning race and parallel attitudes that the individual holds about Black and White as a reference group" (p. 169). Without delving into an extensive discussion of Cross's theory, suffice it to say that what each theme is found to represent is an individual's ever-increasing sense of self as a racial being and an ever-deepening sense of understanding regarding the establishment of a healthy racial identity.

For gifted African American males, identity development, particularly racial identity development, has a significant impact on achievement, motivation, and attitudes toward school (Grantham & Ford, 2003). The gifted African American male is negotiating multiple and competing identity formations. This student finds himself at the intersection of racial, cultural, and academic identity development. As far as racial identity is concerned, negotiating what it means to be African American in the school context presents a unique set of challenges, while at the same time this very same school context can potentially provide a cultural setting that is diametrically opposed to the home or community cultures from which this student emerges. To further problematize this negotiation there are the added complexities of trying to negotiate an academic identity; namely, a gifted identity that oftentimes completely removes the African American male from family, friends, and community. Thus, to isolate and focus solely on one aspect of the identity development process that these gifted African American male students are going through is to offer a severely limited view of how to best create educational programming and policy that will lead to the success of these students.

A prime example of how the intersection and overlap of academic, cultural, and racial identity can impact the development of gifted African American male students is seen in how they address perceptions about their achievement. For this cohort, achievement can be impacted by perceptions of being smart as somehow inferring that they are "acting White" (Fordham & Ogbu, 1986; Ogbu, 2003); as a result, many of these males opt to become class clowns (Ford, Harris, Tyson, & Frazier-Trotman, 2002). Although the concept of acting White is sometimes overextended in its application, it is important to look at how recent research has affirmed the relevance of this concept, particularly as it relates to high-achieving African American students. Recent research conducted by William Darity, an economist, and Karolyn Tyson, a sociologist, both faculty members at the University of North Carolina at Chapel Hill, revealed that the concept of acting White was found to exist primarily in school settings where White students were over-represented in gifted programming and African American students were found to be significantly underrepresented (Tyson, Darity, and Castellino, 2005). Hence, for African American males, the stigma associated with being gifted, especially in contexts where there are few African American peers who are also designated as gifted could potentially lead to this masking (i.e. becoming the class clown) of their abilities (Ford, Harris, Tyson, & Frazier-Trotman, 2002).

MILLENNIAL STUDENT CULTURE

Discussions related to students and student culture should take into account generational cohort influences. The current populations of students in our nation's schools are referred to in the works of the leading generational researchers, Neil Howe and William Strauss, as Millennials. In their 2000 book, *Millennials Rising,* these authors describe Millennials as individuals who were born during the 1982 to 2000 time span. Additionally, these authors report that perhaps what makes this generation one of the most distinctive generations we have seen in history is its sheer size: its members represent the largest generational cohort ever experienced in history. Another major distinction is that this group is the most ethnically and culturally diverse group that history has witnessed (Coomes & Debard, 2004; Debard, 2004; Howe & Strauss, 2000). When referring to Millennials, many use the seven descriptive terms that Howe and Strauss applied to describe this population: *special, sheltered, confident, team oriented, conventional, pressured, and achievers.* Each one of these seven descriptors connects in complex ways to create a unique generational cohort experience.

Even Morley Safer in a recent segment of the popular news documentary *60 Minutes* took on this new generation, reporting, "They think your business as usual ethic is for the birds. . . . The workplace has become a psychological battle-field and the Millennials have the upper hand." What this segment and others like

it provide is some sense of understanding regarding the differences that generational variations in general and contemporary Millennial culture in particular are
bringing to the workplace and the world. For educators and school officials, it
will be increasingly important to recognize that this population of students brings
a strikingly unique set of circumstances to the teaching and learning context.
Most noted has been the technological facility they possess and in turn demand
from the institutions with which they interface. When they were 12–17 years old,
94 percent of this population had "Use[d] the internet for school research and 78%
believe[d] the internet help[ed] them with schoolwork" (Oblinger, 2003, p. 39).
Conventional classroom structures and delivery systems if not updated to capitalize on the technological interests and skills of this generation can potentially be
rendered obsolete.

   While Howe and Strauss's work has served as the primary guide on Millennial
student culture, these authors have both commented along with other scholars
(Broido, 2004; Coomes & Debard, 2004; Dilworth & Carter, 2007) on the limitations of their works on this topic—mainly specifying that their research has tended
to narrowly focus on majority populations. According to Bonner and Hughes
(2007) in their coedited compendium on issues impacting African American
Millennials,

> Recent higher education literature highlighting this generational cohort has lacked
> a specific emphasis on critical issues such as culture, ethnicity, and race—leaving a
> number of questions unanswered. Namely, does the term "Millennial" apply to Afri-
> can American college students? What role does pop culture (e.g., hip hop) play in the
> development of identity for this population? Are our current development theories
> applicable to this group?

If the experiences of African American Millennials are disaggregated from the
experiences of majority Millennial cohorts, it becomes readily apparent that the
universal template used to describe this generation becomes less reliable in its
heuristic abilities. For example, Dilworth and Carter (2007), in contrasting the
experiences of White (majority) and African American Millennials, which they
described as Generation M and Black Generation M respectively, reveal in Table 1
the different social features found in these two groups.

   Scholarly works that connect the threads between what many would view as
disparate strands are needed. Culture, giftedness, identity, and generational status should be woven on this same loom of critical educational consciousness.
Additionally, practitioners need to understand that who these students are and
how they conceptualize their worlds have profound implications for how schools
should go about delivering education. Schools have consistently struggled to
remain relevant to gifted students who often view these enclaves as restrictive
and incongruent with their interests and intellectual abilities. While consideration of generational status might add another layer of complexity, clearly it is an
important component in the efforts to better address the unique needs of gifted
African American males.

Table 1 Enrollment of African American Males at Each Grade Level, Inclusive of Additional Categories (Charter School #1, Charter School #2, and Charter School #3)

Generation M (McGlynn, 2005)	***Black Generation M* (Dilworth & Carter, 2007)**
Grew up in economically stable conditions	Did not grow up in economically stable conditions
Felt protected by the government	Did not feel protected by the government
Have been indulged by their parents	Have not been indulged by their parents
Have been sheltered from the harsh realities of life	Have not been sheltered from the harsh realities of life

GIFTED AFRICAN AMERICAN MILLENNIAL MALES IN SCHOOL CONTEXTS

As articulated in the previous section, focusing on differences found to exist across various generational cohorts is not a new concept; however, applying these generational foci to populations of color has been rather a recent development (Bonner & Hughes, 2007). For African Americans in general and African American gifted males in particular, utilizing the existing literature but in new and profound ways to better understand the various nuances that this cohort brings to the school context could provide some potentially ground-breaking information. One way of addressing the question of how Millennial student culture could be understood through the lenses of gifted African American males is to present each of the seven descriptive factors included in the prevailing framework introduced by Howe and Strauss (2000) and to offer relevant counterpoints (Bonner & Hughes, 2007; Dilworth & Carter, 2007; Hughes & Bonner, 2006; Jennings, Bonner, Lewis, & Nave, 2007; Marbley, Hull, Polydore, Bonner, & Burley, 2007) for each that serve to more aptly illustrate the realities experienced by these students.

According to Howe and Strauss (2000), Millennials have been described as being *special, sheltered, confident,* team oriented, *conventional, pressured, and* a*chievers.* For gifted African American millennial males, each one of these descriptive terms requires a close reexamination based on their unique characteristics and experiences in P-12 education. For example, to use the term *special* as a descriptor to describe the gifted African American male's experience would potentially be at best incongruent and at worst incorrect. According to the extant literature (Howe & Strauss, 2000), Generation M (i.e., majority Millennials), have been told all of their lives that they are special; they have occupied center stage in the lives of parents, society, and agents both internal and external to the school context. However, their peers of color, especially Black Generation M, have been to a lesser extent designated and treated as special Monroe (2005) found that "Although attempting to assert self-affirming identities in adverse environments, behaviors among African American youths often fuel pejorative stereotypes that distinguish black males as troublesome and threatening" (p. 46).

A second example of the lack of fit of Black Generation M with the Howe and Strauss (2000) template depicting the seven descriptive factors is also observed in very profound ways though the use of the term *sheltered*. While gifted Generation M members might have enjoyed the advantages of life in sheltered and safe surroundings, for gifted Black Generation M members, life has not been quite as serene. According to Lowery (2004), society has attempted to shelter Generation M from every imagined danger or threat. Yet for Black Generation M, particularly for African American males, "A black man is more than six times as likely as a white man to be slain. The trend is most stark among black men fourteen to twenty-four years old: They were implicated in a quarter of the nation's homicides and accounted for 15 percent of the homicide victims in 2002, although they were just 1.2 percent of the population" (p. 2). Hence, for many gifted African American males who belong to Black Generation M, visions of being sheltered are more fanciful than factual.

To further problematize Howe and Strauss's (2000) descriptive factors, aggregating three of these terms yields yet another complex congeries of issues between Generation M and Black Generation M cohorts. Generation M descriptors have labeled the group as *confident, pressured,* and *achievers.* The aggregation of these terms collectively paints a picture of a student who is resolute in his or her abilities due to a record of scholastic achievement amassed during elementary and secondary school. According to Elam, Stratton, and Gibson (2007), "Long pressured to excel, Millennial students will have high expectation for their own success" (p. 24). But, for the Black Generation M student, this combination of terms too often plays out in a very different way. More pointedly, what the gifted Black Generation M student experiences is being pressured to fit into a prescribed mold of school culture that is based on Eurocentric cultural norms, especially if the student desires recognition as an achiever. Subsequently, the gifted Black Generation M student is left feeling less confident and self-efficacious in his abilities.

Finally, counterpoints to Howe and Strauss's (2000) factors can be observed through the application of the terms *team oriented* and *conventional*—another pair of descriptors used to codify the Generation M collective. While members of Generation M have flourished under a team-oriented approach to their personal and professional engagements as well as a conventional "back-to-tradition" style of self-expression, their Black Generation M peers have often suffered when these appellations have been applied to them. For the gifted Black Generation M student, opportunities for team-oriented approaches with other gifted Black Generation M students—principally other African American males—represents more the exception than the norm. Also, while the use of the term *conventional* represents Generation M's return to a time of "age old tradition," for gifted Black Generation M students, a return to tradition may represent a time of even more pointed oppression and marginalization for people from their communities.

In summary, it is critical that those who seek to better comprehend the experiences of gifted African American males take a more informed look at the generational influences that impact this population. Employing a generational lens will allow administrators, teachers, parents, and policymakers to better attend to the unique circumstances that these learners bring to the school context. It is also critical that the use of this generational lens take into account important cultural differences. To retrofit Howe and Strauss's (2000) model in total without a serious investigation of the unique experiences that each gifted Black Generation M male brings to the school context will continue to yield many of the same results: nonidentification, underachievement, and underrepresentation.

A CASE IN POINT: GIFTED AFRICAN AMERICAN MALES IN ONE MIDWESTERN SCHOOL DISTRICT

Data were collected during the 2005 and 2006 academic school years at a large Midwestern school district, referred to hereafter by the pseudonym Cascade Independent School (CISD) district. Cascade Independent School District (CISD) during the 2005–2006 academic school year had a total student population of 33,213, of which 3,587 were African American males. The numbers of males from other ethnic groups were as follows: (a) 8,311 Hispanic males; (b) 4,389 White males, and (c) 683 Asian males. Table 2 documents the total number of African American males in CISD in 2005–2006 by grade level throughout the district.

In examining Table 2, we find the actual enrollment of African American males at each grade level and in additional categories (Charter School #1, Charter School #2, and Charter School #3). According to Table 2, during the 2005–2006 academic school year, there were 3,587 African American males enrolled at all levels in CISD, which is approximately 10.8 percent of the total school district population. However, even though the focus of this article is on African American males in gifted programs, we must point out how many African American males have been identified as special education students at the Pre-Kindergarten level. For example, of the 266 students enrolled in Pre-Kindergarten in CISD, 45 (17%) African American males have been identified as special education students—this identification comes before they reach Kindergarten. This number of African American males in special education is approximately 7 percentage points higher than the African American male total population in the school district and in this grade level as well. This also has direct implications for the representation of African American males in gifted/talented/advanced placement programs in CISD at the middle and high school levels.

African American Male Middle School Students in Gifted/Talented/Advanced Programs in CISD

The researchers conducted a detailed analysis of the representation of African American males in all gifted/talented programs at the middle school level in CISD. In 2005–2006, CISD had the following advanced and gifted/talented/advanced

Table 2   African Americans' Enrollment: Summary by Grade Level 2005–2006

Grade	Total African American Male Enrollment	% of Total Enrollment in Grade Level
Pre-Kindergarten—Regular	1	
Pre-Kindergarten—Special education	45	10%
Pre-Kindergarten—CPP	23	
Kindergarten	271	9.6%
Grade 1	283	10.5%
Grade 2	266	10.1%
Grade 3	264	10.7%
Grade 4	280	10.9%
Grade 5	271	11.0%
Grade 6	245	10.2%
Grade 7	290	12.3%
Grade 8	294	12.6%
Grade 9	345	12.5%
Grade 10	269	11.8%
Grade 11	187	10.9%
Grade 12	176	11.5%
Charter school #1	9	1.4%
Charter school #2	52	11.0%
Charter School #3	16	3.6%
Total	**3,587**	**10.8%**

Source: CISD Research Department.

placement programs for all students to participate in at the middle school level: (a) AGATE (Advanced Gifted and Talented Education); (b) AVID (Advancement via Individual Determination); (c) Honors courses; and (d) IB (International Baccalaureate). In the analysis, the researchers focused on the representation of African American males at the middle school level (Grades 6–8; $n = 829$; 22.3% of the total male middle school population) that were participating in any of the gifted/talented/advanced placement programs. Table 3 illustrates the findings.

After completing our examination of Table 3, we find the representation of African American males in AGATE, AVID, Honors, and IB classes at the middle school level to be dismal. First, in the AGATE program, there were a total of 8(0.0096%) African American males enrolled during the 2005–2006 academic school year at the middle school level. Second, in the AVID program at the middle school level, there were only 14 African American males (0.017%) enrolled during

Table 3 *African American Male Students Enrolled in AGATE, AVID, Honors, and IB Classes at the Middle School Level*

Program	N	% of Total African American Male Enrollment at the Middle School Level
AGATE	8	0.0096%
AVID	14	0.017%
Honors	4	0.0048%
IB	0	0%

Source: CISD Research Department.
Note: Total African American male enrollment in CISD at the middle school level in 2005–2006 was 829.

the 2005–2006 academic school year. In the Honors program at the middle school level, we find only 4 African American males (0.0048%) enrolled during this same time period. It is also noteworthy that no African American males were enrolled in the IB program at the middle school level in CISD in 2005–2006. In sum, only 18 African American males (0.005% of the total male middle school population) participating in any gifted/talented/advanced placement programs at the middle school level.

African American Male High School Students in Gifted/Talented/Advanced Programs in CISD

To delve further into the representation of African American males in gifted/talented/advanced placement programs in CISD, the researchers conducted a detailed analysis of the representation of African American males in all gifted/talented/advanced placement programs at the high school levels in CISD. In 2005–2006, CISD had the following gifted/talented/advanced placement programs for all students to participate in at the high school level: (a) Advanced Placement courses; (b) Honors courses; and (d) IB (International Baccalaureate) courses. In the analysis, the researchers focused on the representation of African American males at the middle school level (Grades 9–12; $n = 977$; 21.6% of the total male high school population) that were participating in any of the gifted/talented/advanced placement programs in CISD in 2005–2006. Table 4 documents the analysis of African American male representation.

In an examination of Table 4, we find the representation of African American males in Advanced Placement, Honors, and IB at the high school level to be at best dire and at worst appalling. First, in the Advanced Placement program, there were 24 (0.0245%) African American males enrolled during the 2005–2006 academic school year at the high school level. Second, in the Honors program at the high school level, there were 137 African American males (0.0378%) enrolled during the 2005–2006 academic school year. In the IB program at the high school level, we find only 56 African American males (0.0573%) enrolled during this same time

Table 4   *African American Male Students Enrolled in AGATE, AVID, Honors, and IB Classes at the High School Level*

Program	N	% of Total African American Male Enrollment at the High School Level
Advanced Placement	24	0.0245%
Honors	137	0.0378%
IB	56	0.0573%

Source: CISD Research Department.
Note: Total African American male enrollment in CISD at the high school level in 2005–2006 was 977.

period. It is also noteworthy that in all gifted/talented/advanced programs at the high school level in CISD in 2005–2006, African American males' representation was less than 1 percent of all students (0.042% of the total male high school population) in these programs.

SUMMARY AND CONCLUSION

For change to occur that stems the tide of underachievement and underidentification of African American males for gifted programming, a radically different approach must be taken by administrators, teachers, parents, and policymakers. Too often the remedies offered have been developed to cure specific symptoms; however, what is needed is an elixir that has the potency to address multiple and varying symptoms—many that defy simple responses. Based on the discussions outlined in this article, several recommendations are offered to practitioners and researchers to address the complexities associated with each one of the issues cited above.

(1) *Seek definitions for giftedness that are more encompassing or representative of the nuances found to exist within African American male cohorts.* Current definitions of giftedness are at best only slightly representative and at worst nonrepresentative of the cultural mores and traditions found to exist among African American male cohorts. According to Sternberg (2007), "Different cultures have different conceptions of what it means to be *gifted*. But in identifying children as *gifted*, we often use only our own conception, ignoring the cultural context in which the children grew up" (p. 160). Therefore, it is critical to recognize that definitions of giftedness should seek to be more inclusive. This approach to inclusion should start with an emphasis on ability areas beyond a sole focus on academic ability. Researchers (Bonner & Jennings, 2007; Bonner, Jennings, Marbley, & Brown, in press; Matthews, 2004; Roach, Adelma, & Wyman, 1999) have recently highlighted leadership potential as one of the untapped areas of focus that offers a viable alternative when seeking to identify gifted African American males.

(2) *Identify key constraints and gate-keeping functions that lead to the underidentification of African American males for gifted programming.* Issues ranging from teacher nominations to standardized testing have been viewed as factors contributing to the underidentification of African American males for gifted programming (Ford, Harris, Tyson, & Frazier-Trotman, 2002). These factors need to be identified and subsequently addressed as they materialize across the P-12 continuum; while some factors are more acute at early stages in schooling, others become more pervasive in later contexts. A concerted effort among administrators, parents, teachers, and gifted educators should be undertaken not only to highlight but also to seek viable solutions that are cohort and context specific. Additionally, a body of literature is beginning to emerge that focuses on gifted minority populations and poverty (Bonner, Lewis, Bowman-Perrott, Hill-Jackson, & James, in press; Cross, 2003; Cross & Burney, 2005; Swanson, 2006; VanTassel-Baska, 2009); the intersection of these two areas is necessary in understanding the educational experiences for many gifted African American males.

(3) *Recognize the importance of identity development among gifted African American male students.* Gifted African American males are negotiating the development of their multiple identities. Not only are they tasked with facing their identity as gifted but they are also challenged by the task of integrating their identities as both African American and male. Each identity strand presents a unique set of issues. For an African American student who is also male, school settings are often incongruent with home settings or cultures. For a gifted student, issues associated with establishing a scholar-oriented identity (Whiting, 2006) or an identity based on academic prowess could potentially initiate challenges. Thus, it is important to deal with all facets of the identity development process to promote African American male students' success. Schools could also partner with groups or organizations that are aware of valid measures to encourage the success of high-achieving African American males. According to Whiting (2006), "Such organizations as fraternities, the Boys and Girls Clubs, 100 Black Men, National Urban League, YMCA, and others recognize that one person can make a difference in a child's life" (p. 226).

(4) *Recognize the impact of the generational influence, particularly the Millennial student culture, on student behavior and performance.* Certain characteristics and traits that gifted African American male students bring to the educational setting are strongly associated with their connections to their generational cohort—the Millennial generation (Coomes & Debard, 2004). Understanding how these students learn and process information, having a clearer perspective on the major influence that technology has had on their lives, and developing a better sense of their work ethic and how they approach various tasks is critical. Scant literature is available (Bonner & Hughes, 2007) that focuses specifically on African American Millennial students; more information is needed, particularly from a P-12 perspective.

This article has focused on several complex issues that continue to impede the progress of African American male populations, particularly as they seek entrance into P-12 education's inner sanctum—programs designed for the gifted and talented. What the authors attempted to uncover were a number of the issues that have been recapitulated over the years, such as widespread underidentification and extant definitions of giftedness; however, the focus was also on more contemporary barriers to success like identity development and student generational influence. To truly seek viable outcomes and solutions to these issues, it is readily apparent that remedies can not serve a singular focus. Current approaches reveal the importance of intersectionality (Collins, 1998; Davis, 1983; Crenshaw, 1994; Pastrana, 2004) and the critical need to look at how these issues converge to produce outcomes for these students. At no one time are these students solely gifted, African American, or male, but they are collectively all of these identities at the same time. Thus, to artificially separate out their various identities is at best short-sighted and at worst woefully inappropriate. Despite its focus on a single school district, the case study provided at the end of the article serves as but one glaring example of the need to develop complex solutions to this complex problem of underidentification. Are the numbers of African American students in gifted and talented programs at Cascade reflective of a lack of understanding of African American male identity development? Could the problem be associated with African American males' connections to their Millennial generational cohort? Is the problem attributable to the way the school district defines giftedness (i.e., does the definition overlook cultural mores and traditions)? These are but a few of the questions that must be answered together, not in isolation; then perhaps we can better understand why gifted African American males have been so misunderstood.

REFERENCES

Arnold, M., & Lassmann, M. E. (2003). Overrepresentation of minority students in special education. *Education, 124*(2), 230–236.

Asante, M. K. (1988). *Afrocentricity.* Trenton, NJ: Africa World Press.

Bonner, F. A., II. (2000, May). African American giftedness. *Journal of Black Studies, 30*(5), 643–664.

Bonner, F. A., II. (2001). Making room for the study of gifted African American males. *Black Issues in Higher Education, 18*(6), 80.

Bonner, F. A., II, & Hughes, R. L. (Eds.). (2007). African American millennial college students [Special issue]. *National Association of Student Affairs Professionals Journal, 10*(1).

Bonner, F. A., II, & Jennings, M. (2007). Never too young to lead: Gifted African American males in elementary school. *Gifted Child Today, 38*(2), 30–36.

Bonner, F. A., II, Jennings, M., Marbley, A. F., & Brown, L. (in press). Capitalizing on leadership capacity: Gifted African American males in high school. *Roeper Review.*

Bonner, F. A. II., Lewis, C. W., Bowman-Perrott, V. Hill-Jackson, L. & M. James. (in press). Definition, identification, identity and culture: A unique alchemy impacting the success of gifted African American males in school. *Journal for the Education of the Gifted.*

Broido, E. M. (2004). Understanding diversity in millennial students. *New Directions for Student Services. 106,* 73–85.

Collins, P. H. (1998). It's all in the family: Intersections of gender, race and nation, *Hypatia, 13*(3), 62–82.

Coomes, M. D., & Debard, R. (2004). A generational approach to understanding students. *New Directions for Student Services, 106,* 5–16.

Crenshaw, K. (1994). Mapping the margins: Intersectionality, identity politics, and violence against women of color. In M. Albertson Fineman & R. Mykitiuk (Eds.). *The public nature of private violence.* New York: Routledge.

Cross, T. L. (2003). Leaving no gifted child behind: Breaking our educational system of privilege. *Roeper Review, 25,* 101–104.

Cross, W. E. (1971). Negro-to-Black conversion experience: Toward a psychology of black liberation. *Black World, 20*(9), 13–27.

Cross, W. E. (1991). *Negro to Black conversion experience: Toward a psychology of Black liberation.* Temple University Press. (Reprinted from *Black World, 20*(9), 13–27)

Cross, T. L., & Burney, V. H. (2005). High ability, rural, and poor: Lessons from Project Aspire and implications for school counselors. *Journal of Secondary Gifted Education, 16,* 148–156.

Davis, A. Y. (1983). *Women, race, & class.* New York: Random House.

Debard, R. (2004). Millennials coming to college. *New Directions for Student Services, 106,* 33–45.

Dilworth, P. P., & Carter, S. M. (2007). Millennial versus hip hop: Exploring Black under-graduate students' perspective on socially constructed labels. *National Association of Student Affairs Professionals Journal, 10*(1), 70–84.

Elam, C, Stratton, T. & Gibson, D. D. (2007). Welcoming a new generation to college: The Millennial Students. *Journal of College Admission.* Retrieved from www.nacacnet.org.

Elhoweris, H., Matua, K., Alsheikh, N., & Holloway, P. (2005). Effects of children's ethnicity on teachers' referral and recommendation decisions in gifted and talented programs. *Remedial and Special Education, 26*(1), 25–31.

Fashola, O. (2005). *Educating African American males: Voices from the field.* Thousand Oaks, CA: Corwin Press.

Ferguson, A. (2000). *Bad boys: Public schools in the making of Black masculinity.* Ann Arbor: University of Michigan Press.

Fine, L. (2002). Disparate measures. *Education Week, 21*(41), 30–35.

Ford, D. Y. (1995). Desegregating gifted education: A need unmet. *Journal of Negro Education, 64*(1), 52–62.

Ford, D. Y., Grantham, T. C., & Bailey, D. F. (1999). Identifying giftedness among African American males: Recommendations for effective recruitment and retention In V. Polite & J. Davis (Eds.), *African American Males in School and Society: Practices and Policies for Effective Education* (pp. 51–67). New York: Teachers College Press.

Ford, D. Y., Harris, J. J., III, Tyson, C. A., & Frazier-Trotman, M. (2002). Beyond deficit thinking: Providing access for gifted African American students. *Roeper Review, 24*(2), 52–58.

Ford, D. Y., Howard, T. C., Harris, J. J., III, & Tyson, C. A. (2000). Creating culturally responsive classrooms for gifted minority students. *Journal for the Education of the Gifted, 23*(4), 397–427.

Ford, D. Y., Moore, J. L., III, & Milner, H. R. (2005). Beyond cultureblindness: A model of culture with implications for gifted education. *Roeper Review, 27*(2), 97–103.

Fordham, S., & Ogbu, J. U. (1986). Black students' school success: Coping with the burden of "acting White." *Urban Review, 18*(3), 176–206.

Grantham, T. C. (2004). Rocky Jones: Case study of a high-achieving Black male's motivation to participate in gifted classes. *Roeper Review, 26*(4), 208–215.

Grantham, T. C., & Ford, D. Y. (2003). Beyond self-concept and self-esteem for African American students: Improving racial identity improves achievement. *High School Journal, 87*(1), 18–29.

Howard, G. (2006). *We can't teach what we don't know: White teachers, multiracial schools.* Teachers College Record. New York: Teachers College Press.

Howard, T. C. (2003). A tug of war for our minds: African American high school students' perceptions of their academic identities and college aspirations. *High School Journal, 87*(1), 4–17.

Howe, N., & Strauss, W. (2000). *Millennials rising: The next great generation.* New York: Vintage Press.

Hughes, R. L., & Bonner, F. A., II. (2006). Leaving Black males behind: Debunking the myth of meritocratic education. *Journal of Race and Policy, 2*(1), 76–90.

Jennings, M., Bonner II, F. A., Lewis, C. W., & Nave, F. M. (2007). The historically Black colleges and university: A question of relevance for the African American millennial college student. *National Association of Student Affairs Professionals Journal, 10*(1), 85–96.

Kearns, T., Ford, L., & Linney, J. A. (2005). African American student representation in special education programs. *Journal of Negro Education, 74*(4), 297–310.

Kunjufu, J. (1985). *Countering the conspiracy to destroy Black boys.* Chicago: African American Images.

Kunjufu, J. (1989). *Critical issues in educating African American youth.* Chicago: African American Images.

Kunjufu, J. (2005). *Hip hop street curriculum.* Chicago: African American Images.

Landsman, J., & Lewis, C. (Eds.). (2006). *White teachers/diverse classrooms: A guide to building inclusive schools, promoting high expectations, and eliminating racism.* Sterling, VA: Stylus.

Lee, C. C. (2005). A reaction to EGAS: An important new approach to African American youth empowerment. *Professional School Counseling, 8*(5), 393–394.

Lowery, J. W. (2004). Student affairs for a new generation. In M. D. Coomes & J. W. Lowery (Issue Eds.), *New directions for student services, Iss. 106. Serving the millennial generation* (pp. 87–99). San Francisco: Jossey-Bass.

Majors, R., & Billson, J. M. (1992). *Cool prose: The dilemmas of Black manhood in America.* New York: MacMillan.

Marbley , A. F., Hull, W., Polydore, C., & Bonner, F. A., II., & Burley, H. (2007). African American millennial college: Owning the technological Middle Passage. *National Association for Student Affairs Professionals Journal, 10*(1), 7–19.

Marland, S., Jr. (1972). *Education of the gifted and talented* (Report to the Congress of the United States by the U.S. Commissioner of Education). Washington, DC: U.S. Government Printing Office.

Matthews, M. S. (2004). Leadership education for gifted and talented youth: A review of the literature. *Journal for the Education of the Gifted, 28*(1), 77–113.

McGlynn, A. P. (2005). Teaching millenials, our newest cultural cohort. *Education Digest, 71,* 12–16.

Milner, R. H. (2007). African American males in urban schools: No excuses—teach and empower. *Theory into Practice, 46*(3), 239–246.

Milner, R. H., & Ford, D. Y. (2005). Racial experiences influence us as teachers: Implications for gifted education curriculum development and implementation. *Roeper Review, 28*(1), 30–36.

Monroe, C. (2005). Why are "bad boys" always Black? Causes of disproportionality in school discipline and recommendations for change. *The Clearing House* (September/October), 45–52.

Morris, J. E. (2002). African American students and gifted education. *Roeper Review, 24*(2), 59–62.

Oblinger, D. (2003). Boomers, gen-Xers and millennials: Understanding the new students. *EDUCAUSE, 38*(4), 37–47.

Ogbu, J. (2003). *Black American students in an affluent suburb: A study of academic disengagement.* Mahwah, NJ: Erlbaum.

Okara, O. (2007). The Afrocentric experience: Afrocentric worldview vs. Eurocentric worldview. Retrieved December 19, 2007, from http://www.swagga.com/wviews.htm.

Pastrana, A. (2004). Black identity constructions: Inserting intersectionality, bisexuality, and (Afro-) latinidad into black studies. *Journal of African American Studies, 8,* 74–89.

Pitre, E., Lewis, C., & Hilton-Pitre, T. (2007). The overrepresentation of African American males in special education: A qualitative analysis of the student perspective. *Journal of the Alliance of Black School Educators, 6*(2), 61–75.

Polite, V., & Davis, J. (1999). *African American males in school and society: Practices and policies for effective education.* New York: Teachers College Press.

Roach, A., Adelma, A., & Wyman, L. T. (1999). Leadership giftedness: Models revisited. *Gifted Child Quarterly, 43,* 13–24.

Rowley, S. J., & Moore, J. A. (2002). Racial identity in context for the gifted African American student. *Roeper Review, 24,* 63–67.

Shaunessy, E., Karnes, A., & Cobb, Y. (2004). Assessing potentially gifted students from lower socioeconomic status with nonverbal measures of intelligence. *Perceptual and Motor Skills, 98*(3), 1129–1138.

Shealey, M. W., & Lue, M. S. (2006). Why are all the Black kids still in special education? Revisiting the issue of disproportionate representation. *Multicultural Perspectives, 8*(2), 3–9.

Skiba, R. J., Poloni-Staudinger, L., Gallini, S., Simmons, A. B., & Feggins-Azziz, R. (2006). Disparate access: The disproportionality of African American students with disabilities across educational environments. *72*(4), 411–424.

Sternberg, R. J. (2007). Cultural dimensions of giftedness and talent. *Roeper Review, 29*(3), 160–165.

Sternberg, R. J. (1985). *Beyond IQ: A triarchic theory of human intelligence.* Cambridge, England: Cambridge University Press.

Swanson, J. D. (2006). Breaking through assumptions about low-income, minority gifted students. *Gifted Child Quarterly, 50*(1), 11–26.

Taylor, G., & Phillips, T. (2006). *Improving the quality of education for African-American males: A study of America's urban schools.* Lewiston, NY: Edwin Mellen Press.

Tyson, K., Darity Jr., W. & Castellino, D. R. (2005). It's not "a Black thing": Understanding the burden of acting white and other dilemmas of high achievement. *American Sociological Review, 70*(4), 582–605.

U.S. Department of Education (USDOE). (1993). *National excellence: A case for developing America's talent.* Washington, DC: Author.

VanTassel-Baska, J. (2009). *Patterns and profiles of promising learners from poverty.* Waco, TX: Prufrock Press.

Watkins, A., & Kurtz, D. (2001). Using solution-focused intervention to address African American male overrepresentation in special education: A case study. *Children and Schools, 23*(4), 223–235.

White, J. L., & Cones, J. H. (1999). *Black man emerging: Facing the past and seizing a future in America.* New York: Routledge.

Whiting, G. W. (2006). From at risk to at promise: Developing scholar identities among Black males. *Journal of Secondary Gifted Education, 17*(4), 222–229.

Capitalizing on Leadership Capacity: Gifted African American Males in High School

Fred A. Bonner II; Michael E. Jennings;
Aretha F. Marbley; Lesley-Ann Brown

DOI: 10.1080/02783190801954965
Publication Frequency: 4 issues per year
Published in: *Roeper Review*, Volume 30, Issue 2, April 2008, pages 93–103

ABSTRACT

Leadership is one of the most underemphasized dimensions of high ability cited in the current federal definition of giftedness. This particular ability area is highlighted here in an effort to offer helpful information and recommendations to administrators, educators, parents, and policymakers who seek usable solutions to the problem of underidentification among gifted secondary African American male student populations. Key topics and issues addressed include definitions of giftedness, school context and environment, identity development, resilience, and leadership potential. The analysis concludes with practitioner- and researcher-focused recommendations.

INTRODUCTION

African American males continue to go underidentified for our nation's gifted programs. This lack of identification has led to underrepresentation by as much

Fred A. Bonner, Michael E. Jennings, Aretha F. Marbley et al., "Capitalizing on Leadership Capacity: Gifted African American Males in High School," *Roeper Review*, Volume 30, Issue 2 (January 2008): 93–103. Taylor & Francis Group, reprinted by permission of the publisher (Taylor & Francis Group, http://www.informaworld.com).

as 50 percent nationally (Office of Civil Rights, 2002). According to Lee (1996), "Black males encounter formidable challenges to their educational development and many of them experience a serious stifling of achievement, aspiration, and pride in school systems throughout the country" (p. 5). Both current and historical arguments (e.g., Bennett, 1992; D'Souza, 1996; Herrnstein & Murray, 1994; Simon, 2007), much like Armstrong Williams's dire report on African American male crime statistics cited in a 2004 column in the *New York Amsterdam News*, would have many of us believe that Black males are pathological and failing miserably in our nation's schools, when, in actuality, our nation's schools seem to be the purveyors of pathology and are miserably failing our Black males (Dunbar, 2001; McNally, 2003).

Despite our efforts at expanding the definition of giftedness to include several categories and criteria in the identification process, we continue to see a high degree of underrepresentation among African American male cohorts. The literature in the past two decades has been noteworthy (e.g., Fashola, 2005; Ferguson, 2000; Ford, 2003; Ford, Moore, & Milner, 2005; Grantham, 2004; Hopkins, 1997; Hrabowski, Maton, & Greif, 1998; Kunjufu, 1990, 2005a; Lee, 2005; Morris, 2002; Ogbu, 2003; Polite & Davis, 1999; Porter, 1998; Taylor & Phillips, 2006; Watson & Smitherman, 1996; Whiting, 2006; Wynn, 1992) regarding the "underachievement" and underrepresentation of African American males in U.S. schooling. According to the literature on these phenomena, African American males have been disproportionately placed in special education classrooms (Harry & Anderson, 1994; Kearns, Ford, & Linney, 2005; Watkins & Kurtz, 2001) and underrepresented in gifted and talented programs (Bonner, 2001; Ford, 1995; Ford, Grantham, Bailey, Polite, & Davis, 1999; Polite, & Davis, 1999).

In this article, we discuss the promise offered by one of the ability areas cited in the federal definition of giftedness—*leadership ability*—to address and circumvent this cycle of underrepresentation. An examination of an array of contributing factors found to impact African American male readiness and identification for gifted programming is explored: definitions of giftedness, secondary school contexts, identity development, resilience, and leadership potential each are considered in turn. Perhaps by considering this often overlooked form of giftedness among African American male populations, we can "increase the representation of Black males in gifted education. Maybe then these young men can have the opportunity to fulfill their potential" (Whiting, 2006, p. 227).

DEFINING GIFTEDNESS

What have historically and currently served as formidable barriers to the identification of African American males for gifted and talented programs are the definitions of giftedness used by most states. These definitions tend to focus narrowly on giftedness as a construct measured overwhelmingly, if not solely, by academic ability. According to Sternberg (2007), "Different cultures have different conceptions of what it means to be *gifted*. But in identifying children as gifted, we often use only our own conception, ignoring the cultural context in which the children grew up" (p. 160). Hence, an unfortunate outcome of our truncated views regarding the necessary and sufficient attributes to be identified as gifted is that they create a template that not all children fit neatly. Even more problematic have been the attempts at identifying a definition that is parsimonious, inclusive, and flexible while also being heuristic.

Hence, finding a definition that adequately describes an elusive and multifaceted concept like giftedness has been an ongoing task since work in the field began. Posing the greatest challenges to this process are the many ways that giftedness can be operationalized (Gardner, 1983; Renzulli, 1981; Sternberg, 1985) nationally and in various cultures (Bonner, 2001; Ford, 1995; Hilliard, 1976). Matthews (2004) stated,

> Beginning with its origins in the early history of psychology, giftedness was defined primarily in terms of intellectual ability. By the 1950s, however, spurred by factors that included the multifaceted model of intelligence developed by J. P. Guilford and the elaboration by DeHann and Kough of 10 categories of gifts and talents, a variety of efforts began leading toward a broader conceptualization of giftedness. (p. 77)

A first step in expanding how giftedness was defined came by way of congressional mandate and the subsequent efforts of Commissioner of Education Sydney Marland (1972), who published the first federal definition of giftedness. According to Marland, giftedness was defined as follows:

> Gifted and talented children are those identified by professionally qualified persons, who by virtue of outstanding abilities are capable of high performance. These are children who require differentiated educational programs and/or services beyond those normally provided by the regular school program in order to realize their contribution to self and society. Children capable of high performance include those with demonstrated achievement and/or potential ability in any of the following areas singly or in combination: (a) General Intellectual Ability, (b) Specific Academic Aptitude, (c) Creative or Productive Thinking, (d) Leadership Ability, (e) Visual and Performing Arts, and (f) Psychomotor Ability [This was dropped from the definition. It was thought that students with great athletic talent were being discovered.] (p. 10)

Successive refinements of the Marland definition have since been developed. Theorists have acknowledged the multifaceted, complex nature of intelligence and the fact that contemporary tests (often overly simplistic and static) fail to do justice to this construct (Ford, 2003; Frasier, 1989; Grantham & Ford, 2003; Hilliard, 1976; Sternberg, 2007). Thus, the U.S. Department of Education (1993) broadened the definition of giftedness:

> Children and youth with outstanding talent perform or show the potential for performing at remarkably high levels of accomplishment when compared with others of their age, experience, or environment. These children and youth exhibit high performance capacity in intellectual, creative, and/or artistic areas, and unusual leadership capacity,

or excel in specific academic fields. They require services or activities not ordinarily provided by the school. Outstanding talents are present in children and youth from all cultural groups, across all economic strata, and in all areas of human endeavor. (p. 19)

Readily apparent across the states is the wide variation in the use of this definition (Davidson Institute, 2007; National Association for Gifted Children, 2005); consequently, depending on state mandates and local norms, how and whether this definition is used in its current form is debatable. It is important to note that states are not required to use the federal definition and can opt for their own definitions. According to the Education Commission of the States (2004), "The states vary in how they identify gifted and talented students. . . . Twenty-five states use 'gifted and talented,' or some variation, as the classifying term. Eighteen states have chosen to only use the term 'gifted,' or some variation and not mention the word 'talented.' Finally, three states use the term 'high ability student'" (p. 1). Also, it is important to note that some states embrace more traditional definitions of giftedness, those focusing on academic ability and intelligence, while others use more multifaceted and fluid criteria.

Although there is great variability across the states' definitions, many have been consistent in employing leadership capacity or leadership potential as an area of importance. According to the *2004–2005 State of the States Report* provided by the National Association for Gifted Children and the Council of State Directors of Programs for the Gifted, 13 states included leadership in their definition of giftedness (2005). Matthews's (2004) observation that "Leadership has been retained in the federal definition of giftedness across major revisions, since its inclusion in the Marland Report (1972) definitions more than 30 years ago" (p. 77) is significant.

Gifted African American Males: The Secondary School Context

A number of factors have been cited as contributing to the widespread underrepresentation of African American males in gifted programs. According to Ford, Harris, Tyson, and Frazier-Trotman (2002), lack of teacher referral, low test scores, and student and family choice are the three most significant factors. Hughes and Bonner (2006) found that structural inequalities also serve as major barriers. These barriers include teacher propensities to pathologize African American males in their early school experiences, education tracking that locks African American males into substandard classes, and ineffective classroom learning environments. Hughes and Bonner (2006) asserted that

For Black males, the acquisition of an education is often a catch-22 situation in which to fully understand what academic accoutrements are necessary for success they must possess certain cultural capital (Bourdieu, 1997). Yet, the Black male is expected to have certain cultural capital in order to understand what academic accoutrements are necessary for success. (p. 4)

This conundrum has often resulted in findings akin to what the Office of Civil Rights (2002) reported: namely, that the representation of racial and ethnic groups in gifted and talented programs favors some groups more than others. The study found that gifted and talented programs were composed of 7.64 percent Asian/Pacific Islander students, 72.59 percent White students, 8.43 percent African American students, 10.41 percent Hispanic/Latino students, and 0.93 percent American Indian/Alaskan American students. However, when these data are juxtaposed with data highlighting the representation of each group across the entire public school education spectrum during the same year (U.S. Department of Education, 2004), disparities become readily apparent: 4.30 percent were Asian/Pacific Islander students, 59.50 percent were White students, 17.30 percent are African American students, 17.80 percent were Hispanic/Latino students, and 1.20 percent were American Indian/Alaskan American students.

Most noteworthy are the data that report White students as representing 59.50 percent of the overall student population in the nation's schools during the 2002 fall term while garnering a whopping 72.59 percent of the spots in gifted and talented programs. These data are but one indicator of the need to identify additional and alternative measures to ensure that all students are fairly represented and have an equitable opportunity to participate in gifted and talented programs.

For the African American male student, the secondary school period is a time in which giftedness should be cultivated and honed for the critical next step in the educational journey—higher education. We must take measures to ensure that these individuals are successful. To address this problem head-on, one viable strategy is to focus on areas in which giftedness is promoted and valued among African American populations. From W.E.B. Du Bois's (1903) notion of the Talented Tenth to some of the contemporary initiatives enacted by civic, Greek-letter, and clergy-based organizations, leadership or leadership capacity as it is codified in the federal definition of giftedness serves as an excellent starting point.

Gifted African American Males: Identity Development

Perhaps one of the most complex topics associated with gifted African American male cohorts stems from their development of identity—that is, how these individuals develop an identity that embraces their multiple statuses as gifted, African American, and male. For African American gifted males, *identity development* (which includes forging a coherent and strong sense of who they are, where they are heading, and where they "fit" in) is closely aligned with their sense of *self-concept*: that is, a holistic and realistic awareness of their unique attributes and traits. In this manner, gender, race, and ethnicity each becomes an integral part of their identity development (Hughes & Bonner, 2006; Majors & Billson, 1992).

Thus, for African American gifted males, embracing their multiple identities—Black, male, and gifted—impacts their peer interactions as well as their psychosocial and personal development (Allen, 1986; Fleming, 1984; Hughes, 1987; Sedlacek, 1987; Thomas, 1981). In essence, embracing their race, culture, ethnicity, and gifted status is critical in fostering a positive self-concept and identity.

Further, it could be argued that the very meaning of identity, particularly as it is associated with such constructs as ethnicity, gender role norms, and giftedness, evolves into internalized attitudes and cultural constructions among African male cohorts (Akbar, 1979, Akbar, Smith, Burlew, Mosley, & Whiteney, 1979; Asante, 1988, 2000; Cross, 1991a, b; Helms (as cited in Ponterotto, Casas, Suzuki, & Alexander, 1995; Kunjufu, 1987, 2005a, 2005b; Monroe & Goldman, 1988; Wilson & Constantine, 1999). In fact, a widely held belief is that the development of a positive identity among gifted African American males helps to create simultaneously a healthy attitude toward and confidence in their academic abilities and, we believe, possibly leads to the cultivation of leadership ability.

In terms of giftedness, many African American students find that their abilities and academic successes move them farther away instead of closer to members of their peer groups and home communities. As Bonner (2001) reported, "In the school setting, students are expected to achieve and perform at levels commensurate with their gifted and talented designation. At home, students are expected to act in a manner that conforms to their environment and social climate" (p. 651). What often happens is that the student, especially the African American male, becomes caught in this unforgiving middle position—not "real enough" and "too smart" to be part of the home community and not "cultured enough" and "too foreign" to be part of the mainstream. Thus, many of these students are left to their own devices and experience profound difficulties in navigating these two worlds.

The members of this cohort encounters an additional set of complexities in their attempts to develop their racial and ethnic identities. According to Grantham and Ford (2003), gifted African American students experience numerous barriers associated with identity development, especially in terms of their racial identity development. Additionally, Grantham and Ford state, "Racial identity concerns the extent to which people of color are aware of, understand, and value their racial background and heritage. The main premise of this theory is: Do people of color recognize and value their background and appearance?" (p. 20)

Although not all gifted African American male students develop their cultural values and belief system within a purely African or African American cultural and historical framework, the development of identity for the majority of this group continues to be heavily impacted by these structures. Therefore, the models found in Asante's (1988) *Afrocentric Cultural Identity* and Cross's (1991a) *Negro to Black Conversion* are two of the of the major cultural identity typologies found useful in providing a theoretical and empowerment identity model for understanding gifted African American male students.

William E. Cross, Jr., first introduced one of the primary theories used to frame the racial identity development process found to occur among African Americans in 1971. The four stages or themes as they are sometimes referred to in Cross's model (preencounter, encounter, immersion, and internalization) "each describes 'self-concept' issues concerning race and parallel attitudes that the individual holds about Black and White as a reference group" (p. 169). Without providing an exhaustive discussion here of Cross's theory, worthy of note is that each theme is found to represent an ever-increasing sense of self as a racial being and an ever-deepening sense of understanding regarding the establishment of a healthy identity.

What can be problematic for the African American male who seeks to establish his racial identity in a school context is that these enclaves are ill-prepared to provide the necessary encouragement and space for this process to unfold. Additionally, as institutions they are generally opposed to a developed sense of identity that does not readily embrace all aspects of the Eurocentric frameworks upon which American education is based. According to Howard (2003), "Some researchers posit that the dissonance that exists between school and student culture is the primary reason for the academic underachievement and social maladjustment of racially diverse students" (p. 6). Without a better alignment between cultural, gender, racial, and academic identity development, the typical outcome for the gifted African American male is often underachievement, primarily associated with feelings of alienation and incongruence with the educational environment.

Asante's (1988) Afrocentric model readily addresses many problems stemming from cultural misalignment. This model engenders a worldview aimed at constructing a collective Black consciousness leading to a new sense of empowerment and identity. The cultural values of the Afrocentric model are consistent with the basic principles of the African American worldview, characterized by interdependence, cooperation, unity, mutual responsibility, and reconciliation. There is a constant interplay among systems and subsystems where the focus is on cooperation and group cohesiveness, on the corporate whole (the African American community), rather than the individual. This means that the gifted African American male is not seen as alone, but rather as an intricate part of the African American community.

GIFTED AFRICAN AMERICAN MALES: RESILIENCE FACTORS

A question that often plagues the minds of scholars and the broader education community is often stated thus: Why is it that some African American males overcome various education and non-education-related obstacles (i.e., academic integration, social integration, family pressure and influence, peer pressure and influence, self-esteem, identity development) during their P-12 experiences while others fail to prevail? These obstacles are found to be somewhat surmountable according to Ford and Moore (2004), who refer to the challenges encountered by gifted African American males in assimilating and forming key relationships in school contexts as paying a "Black tax." Defined as incessant psychological and social stress faced by African Americans, as a result of being the minority member or pioneer in nontraditional domains (e.g., gifted education programs), the Black tax often leads these students to feel isolated, excluded, and depressed (Bailey & Moore, (as cited in C. Rabin, 2004; Flowers, Milner, & Moore, 2003; Moore, Flowers, Guion, Zhang, & Staten, 2004; Moore, Ford, & Milner, 2005; Moore, Madison-Colmore, & Smith, 2003).

Students who have the ability to rise despite the many obstacles (including the Black tax) they encounter develop protective processes that neutralize and in many ways offset these challenges that inhibit their pursuit of success. Identified by Zimmerman, Ramirez-Valles, and Maton (1999) as the maintenance of healthy development despite the presence of external and internal threats or the ability to recover from major traumatic life events, *resilience* is a concept that should be viewed as evolving and worthy of cultivation across the student's life continuum; this cultivation can mainly be facilitated by offering the student protective processes at critical life junctures (Garmezy, Masten, Cummings, Greene, & Karraker, 1991; Staudinger, Marsiske, & Baltes, 1993; Winfield, 1994). These protective processes that operate at turning points in the individual's life enable him to respond positively to perilous situations (Winfield, 1994). Rutter (1987) summarized this point:

> Protection does not reside in the psychological chemistry of the moment but in the ways in which people deal with life changes and in what they do about their stressful or disadvantageous circumstances. Particular attention needs to be paid to the mechanisms operating at key turning points in people's lives when a risk trajectory may be redirected onto a more adaptive path. (p. 329)

Protective processes, which include supportive families and communities, school staff, and an internal locus of control, compared to the risks experienced in external environments determine the level of resilience that one possesses (Winfield, 1994). A key example is Floyd's (1996) study of 20 high-achieving African American high school seniors with families from disadvantaged socioeconomic backgrounds. Floyd found that family support, the influence of teachers and school counselors, and personal beliefs of optimism and persistence were positively associated with resilience and academic success (L. A. Flowers, Zhang, Moore, & T. A. Flowers, 2004).

Family support was noted in several studies as one of the most influential factors in determining the resilience of gifted African American males. Winfield (1994) asserted that parents of resilient children give their adolescents structure in their everyday tasks, actively participate in their educational pursuits, and show an interest in their children's ambitions. Likewise, Maton, Hrabowski, and Grief (1998) affirmed that African American males who are academically successful were reared in families characterized by "high levels of academic engagement, strictness, nurturance, and community connectedness" (p. 662). While the belief that "it takes a village to raise a child" is still very prevalent within the African American community, one viable way to possibly offset negative the peer, neighborhood, and societal challenges associated with being gifted, African American, and male is for parents to encourage and nurture resilience among these young people.

Additionally, teachers play an integral role in the academic success of gifted program participants. Teaching styles, cultural sensitivity, and expectation levels have also been cited as influential factors in the resilience of gifted students. In a phenomenological study of African American high-school students in gifted education programs, T. A. Flowers et al. (2003) noted that teachers and school counselors needed to improve their level of cultural awareness, make their behaviors and teaching styles congruent with those of the population and environment of the school, and display care for the constituencies of their classrooms by appropriately managing classroom discipline. Teachers are primarily responsible for the learning experiences of students; therefore, if they in collaboration with school counselors encourage true learning and achievement, then both the intended and unexpected outcomes of resilient behavior will persist among the members of this cohort as they transition into higher education.

AFRICAN AMERICAN MALES AND LEADERSHIP POTENTIAL: THE SECONDARY CONTEXT

The academic literature of the past 20 years has revealed much about the experiences of African American males in educational institutions. While the overrepresentation of African American male students in special education has received a great deal of attention in academic literature, there has been less attention paid to the underrepresentation of African American males in gifted and talented programs. Several reasons have been given to explain this underrepresentation (Ford, Grantham, & Bailey, 1999; Polite, & Davis, 1999). However, many of the explanations are related to the definition(s) utilized in defining what constitutes *gifted and talented*. Specifically, Bonner (2000) found that the unique attributes, learning styles, and cultural backgrounds of African American male students were not taken into account by the existing definitions of giftedness utilized by most school districts. Hebert (1998) found that the underachievement pattern can be reversed through modification of the instructional program to increase the student's motivation to participate in school and achieve at higher levels of performance. Additionally, Ford, Grantham, Bailey, Polite, & Davis (1999) stated that educators may work diligently to provide a learning environment that is culturally responsive. Such a classroom or school is characterized by positive student-teacher relationships, multicultural curricula, and culturally compatible instructional styles.

One of the primary ability areas used to define giftedness that shows great promise in increasing the numbers of African American males identified is leadership. The use of this ability area has, to date, proven to be especially difficult because leadership remains the most underinvestigated aspect of the several domains that define giftedness (Matthews, 2004). However, given the importance of leadership ability in definitions of giftedness, it is critical that the leadership potential of African American male students be recognized and developed as part of the secondary educational experience. Developing leadership ability among African American male high-school students is of particular importance due to its implications and to the translation of this ability into future adult contexts (Roach, Adelma, & Wyman, 1999).

An examination of the existing literature on leadership and its connection to gifted and talented youth identifies several specific studies as particularly compelling (Matthews, 2004). In particular, Matthews (2004) described the research of Roach et al. (1999) as "monumental" and stressed that their work is "the only study addressing the long-term development of youth leadership and its relationship with adult leadership" (p. 94). This relationship is of special importance because Roach et al. noted that theories of adult leadership tend to focus on individual abilities, whereas theories of youth leadership are primarily situational, thus inviting a focus on "responding to challenges posed by particular situations" (Matthews, 2004, p. 94). A central focus of this situational orientation is the idea that self-knowledge is a primary component of youth leadership (Roach et al., 1999). This emphasis on self-knowledge stands in contrast to the emphasis on the charisma and influence of individuals that permeates theories of adult leadership (Matthews, 2004).

The importance of self-knowledge thus stands as a potentially important component in the development of youth leadership. While there is only a limited amount of academic literature focusing on leadership as a component of giftedness, there is an even greater scarcity of literature specifically focused on leadership and African American gifted students. However, there is a set of writings (see Aronson & Inzlicht, 2004; Brown & Dutton, 1995; Howard, 2003; Kuriloff & Reichert, 2003; Steele, 1997; Tillman, 2003) related to self-knowledge that potentially informs leadership development models for African American secondary students. Literature in the field of gifted and talented education has also largely overlooked contemporary mentoring and Rites of Passage programs aimed at African American male cohorts (Cooper, Groce, & Thomas, 2003).

ENCOURAGING LEADERSHIP POTENTIAL

As a primary means of building self-esteem, developing ethnic pride, transitioning into independence, developing identity, and helping to negate the risk factors faced by African American male adolescents (Alford, 2003; Campbell-Whatley & Algozzine, 1997; Futrell, 2004; Grantham, 2004; Utsey, Howard, & Williams, 2003; Vanderslice, 1998), culturally specific Rites of Passage programs, particularly those with strong mentoring components, have been advanced. Within such programs, mentoring is offered as a means to aid African American males who are struggling with academic achievement (Hrabowski et al., 1998; Price, 2002; Struchen & Porter, 1997). A number of long-standing organizations, including the Boy Scouts of America, 100 Black Men of America, Inc., and the Urban League have offered mentoring activities for young men throughout the country. African American fraternal organizations have offered mentoring programs targeting African American males for several decades. Specifically, Alpha Phi Alpha Fraternity, Inc. (Wesley, 1981) and Kappa Alpha Psi Fraternity, Inc. (Crump, 1991) have established mentoring opportunities that continue to focus on leadership development among adolescent African American males. These types of programs have existed for many years; however, they have generally operated in isolation from one another without a unified program or clear method of developing and managing emerging models of mentorship.

One leadership development framework found to be highly effective in promoting successful achievement among African American males (Alford, 2003; Hare & Hare, 1985; Harvey & Hill, 2004; Hill, 1992) is the African American Rites of Passage (AA-RITES) program. The focus on skills related to the development of self-knowledge and mentoring inherent in the AA-RITES program offers a unique opportunity for African American secondary students to develop a set of effective leadership skills. In many cases, African American males have not been provided with opportunities to master crucial developmental tasks during childhood and adolescence, and this in turn negatively influences their academic, career, and social success in later stages of life (Lee, 1991b). Therefore, the development of these skills has implications for the transition from adolescence to adulthood as well as for increasing the inclusion of African American male secondary students in gifted and talented programs.

According to Alford (2003), Rites of Passage can be defined as "symbolic and meaningful events that mark transitional periods for individuals as specified stages of life occur" (p. 3). Utilizing the work of Warfield-Coppock (1990), Alford (2003) characterizes Rites of Passage Programs as bringing "stability, ease of transition, and continuity to life, as well as groundedness, balance, and order" (p. 6). In essence, Rites of Passage are a part of every human society and have their earliest roots in ancient African societies, particularly those developed in the Nile Valley of present-day Egypt (Warfield-Coppock, 1992). Traditional cultures utilize Rites of Passage to mark the important transition from adolescence to adulthood (Eliade, 1958, 1994). Although the roots of these rites are centuries old, they remain a primary cultural activity for many African cultural communities throughout the world (Goggins, 1998; Hare & Hare, 1985; Hill, 1992; Maye & Maye, 2000).

Warfield-Coppock (1992) noted that Rites of Passage programs for African American males have existed for at least several decades. However, she discussed the contemporary revitalization of these programs and traced their recent resurgence to the Black Nationalist Movement of the 1960s and early 1970s (Warfield-Coppock, 1990; 1992). Although the historical connections discussed by Warfield-Coppock (1992) are valid, she failed to consider that the contemporary use of Rites of Passage programs for African American male adolescents has been heavily influenced by the hip-hop culture that emerged nationwide in the 1980s.

In describing the goals of Rites of Passage programs, Warfield-Copppock (1992) described the development of a "strong, positive sense of self and achievement" (p. 472) as being of primary importance in the personal growth of African American young men. However, conducting research on the effectiveness of these programs for African American male adolescents has been difficult because most Rites of Passage are historically private in nature and are usually tightly controlled by local community and fraternal organizations (Warfield-Coppock, 1992). Despite this, research on Rites of Passage programs for African American males across the country revealed that (a) most of these programs had improvement of self-concept as one of the major indicators of success of the program, and (b) self-knowledge was a crucial attribute for African American youth making the transition to adulthood (Warfield-Coppock, 1990; 1992).

Individuals who are responsible for designing curricula or implementing effective programming to encourage the leadership potential among gifted African American males should address both areas. A good example of these tenets is revealed in the model introduced in Courtland Lee's *Black Manhood Training* (1987), designed to emphasize not only the importance of understanding Black history but also the contemporary societal challenges facing African American males (e.g., incarceration, unemployment, teenage fatherhood, drugs, violence, education). Programs such as this not only provide an opportunity for gifted African American males to develop a better understanding of their cultural history and tradition but also allow them to tackle thorny contemporary issues of importance in a "safe space."

CONCLUSION

Targeting both mentoring and Rites of Passage programming initiatives is a means of cultivation of leadership potential in secondary school contexts. To offer administrators, faculty, and parents viable information on how to effectively meet the needs of gifted African American male students, we offer the following recommendations:

1. *Avoid treating African American males as a monolithic group.* The development of programs emphasizing leadership for African American gifted males must take into account the range of background experiences these students bring to the educational context. Some students will have had many opportunities to be exposed to leadership and decision making in home or community settings. Others will not have been exposed to such opportunities and may flounder when first presented with them.

2. *Infuse "real-world" experiences into the leadership curriculum and provide "authentic" training opportunities.* It is crucial to avoid a purely academic approach to leadership, one in which students learn lessons in leadership processes only through theoretical exercises. At the secondary level, a wealth of opportunities is available in academic and sports-related venues for students to develop and display their leadership abilities in meaningful ways. Examples include student council, special interest clubs, and various team sports (i.e., sports emphasizing camaraderie, esprit de corps, and teamwork).

3. *Include civic, clergy-based, community and historically Black Greek letter organizations (HBGLOs) in the planning and development of the curriculum emphasizing leadership ability.* These groups have a history and tradition of cultivating and providing leadership experiences for African American males. To capture important cultural nuances and idiosyncrasies, it is important to

get input from individuals who are indigenous to these communities. According to Whiting (2006), "Such organizations as fraternities, the Boys and Girls Clubs, 100 Black Men, National Urban League, YMCA, and others recognize that one person can make a difference in a child's life" (p. 226).

4. *Develop more seamless connections between youth leadership behavior and adult leadership performance* (Roach et al., 1999). Students at the secondary level are not afforded the opportunity to see how current leadership training will become manifest. *Proximal peers* are essential—college is viewed as a next step; therefore, connections to college student leaders who could serve as proximal-peer mentors would be beneficial. Additionally, college graduates and working professionals could serve as mentors and role models to expose students to leadership expectations and roles.

5. *Establish clear criteria for how leadership ability is to be used in the evaluation of giftedness.* The literature affirms the confusion and lack of specificity related to defining this particular form of giftedness (Matthews, 2004; Roach et al., 1999). Thus, it is important for administrators, teachers, and personnel responsible for identifying gifted African American males not only to establish effective programs to enhance these abilities but also to recognize them as viable identification constructs.

6. *Recognize the barriers that may potentially prohibit African American male participation in leadership development initiatives.* The literature addresses the structural inequities that are imposed on African American male populations in schools (Bonner, 2000; Ford, 2004; Ford, Grantham, Bailey, Polite, and Davis, 1999; Grantham, 2004). Additionally, a number of other sources, such as family and peers, can be equally prohibitive. As a result, many African American males adopt an oppositional stance toward anything "scholarly." Thus, it is important to note that "The earlier we focus on the scholar identities of such males, the more likely we are to develop a future generation of Black male scholars who are in a position to break the vicious cycle of underachievement" (Whiting, 2006, p. 223).

7. *Recognize and encourage resilience among gifted African American male cohorts.* Even being afforded the opportunity to participate in the school context is a major achievement for many gifted African American males. Many have overcome numerous barriers and obstacles from both externally and internally motivated sources; thus, their resilience in the face of these impediments should be recognized. Notwithstanding their giftedness, it is critical to understand that not all students are operating on a level playing field.

Additionally, the lack of empirical data focusing on gifted African American males and leadership has prompted us to offer several implications and recommendations for future research. The following research initiatives should be undertaken or expanded:

1. *Research focusing on how leadership development theories and leadership development models interface with models of identity development among gifted*

African American male cohorts. There are a number of leadership development theories and models that have been uncovered in the extant literature
(Burns, 1978; Greenleaf, 1977; Kouzes & Posner, 1989; Moxley, 2000; Northouse, 2001; Owen, 2000; Prewitt, 2004). Each provides a unique perspective
on this construct. Additionally, there are several theories and models that have
been made available to explain identity development (Allen, 1986; Evans, Forney, & Guido-DiBrito, 1998; Robinson & Howard-Hamilton, 1994; Salazar &
Abrams, 2005), both as content and process. Thus, research aimed at revealing how leadership and identity development interface is critically needed.
For example, one potential question that might be addressed by this research
is the following: Are there particular stages along the identity development
continuum that are ideal for particular approaches to leadership development
among gifted African American male cohorts?

2. *Research focusing on the roles that faith-based, fraternal, and civic institutions
   play in the cultivation of leadership competences and skills for gifted African
   American males.* Research to determine the relative impact of key organizations and institutions on leadership development and potential specifically
   for gifted African American males should be undertaken. According to Bonner and Jennings (2007), "These groups have a longstanding history of cultivating and providing leadership experiences for African American males"
   (p. 34).

3. *Research highlighting the unique characteristics of the African American family,
   particularly characteristics that foster leadership among gifted African American males.* The primacy of the family, although at times contested, continues
   to serve as the main unifying force within the African American community.
   Notwithstanding the contestation, particularly for the gifted African American male, the family provides an important source of ongoing support. Tar-
   geted research aimed at exploring how the family contributes to the success
   of these gifted males speaks to what Grantham and Ford (2003) alluded to in
   their work as the critical need to focus on and avoid overlooking the important role that the African American family plays.

4. *Research is needed that focuses on Rites of Passage Programs specifically targeting gifted African American males.* The goal of Rights of Passage Programs
   is "To prepare African American youth to reclaim their history and transform the circumstances of their lives" (Cooper et al., 2003, p. 4). How these
   programs intersect with their multiple identities (i.e., gifted, African, and
   male) is critical in understanding how their leadership potential can be cultivated.

The federal definition of giftedness highlights leadership as one of the key ability areas of focus. A wealth of opportunity is afforded to those responsible for
the identification of gifted students, particularly among African American male
populations. With the longstanding tradition of leadership in the African American community via civic and clergy-based organizations as well as HBGLOs,

targeting leadership ability as an area of emphasis could only provide tangible benefits.

Giftedness at its highest levels can be found across all ethnic and racial groups (Bonner, 2000; Bonner & Jennings, 2007; Delpit, 1995; Ford, Grantham, Bailey, Polite and Davis, 1999; Sternberg, 2007). However, the manifestations of giftedness differ from group to group due to differing values, attitudes, and opportunities. Essentially, what is valued in the culture is produced by the culture. Therefore, because leadership is cultivated and promoted as a from of giftedness within the African American culture, it is incumbent on schools and school officials to recognize and honor this form of ability in an effort to ensure the development of the unique talents of all gifted and talented students.

REFERENCES

Akbar, N. (1979). *Visions for Black men.* Nashville, TN: Winston-Derek.

Akbar, N., Smith, W., Burlew, K., Mosley, M., and Whiteney, W. (Eds.). (1979). African roots of Black personality. *Reflections on Black psychology* (pp. 79–87). Washington, DC: University Press of America.

Alford, K. (2003). Cultural themes in rites of passage: Voices of young African American males. *Journal of African American Studies, 7*(1), 3–26.

Allen, W. R. (1986). *Gender and campus race differences in Black student academic performance, racial attitudes and college satisfaction.* Atlanta, GA: Southern Education Foundation.

Aronson, J., and Inzlicht, M. (2004). The ups and downs of attributional ambiguity: Stereotype vulnerability and the academic self-knowledge of African-American students. *Psychological Science, 15,* 829–836.

Asante, M. K. (1988). *Afrocentricity.* Trenton, NJ: Africa World Press.

Asante, M. K. (2000). Afrocentricity and history: Mediating the meaning of culture in western society. *Souls, 2*(3), 50–62.

Bailey, D. F., & Moore, J. L., III. (2004). Emotional isolation, depression, and suicide among African American men: Reasons for concern. In C. Rabin (Ed.), *Linking lives across borders: Gender-sensitive practice in international perspective* (pp. 186–207). Pacific Grove, CA: Brooks/Cole.

Bailey, D. F., Moore, & J. L., III, Rabin, C. (2004). Emotional isolation, depression, and suicide among African American men: Reasons for concern. In C. Rabin, (Ed.), *Linking lives across borders: Gender-sensitive practice in international perspective* (pp. 105–120). Pacific Grove, CA: Brooks/Cole.

Bennett, W. J. (1992). *The de-valuing of America: The fight for our culture and our children.* New York: Touchstone.

Bonner F. A., II. (2000). African American giftedness. *Journal of Black Studies, 30*(5), 643–664.

Bonner F. A., II. (2001). Making room for the study of gifted African American males. *Black Issues in Higher Education, 18*(6), 80.

Bonner F. A., II, & Jennings, M. (2007). Never too young to lead: Gifted African American males in elementary school. *Gifted Child Today, 38*(2), 30–36.

Bourdieu, P. (1997). *The forms of capital.* Oxford, England: Oxford University Press.

Brown, J. D., & Dutton, K. A. (1995). The thrill of victory, the complexity of defeat: Self-esteem and people's emotional reactions to success and failure. *Journal of Personality and Social Psychology, 6,* 712–722.

Burns, J. M. (1978). *Leadership.* New York: Harper & Row.

Campbell-Whatley, G. D., & Algozzine, B. (1997). Using mentoring to improve academic programming for African American male youths with mild disabilities. *School Counselor, 44*(5), 362.

Cooper, R., Groce, J., & Thomas, N. D. (2003). Changing direction: Rites of passage programs for African American older men. *Journal of American Studies, 7*(3), 3–14.

Cross, W. E. (1991a). Negro to Black conversion experience: Toward a psychology of Black liberation. *Black World, 20*(9), 13–27.

Cross, W. E. (1991b). *Shades of Black: Diversity in African American identity.* Philadelphia: Temple University Press.

Crump, W. L. (1991). *The story of Kappa Alpha Psi: A history of the beginning and development of a college Greek letter organization, 1911–1991.* Philadelphia: Kappa Alpha Psi Fraternity.

Davidson Institute. (2007). *Gifted education state policy database.* Retrieved August 7, 2009, from http://www.gt-cybersource.org/StatePolicy.aspx?NavID=4_0.

Delpit, L. (1995). *Other people's children.* New York: New Press.

D'Souza, D. (1996). *The end of racism.* New York: Free Press.

Du Bois, W. E. B. (1903). *The souls of Black folk.* Chicago: A. C. McClurg.

Dunbar, C. (2001). *Alternative schooling for African American youth: Does anyone know we're here?* New York: Peter Lang.

Education Commission of the States. (2004). *State gifted and talented definitions.* Retrieved August 7, 2009 from http://www.ecs.org/clearinghouse/52/28/5228.doc

Eliade, M. (1958). *Rites and symbols of initiation: The mysteries of birth and rebirth* (W. Trask, Trans.) New York: Harper & Row.

Eliade, M. (1994). *Rites and symbols of initiation: The mysteries of birth and rebirth.* Putnam, CT: Spring Publications

Evans, N. J., Forney, D. S., & Guido-DiBrito, F. (1998). *Student development in college: Theory, research, and practice.* San Francisco: Jossey-Bass.

Fashola, O. (2005). *Educating African American males: Voices from the field.* New Thousand Oaks, CA: Corwin Press.

Ferguson, A. (2000). *Bad boys: Public schools in the making of Black masculinity.* Ann Arbor: University of Michigan Press.

Fleming, J. (1984). *Blacks in college: A comparative study of students' success in Black and in White institutions.* San Francisco: Jossey-Bass.

Flowers, T. A., Milner, H. R., & Moore, J. L., III. (2003). Effects of locus of control on African American high school seniors' educational aspirations: Implications for preservice and inservice high school teachers and counselors. *High School Journal, 87,* 39–50.

Flowers, L. A., Zhang, Y., Moore, J. L., III, & Flowers, T. A. (2004). An exploratory phenomenological study of African American high school students in gifted education programs: Implications for teachers and school counselors. *E-Journal of Teaching and Learning in Diverse Settings, 2,* 39–53. Retrieved August 7, 2009, from http://www.subr.edu/coeducation/ejournal/EJTLDS.Volume%202%20Issue%201.Flowers%20et%20al.pdf.

Floyd, C. (1996). Achieving despite the odds: A study of resilience among a group of African American high school seniors. *Journal of Negro Education, 65,* 181–189.

Ford, D. Y. (1995). Desegregating gifted education: A need unmet. *Journal of Negro Education, 64*(1), 52–62.

Ford, D. Y. (2003). Two other wrongs don't make a right: Sacrificing the needs of diverse students does not solve gifted education's unresolved problems. *Journal for the Education of the Gifted, 26,* 283–291.

Ford, D. Y. (2004). A challenge for culturally diverse families of gifted children: Forced choices between affiliation or achievement. *Gifted Child Today, 27,* 26–29.

Ford, D. Y., Grantham, T. C., Bailey, D. F., Polite, V., & Davis, J. (Eds.). (1999). Identifying giftedness among African American males: Recommendations for effective recruitment and retention. *African American males in school and society: Practices and policies for effective education.* New York: Teachers College Press.

Ford, D. Y., Harris, J. J., III, Tyson, C. A., & Frazier-Trotman, M. (2002). Beyond deficit thinking: Providing access for gifted African American students. *Roeper Review, 24,* 52–58.

Ford, D. Y., & Moore, J. L., III (2004). The achievement gap and gifted students of color. Cultural, social, and psychological factors. *Understanding Our Gifted, 16,* 3–7.

Ford, D. Y., Moore, J. L., & Milner, R. H. (2005). Beyond cultureblindness: A model of culture with implications for gifted education. *Roeper Review, 27,* 97–103.

Frasier, M. (1989). Poor and minority students can be gifted, too! *Educational Leadership, 46*(6), 16–19.

Futrell, M. (2004). Anticipating success: Removing the barriers to educational equity and equality. *Harvard Journal of African American Public Policy, 10,* 103–116.

Gardner, H. (1983). *Frames of mind: The theory of multiple intelligences.* New York: Basic Books.

Garmezy, N., & Masten, A. S. (1991). The protective role of competence indicators in children at risk. In E. M. Cummings, A. L. Greene, & K. H. Karraker (Eds.), *Life-span developmental psychology: Perspectives on stress and coping* (pp. 151–174). Hillsdale, NJ: Lawrence Erlbaum.

Goggins, L. (1998). *Bringing the light into a new day: African centered Rites of Passage.* St. Akron, OH: Rest Publications.

Grantham, T. C. (2004). Rocky Jones: Case study of a high-achieving Black male's motivation to participate in gifted classes. *Roeper Review, 26,* 208–215.

Grantham, T. C., & Ford, D. Y. (2003). Beyond self-concept and self-esteem for African American students: Improving racial identity improves achievement. *High School Journal, 87*(1), 18–29.

Greenleaf, R. K. (1977), *Servant leadership.* New York: Paulist Press.

Hare, N., and Hare, J. (1985). *Bringing the Black boy to manhood: The passage.* San Francisco: Black Think Tank.

Harry, B., & Anderson, M. (1994). The disproportionate placement of African American males in special education programs: A critique of the process. *Journal of Negro Education, 63*(4), 602–620.

Harvey, A., & Hill, R. (2004). Africentric youth and family Rites of Passage Program: Promoting resilience among at-risk African American youths. *Social Work, 49*(1), 65–74.

Hebert, T. P. (1998). Gifted Black males in an urban high school: Factors that influence achievement and underachievement. *Journal for the Education of the Gifted, 21,* 385–414.

Helms J. E. (1995). An update of Helm's White and People of Color racial identity models. In J. G. Ponterotto, J. M. Casas, L. A. Suzuki, C. M. Alexander (Eds.), *Handbook of Multicultural Counseling* (pp. 181–198). Thousand Oaks, CA: Sage Publications.

Herrnstein, R. J., & Murray, C. (1994). *The bell curve.* New York: Free Press.

Hill, P. (1992). *Coming of age: African American male rites-of-passage.* Chicago: African American Images.

Hilliard, A. G. (1976). *Alternatives to IQ testing: An approach to the identification of gifted "minority" children* (Report No. PS 009 639). Sacramento: California Department of Education, Special Education Division. (ERIC Document Reproduction Service No. ED147009)

Hopkins, R. (1997). *Educating Black males: Critical lessons in schooling, community, and power.* Albany: State University of New York Press.

Howard, T. C. (2003). A tug of war for our minds: African American high school students' perceptions of their academic identities and college aspirations. *High School Journal, 87*(1), 4–17.

Hrabowski, F. A., III, Maton, K. I., & Greif, G. L. (1998). *Beating the odds: Raising academically successful African American males.* Oxford, England: Oxford University Press.

Hughes, M. S. (1987). Black students' participation in higher education. *Journal of College Student Personnel, 28,* 532–545.

Hughes, R. L., & Bonner, F. A., II. (2006). Leaving Black males behind: Debunking the myth of meritocratic education. *Journal of Race and Policy, 2,* 76–90.

Kearns, T., Ford, L., & Linney, J. A. (2005). African American student representation in special education programs. *Journal of Negro Education, 74,* 297–310.

Kouzes, J., & Posner, B. (1989). *The leadership challenge: How to get extraordinary things done in organizations.* San Francisco: Jossey-Bass.

Kunjufu, J. (1987) *Lessons from history: A celebration of blackness.* Chicago: African American Images.

Kunjufu, J. (1990). *Countering the conspiracy to destroy Black boys.* Chicago: African American Images.

Kunjufu, J. (2005a). *Hip hop street curriculum.* Chicago: African American Images.

Kunjufu, J. (2005b). *Keeping Black boys out of special education.* Chicago: African American Images.

Kuriloff, P., & Reichert, M. (2003). Boys of class, boys of color: Negotiating the academic and social geography of an elite independent school. *Journal of Social Issues,* 751–770.

Lee, C. C. (1987). Black manhood training: Group counselling for male Blacks in grades 7–12. *Journal for Specialists in Group Work, 12,* 18–25.

Lee, C. C. (1991a). Counseling Black males: From theory to practice. In R. L. Jones (Ed.), *Black psychology,* 3rd edition (pp. 559–576) Berkeley, CA: Cobb & Henry.

Lee, C. C. (1991b). A group counseling model for developing manhood among Black male adolescents. *Journal of Health Care for the Poor and Underserved, 2,* 19–25.

Lee, C. C. (1996). *Saving the native son: Empowerment strategies for young Black males,* Greensboro, NC: ERIC Counseling and Student Services Clearinghouse.

Lee, C. C. (2005). A reaction to EGAS: An important new approach to African American youth empowerment. *Professional School Counseling, 8*(5), 393–394.

Majors, R., & Billson, J. M. (1992). *Cool prose: The dilemmas of Black manhood in America.* New York: MacMillan.

Marland S. (1972). *Education of the gifted and talented.* Washington, DC: U.S. Government Printing Office.

Maton, K. I., Hrabowski, F. A., III, & Greif, G. L. (1998). Preparing the way: A qualitative study of high-achieving African American males and the role of the family. *American Journal of Community Psychology, 26,* 639–668.

Matthews, M. S. (2004). Leadership education for gifted and talented youth: A review of the literature. *Journal for the Education of the Gifted, 28,* 77–113.

Maye, M., & Maye, W. (2000). *"Orita": Creating rites of passage for today's youth.* New York: Faith Works.

McNally, J. (2003). *A ghetto within a ghetto: African American students overrepresented special education programs. Rethinking Schools Online.* Retrieved April 20, 2009 from http://rethinkingschools.org/archive/17_03/ght179.shtml.

Monroe, S., & Goldman, P. (1988). *Brothers.* New York; Ballantine Books.

Moore, J. L., III, Flowers, L. A., Guion, L. A., Zhang, Y., & Staten, D. L. (2004). Improving the experiences of non-persistent African American males in engineering program: Implications for success. *National Association of Student Affairs Professionals Journal, 7,* 105–120.

Moore, J. L., III, Ford, D. Y., & Milner, H. R. (2005). Recruiting is not enough: Retaining African-American students in gifted education. *Gifted Child Quarterly, 49,* 49–65.

Moore, J. L., III, Madison-Colmore, O., & Smith, D. M. (2003). The prove-them-wrong syndrome: Voices from unheard African-American males in engineering disciplines. *Journal of Men's Studies, 12,* 61–73.

Morris, J. E. (2002). African American students and gifted education. *Roeper Review, 24,* 59–62.

Moxley, R. (2000). *Leadership and the spirit: Breathing new vitality and energy into individuals and organizations.* San Francisco: Jossey-Bass.

National Association for Gifted Children. (2005). *2004–2005 state of the states: A report by the National Association for Gifted Children and the Council of State Directors of Programs for the Gifted.* Washington, DC: Author.

Northouse, P. G. (2001). *Leadership: Theory and practice.* Thousand Oaks, CA: Sage.

Ogbu, J. (2003). *Black American students in an affluent suburb: A study of academic disengagement.* Mahwah, NJ: Erlbaum.

Owen, H. (2000). *The power of spirit: How organizations transform.* San Francisco: Berret-Koehler.

Polite, V., & Davis, J. (1999). *African American males in school and society: Practices and policies for effective education.* New York: Teachers College Press.

Ponterotto, J. G., Casas, J. M., Suzuki, L. A. & Alexander, C. M. (Eds.). (1995). *Handbook of multi-cultural counseling.* Thousand Oaks, CA: Sage.

Porter, M. (1998). *Kill them before they grow: The misdiagnosis of African American boys in America's classrooms.* Chicago: African American Images.

Prewitt, V. (2004). Integral leadership for the 21st century. *World Futures. 60,* 327–333.

Price, H. (2002). *Achievement matters: Getting your child the best education possible.* New York: Kensington Publishing.

Renzulli, J. S. (1981). The revolving door model: A new way of identifying the gifted. *Phi Delta Kappan, 62*(9), 648–649.

Roach, A., Adelma, A., & Wyman, L. T. (1999). Leadership giftedness: Models revisited. *Gifted Child Quarterly, 43,* 13–24.

Robinson, T. L., & Howard-Hamilton, M. (1994). An Afrocentric paradigm: Foundation for a healthy self-image and healthy interpersonal relationships. *Journal of Mental Health Counseling, 16*(3), 327–340.

Rutter, M. (1987). Psychological resilience and protective mechanisms. *American Journal of Orthopsychiatry, 57,* 316–331.

Salazar, C. F., & Abrams, L. P. (2005). Conceptualizing identity development in members of marginalized groups. *Journal of Professional Counseling: Practice, Theory, and Research, 33*(1), 47–59.

Sedlacek, W. E. (1987). Black students on White campuses: 20 years of research. *Journal of College Students Personnel, 28,* 532–545.

Simon, J. (2007). Rise of the carceral state. *Social Research, 74*(2), 471–508.

Staudinger, U. M., Marsiske, M., & Baltes, P. B. (1993). Resilience and levels of reserve capacity on later adulthood: Perspectives from life-span theory. *Development and Psychopathology, 5,* 541–566.

Steele, C. M. (1997). A threat in the air: How stereotypes shape intellectual identity and performance. *American Psychologist, 52,* 613–629.

Sternberg, R. J. (1985). *Beyond IQ: A triarchic theory of human intelligence.* Cambridge, England: Cambridge University Press.

Sternberg, R. J. (2007). Cultural dimensions of giftedness and talent. *Roeper Review, 29,* 160–165.

Struchen, W., & Porter, M. (1997). From role-modeling to mentoring for African American youth: Ingredients for successful relationships. *Preventing School Failure, 41,* 119–123.

Taylor, G., & Phillips, T. (2006). *Improving the quality of education for African-American Males: A study of America's urban schools.* Lewiston, NY: Edwin Mellen Press.

Thomas, G. E. (1981). *Black students in higher education: Conditions and experiences in the 70s.* Westport, CT: Greenwood Press.

Tillman, L. C. (2003). Mentoring, reflection, and reciprocal journaling. *Theory into Practice, 42*(3), 226–233.

U.S. Department of Education. (1993). *National excellence: A case for developing America's talent.* Washington, DC: Author.

U.S. Department of Education. (2002). Elementary and secondary school civil rights survey 2002. Retrieved April 13, 2009, from http://ocrdata.ed.gov/ocr2002rv30a/.

U.S. Department of Education. (2004). *National center for education statistics.* Retrieved April 20, 2009 from http://nces.ed.gov/programs/digest/d04/tables/xls/tabn042.xls.

Utsey, S. O., Howard, A., & Williams, O., III. (2003). Therapeutic group mentoring with African American male adolescents. *Journal of Mental Health Counseling, 25*(2), 126–140.

Vanderslice, R. (1998). Hispanic children and giftedness: Why the difficulty in identification?. *Delta Kappa Gamma Bulletin, 64*(3), 18–23.

Warfield-Coppock, N. (1990). *Afrocentric theory and applications, Vol. I: Adolescent rites of passage.* Washington, DC: Baobab Associates.

Warfield-Coppock, N. (1992). The rites of passage movement: A resurgence of African centered practices for socializing African American youth. *Journal of Negro Education, 61*(4), 471–482.

Watkins, A., & Kurtz, D. (2001). Using solution-focused intervention to address African American male overrepresentation in special education: A case study. *Children and Schools, 23*(4), 223–235.

Watson, C., & Smitherman, G. (1996). *Educating African American males: Detroit's Malcolm X academy solution.* Chicago: Third World Press.

Wesley, C. H. (1981). *The history of Alpha Phi Alpha: A development in college life.* Chicago: Foundation.

Whiting, G. W. (2006). From at risk to at promise: Developing scholar identities among Black males. *Journal of Secondary Gifted Education, 17*(4), 222–229.

Williams, A. (2004). *New York Amsterdam News, 95*(20), p. 8.

Wilson, J. W., & Constantine, M. G. (1999). Racial identity attitudes, self-concept, and perceived family cohesion in Black college students. *Journal of Black Studies, 29,* 354–366.

Winfield, L. F. (1994). *Developing resilience in urban youth.* Oak Brook, IL: North Central Regional Educational Laboratory.

Wynn, M. (1992). *Empowering African American males to succeed: A ten step approach for parents and teachers.* Marietta, GA: Rising Sun.

Zimmerman, M. A., Ramirez-Valles, J. R., & Maton, K. I. (1999). Resilience among urban African American male adolescents: A study of the protective effects of sociopolitical control on their mental health. *American Journal of Community Psychology, 27,* 733–751.

Leaving Black Males Behind: Debunking the Myths of Meritocratic Education

Robin L. Hughes, PhD

Indiana University-Purdue University Indianapolis

Fred A. Bonner II, EdD

Texas A & M University

In a *Washington Post* article, "Degrees of Separation," (June 25, 2002) staff writer Michael Fletcher takes aim at the organizations he deems responsible for creating the ever-growing conundrum faced by our colleges and universities; namely, "Where are all of the men?" He goes on to state that years of tampering with the education of males has led to declining SAT scores and substandard rankings of United States men when compared to their international counterparts. Another national mainstream newspaper, *USA Today*, eloquently states that while girls received extra help in the classroom, boys received prescriptions for Ritalin. These are but a few examples included in recent articles in powerhouse, mainstream newspapers that have taken on the U.S. educational system—specifically with regard to the ways in which it has routinely failed males (Essay staff, 2003).

Academic and scholarly news outlets appear to be more embattled when discussing this topic. Many of these venues claim that boys are conspicuously being shortchanged by the educational system (Hoff-Sommers, 2000), while others maintain that the general population of males is not being neglected at all (Brownstein, 2000; Fuentes, 2003; Gewertz, 2004; King, 2000; Smith, 2005), that in actuality, only boys of color appear to be impacted. To add to this point, in an article in the *Chronicle of Higher Education* more than five years ago, Brownstein (2000) explained that while empirical studies and press releases continued to report the impending national "crisis"—the undermining of education for males—little evidence suggested that all males were represented in these critical discussions. In fact, the author went on to state that the "crisis" was occurring among males in

Robin Hughes and Fred A Bonner II, "Leaving Black Males Behind: Debunking the Myths of Meritocratic Education," *The Journal of Race and Policy* 2, No. 1 (Spring/Summer 2006). Reprinted with permission.

Black and other racial minority populations; other (i.e. ,White) males were found to be "doing just fine" (Fuentes, 2003; King, 2000).

Although some male populations appear to be faring well in higher education, the fact still remains that in general, enrollment among both White and Black males who attend college has decreased (Gewertz, 2004; King, 2000; Smith, 2005). It is important to highlight from this statement the words "in general." According to King, once race is used as a means to disaggregate the male college-going population, we "generally" find significantly fewer Black males left in the pool. Perhaps an even more significant finding is that there is virtually no difference in number between male and female White, traditional-aged undergraduates. Where we do find significant gender gaps is among African American, Native American, and to a lesser degree Hispanic populations. King's research reveals that the true gaps found to exist among males and females in academe are within populations of color—there are simply fewer males of color "in general," which in turn reduces the numbers of males reported overall. Thus, the revelation is that there is really no revelation at all. We have known for quite some time that higher education applicant pools are not reflective of students from low-income and minority statuses (King, 2000).

This article attempts to address the disparities in Black male participation in higher education by exploring several pervasive myths that have been espoused as rationales for the continued low enrollment of this cohort. A critical race theory (CRT) framework will be used to challenge assumptions and offer new insight regarding low collegiate enrollment as an outcome of various structural inequities—that is, teacher propensity to pathologize Black males in their early school experiences and education tracking that locks Black males into substandard classes and ineffective classroom learning environments. The authors will conclude with recommendations for individuals within and outside of educational contexts to assist not only in debunking the identified myths—all the research on Black males is brand new, Black males graduate at a much lower rate, something is wrong with Black males, and those who teach Black males are colorblind—but also in improving the current and future educational status of Black males in the academy.

THE MAKING OF MYTHS

Current research would have many of us believe that Black males are pathological and failing miserably in our nation's schools, when in actuality our nation's schools seem to be the purveyors of pathology and are miserably failing our Black males (Dunbar, 2001; Ferguson, 2000; McNally, 2003). A typical response by K-12 educational institutions when quizzed about the declining academic and social status of Black males has been to speak from a position promoting pathology over inclusion (Kunjufu, 2005) in special education courses; underinclusion in gifted and talented courses (Bonner, 2000; Ford, 1992, 1994); overprescription of behavior-altering drugs (e.g., Ritalin and Aderall); and overutilization of labels such as ADD and ADHD (Dunbar, 2001; Ferguson, 2000; Losen & Orfield, 2002). These same constituencies rarely if ever question or second-guess their decisions or the inequitable social and structural processes that often place Black males in such categories and situations in the first place (Davis, 2002).

When inequities are left to run rampant in the lower schools, the outcome typically results in fewer Black males who have the academic credentials necessary for entry into institutions of higher learning—resulting in low enrollment. According to Lee (1996), "Black males encounter formidable challenges to their educational development and many of them experience a serious stifling of achievement, aspiration, and pride in school systems throughout the country" (p. 5). For Black males, the acquisition of an education is often a catch-22 situation in which to fully understand what academic accoutrements are necessary for success they must possess certain cultural capital (Bourdieu, 1997). Yet the Black male is expected to have certain cultural capital in order to understand what academic accoutrements are necessary for success.

Perhaps a teleological approach that looks at the very essence of why Black males are underachieving from a standpoint that eschews notions of deficiency and pathology would lead to a different outcome for these men. As critical theorists, we argue that low enrollment of Black males is a result of the failure to seriously educate, and in some instances a propensity to *miseducate*, Black males (Woodson, 1990). These inequities are perpetuated by a lack of appreciation and understanding of what these individuals are bringing to the educational context; hence, through CRT we speak to the importance of allowing these individuals to bring their personal and collective narratives as well as their social constructions to the table (Delgado, 1995).

Delgado (1995) further states that "Each of the prime Critical themes—the call for context, critique of liberalism, insistence that racism is ordinary not exceptional, and the notion that traditional civil rights law has been more valuable to Whites than to Blacks" (p. xv) must be used as ground to engage in important discourse—especially in our deliberations about the education of Black males. Through the lens of CRT, we are able to recognize that race is neither real nor is it objective; rather it is a social construction. As critical writers we use the tools of CRT to present *counterstories* to challenge and combat vitriolic metanarratives and beliefs and add voice to those who have been silenced (p. 43).

Additionally, we agree with the conflict theorists who assert that education for the majority has historically undermined the education of minority students. In speaking to this issue, Irvine (1990) states that "As an agent of ideological control, schools preserve their historical purpose—maintaining the existing social order, in which low-income and minority persons are 'educated' for less skilled, routine jobs and conditioned by schools for obedience, the acceptance of authority, and external control" (p. 2).

By blaming Black males for their own school failure (Irvine, 1990; Kunjufu, 2005), schools are essentially blaming themselves; however, to combat this view of oppression, schools must cooperate in the transformation of the educational experiences for Black males, just as in *Pedagogy of the Oppressed*, when Freire (1993) asserts in his diatribe on the problems found to exist among oppressor and oppressed, "Hence the radical requirement—both for the individual who discovers him or herself to be an oppressor and for the oppressed—that the concrete situation which begets oppression must be transformed" (p. 32). This transformation must begin with a radical attack on the myths that shape the thoughts and perceptions of the individuals responsible for our educational systems; these individuals are ultimately responsible for enacting policies and procedures that are anabolic to Black males.

MYTH 1: ALL THE RESEARCH ON BLACK MALES IS BRAND NEW

Perhaps one of the most troubling myths associated with the low enrollment of Black males in higher education is the belief that this phenomenon is a relatively "new" development. Contrary to this view, numerous African American scholars have studied this topic for years (Davis, 2002; Delpit, 2003; Dunbar, 2001; A. Ferguson, 2001; Lopez, 2003). Perhaps an even more troublesome dimension to this myth is the evolving rhetoric that tends to downplay the historically specific origins of oppression of Black males in schools, instead placing these discussions in a more generalized framework for debate. These efforts have essentially served to obliterate the nuances of what it has meant historically to be both Black and male in our nation's school settings (Hoff-Sommers, 2000).

The result has been a sudden interest by the American public in the ways that males have been treated—it has even been elevated to the level of generating the label "male problem." The irony in this situation is that we have only recently begun to pay attention to these problems now that males in mainstream populations have been impacted, when in fact, we should have been paying attention to these problems years ago. According to Hoff-Summers (2000):

> Under the guise of helping girls, many schools have adopted policies that penalize boys, often for simply being masculine. Boys do need help, but not the sort they've been getting. . . . they need help catching up with girls academically, they need love, discipline, respect, and moral guidance. They desperately need understanding. They do not need to be rescued from masculinity. (p. 150)

It was as if the statements of Hoff-Summers (2000) and other educational pundits served as a clarion call, a call that elevated the declining performance of males in school to the level of national crisis. Books were written to help advise and guide teachers to work with male students, national programs were enacted to serve as blueprint initiatives to ameliorate the plight of the disappearing male, and mass media venues showed their support by dedicating popular television and press time to solving the boy problem that was perceived to be taking shape in the nation. Yet, when issues of a similar nature were presented and the relative impact on Black males was used as the raison d'être for the movement of the masses, the reaction took on a quite different tone. In fact, there was no call to arms to address the "Black male problem," especially from a strengths model approach; instead, a deficit model with its propensity for ascribing blame and pathology to these males for their perceived abhorrent behavior was the modus operandi. Prescriptions for behavior-altering drugs, classroom settings designed to control misbehavior (Skiba, Michael, Nardo, and Peterson, 2002), and alternative educational environments (Davis, 2002: Delpit, 2003; Dunbar, 2001; Ferguson, 2000; Lopez, 2003) to sequester the untamable souls were utilized.

It is apparent that the increasingly low enrollment of Black males in higher education is a direct correlate to the ways in which those responsible for providing a fair and equitable education in the lower schools have treated this group. This continued malfeasance has also indirectly led to a number of other social ills for Black male populations, not the least of which is the ever-widening gap in educational attainment between Black male and Black female populations. Hoff-Summers (2002) highlighted this problem with her question: What does it mean in the long run that we have females who are significantly more literate, significantly more educated than their male counterparts? We know from history and lived experiences in the United States that educating only one segment of the population creates severe social problems (Lopez, 2003). The low enrollment of Black males in higher education is not new—only our excuses for ignoring this problem tend to be.

MYTH 2: BLACK MALES GRADUATE AT MUCH LOWER RATES

Some would argue that since the American education system is based on the ideals of meritocracy, Black males, just like their White male counterparts, have had equal access and opportunities to take whichever courses they deem useful for their current and future success (Bennett, 1992; D'Souza, 1996). Many would add that Black males are obviously choosing not to take college preparation courses due to inherent deficiencies or cognitive limitations (Herrnstein & Murray, 1994) in their capacity to achieve—both notions serving as fodder for the myth that Black males underachieve and subsequently graduate at lower rates than the mainstream masses.

A most cursory look at the literature highlighting the experiences of Black males in K-12 institutions will reveal the overwhelming collection of obstacles this group must overcome just to don a cap and gown on graduation day: obstacles such as pedagogical practices that overlook and often downplay their unique learning styles (Bonner, 2000; Delpit, 2003; Irvine, 1990; Kunjufu, 2005; Lee, 1996; Mincy, 1994; Murrell, 2002); curriculum content that obliterates the contributions of their ancestors (Delpit, 2003; Hilliard, 1976; Hollins, 1996); and social practices that continually remind them that they are not part of the "norm" (Gordon, 1999; hooks, 2004; Irvine, 1990; Murrell, 2002). Although Black males are graduating from high school at rates commensurate with their White male counterparts and we are continuing to see increases in the overall numbers of Black male high school graduates (King, 2000, Smith, 2005), this is but a small victory when the real battle begins once these individuals are able to acquire a college degree.

It is a widely espoused myth that Black males graduate from high school at significantly lower rates than other groups, especially their White male counterparts. On the contrary, King (2002) found that close to 90 percent of White and African American males age 25–29 had earned a high school diploma. One would assume that if Black males and White males are graduating from high school at roughly the same rates, then the pool of applicants to institutions of higher education should be roughly equivalent. The reality is that the numbers of Black males choosing to enter college are at significantly lower numbers than the numbers of their White male peers. Is it safe, therefore, to assume that there is a proverbial "fly in the ointment"—or a flaw in the available applicant pool argument made by many educational conservatives?

A cogent point of departure for this argument might be disabusing individuals of the notion that Black males and White males receive the same K-12 education and educational experiences. The truth is that although Black males are graduating from K-12 at roughly the same rates as their White male peers, they are not graduating from the same types of programs: that is, Black males are graduating from special education programs, attending alternative schools, and being tracked into less rigorous vocational programs (Kunjufu, 2005). At the same time, their White male counterparts are graduating from gifted and talented programs, enrolling in Advanced Placement (AP) courses, and attending summer enrichment sessions for talented and precocious youth. In other words, the graduation rates for these two groups may reveal, at first glance, that all things are equal; however, once these data are disaggregated and mined for potential solutions to the problem under discussion, a different story is uncovered.

We know that the best predictor of both enrollment and success in college is the rigor of the high school curriculum (Horn & Kojako, 2001). In fact, students who take rigorous coursework in high school account for more than 80 percent of those students who either stay on the persistence track to a bachelor's degree or who are retained at their initial institution (Warburton, Bugarin, & Nuñez, 2001). In addition, data supplied by King (2000) suggest that young, low-income Black males are more likely than any of their counterparts to leave high school without completing the necessary course work in preparation for college.

MYTH 3: SOMETHING IS WRONG WITH BLACK MALES

Despite our nation's supposed rejection of cultural deficit models, Darwinian theoretical frameworks, and eugenics as plausible explanations for school failure among populations of color, we continue to rely heavily on deficiency theories as a means to explain underachievement among these groups (Bonner, 1999; Herring, 1995). One of the most pervasive sets of tools used to lead the way in this malevolent means of codifying populations of color, especially Black males, has been standardized tests. It was Asa Hilliard who posited that these assessments seek to ask two fundamental questions and lead to two fundamentally different approaches to understanding human behavior:

1. Do you know what I know?
2. What is it that you know?

According to Bonner (2000),

> The first approach is what most standardized tests measure. The language, culture, and experiences of the individuals who construct these tests become the prevailing benchmarks of success. The tests then become a measure of which students have a better grasp of White, middle-class culture—not what knowledge and information they have acquired. (p. 646)

The misuse of assessment measures and standardized tests often serves to initiate the downward spiral for Black males in the education system. These standardized tests are like a hydra, touching all parts of the student's school experience, often resulting in dire outcomes:

- Black males have a 3.26 greater chance of being labeled mentally retarded than White females, a 2.34 greater chance of being placed in a Learning Disabled (LD) classroom, and an astronomical 5.52 greater chance of being placed in an emotional disturbed classroom (Kunjufu, 2005).
- Black males are three times more likely to be placed in classes for the educable mentally retarded than in gifted and talented classes (Lee, 1996).
- Black males are far more likely than other ethnic/gender groups to be placed in general education and vocational high school curriculum tracks than in academic tracks (Lee, 1996).

What are the consequences and outcomes of these disparities?

> Black males are 67% more likely than Whites with emotional behavior problems to be removed from school on the grounds that they are a danger to other students. Black male students were 13 times more likely than White students with emotional behavior problems to be arrested in school. . . . In addition, of the number of Black males who are diagnosed as emotionally disturbed, 58% drop out of school, and of that group, 73% are arrested within three to five years of dropping out. (Losen &Orfield, 2002, p. 150)

The literature affirms the fact that not only are Black males overrepresented in special education classrooms in every state (Herrera, 1998; Skiba et al., 2002; Smith, 2005) but that they are also overrepresented in our penal systems and constitute the highest number of per capita murder victims in our country (Losen & Orfield, 2002; Smith, 2005). And we cannot ignore the fact that this cohort represents the most underemployed population in the country (Economic Policy Institute, 2005; Herring, 1995).

Given these grim statistics, one could tacitly accept as fact the notion that Black males disproportionately suffer from some sort of "mysterious pathology," a condition that defies conventional wisdom on offering viable remedies. Yet, the statistics must be couched in terms of the background experiences and lived realities of these men. It is important to talk about such issues as the African American worldview (Parham, White, & Ajamu, 2000) and how Black males function differently in academic and social contexts based on the different psychological and psychosocial perspectives they bring to the table.

Also, one cannot, perhaps, ignore the most significant disparity found to exist between Black populations and their White counterparts, namely, the vast gap in socioeconomic status. According to data from the U.S. Census Bureau's Current Population survey, the Children's Defense Fund found that "Black children are far more likely than Whites to grow up in extreme poverty—nearly one million Black children live in extreme poverty (with after-tax income (including food and housing benefits) below *half* the poverty line. The number of extremely poor Black children is now at its highest level in the 23 years for which such data exist" (p. 1). In light of the data and statistics presented in this section, the myth that something must be inherently wrong with Black males should prompt us to recall the old adage, "When you point the finger of blame at others, four fingers are pointing back at you." Is something wrong with them—or is something wrong with us?

MYTH 4: THOSE WHO TEACH BLACK MALES ARE COLORBLIND

There has been little evidence to support the colorblind philosophy, namely, the idea of a mystical trait possessed by some that allows them to see beyond skin color in an effort to combat ethnic and racial discrimination (Chemers & Murphy, 1995). In fact, recent documented evidence reveals the direct opposite of this claim, uncovering the importance of not only seeing color but also attempting to connect race and ethnicity with such important concepts as learning preferences, learning styles, and teaching modalities (Dunn & Dunn, 1992; Hollins, 1996; Murrell, 2002; Shade, 1982; Witkin & Moore, 1975).

To say that we do not see color is to say that we are ignoring critical differences and noteworthy nuances that can potentially mean success or failure for Black males (Cose, 1997). In support of this claim, Lowe (2002) says in "Color Blindness: Anti-Discrimination Doctrine or Hegemonic Reproduction of Racial Inequality?" that "color blindness and race neutrality are little more than hegemonic mechanisms designed to reproduce the same, historical social inequalities at the expense of America's non-Whites, immigrants, women, and other historically underrepresented and oppressed groups to the economic benefit of a White power elite" (p. 1).

Efforts to address the colorblind philosophy must begin with those who so readily espouse it—teachers. In a recent study, Hanushek, Kain, O'Brien, and Rivkin (2005) found that when students were taught by teachers of their own race, their performance levels were significantly higher. However, we find a different set of circumstances in schools systems or cities in which the teaching population and student population appear to be at ethnic and racial odds. Kunjufu's (2005) work provides a key example: "In New York City, 36% of students are Black, but 67% of the special education students are Black males. At the same time, White teachers are counted at 77% of the teachers in New York City" (p. 24).

Other data from the U.S. Department of Education, *National Center for Education Statistics Mini-Digest of Education Statistics* (2003), report that the majority of elementary and secondary school teachers in the nation are both female (74%) and White (87%), whereas the population of African American teachers accounted for a mere 7% of the total. For Black males, this could place them at a greater risk for school failure due to the cultural incongruence that potentially exists between them and their teachers (Herrera, 1998; Hanushek, et al., 2005). Data also reveal that a relationship exists between the race of the student, the race of the teacher, and placement in special education classrooms (Herrera, 1998). Also, the work of Hilliard (1976) highlights the constant and disproportionate increases in the numbers of Blacks who were placed in special education courses after desegregation, post *Brown 1954*. Taken in the aggregate, promoting a colorblind approach to educating Black males does not surreptitiously remove color—it only makes us blind.

RECOMMENDATIONS AND CONCLUSION

A concerted and dedicated effort to address each of the myths articulated in this article has to become the goal of those who are committed to improving the educational opportunities for Black males. Simply stating that education is meritocratic is not enough, given the reality of the conditions for certain populations and the fact that their access to social and cultural capital is often severely constrained. Although myriad approaches can be implemented to catalyze the efforts to support Black males, perhaps debunking these myths and offering means to allay them provide a good start.

We know from the research that Myth 1, all the research on Black males is brand new, is a gross misrepresentation of reality. Although scant, data do exist that profile the learning, growth, and development among Black male populations. Unfortunately, movement across the data to elicit action has not been readily forthcoming. Our best research uncovers important findings regarding the overinclusion of Black males in special education and the underinclusion of this population in gifted and talented courses. Yet we fail to get at the root cause of these maladies. Perhaps task forces or groups at a grassroots level—composed of individuals who work on the front lines in the educational system and have a concomitant interest in enhancing the status of Black males—could be used to offer new insight. The insight offered must not be added to the ever-growing piles of data collected on this population but must be transformed into practical items that can ultimately make a difference in policy and programming.

Myths 2 and 3, Black males graduate at lower rates and something is wrong with Black males, are acutely linked in many ways. The constant reminders that they (Black males) as a group are deficient and pathological—that something is wrong with them—results in these men becoming circumscribed by the negative perceptions of those who operate within the educational system. In truth, these men graduate from high school at rates closely paralleling those of their White male counterparts, but they are grossly underrepresented in the numbers of those who go on to seek postsecondary education. Therefore, it appears that the negative self-perceptions held by Black males are yielding bitter fruit far past their K-12 experiences, impacting their aspirations for future achievement. A countervailing course of action might be to create opportunities for empowerment and for these individuals to show, in their own terms, their natural talents and abilities, akin to what Jerome Bruner in his book *The Culture of Education* (1996) calls an *oeuvre,* a celebration of their creative works and accomplishments.

Finally, Myth 4, those who teach Black males are colorblind, is an impossibility. To assume the position of colorblindness is to assume a position of ignorance—all cultural distinctions and group traditions, not to mention social mores and taboos, would have to be held in abeyance. Yet the harsh reality of our very present situation in American schools is that students are bringing their lives from their communities and homes as well as the street into the classroom context. To ignore these realities is to suffer severe and dire consequences. Just as we cannot disaggregate gender from the teaching and learning equation, we must not remove such elements as ethnicity and race. From a strengths perspective, these elements add to the richness of the instructional setting, providing our students with an authentic view of the very concepts we attempt to teach through formal course content. In essence, multicultural approaches reveal to students the importance of diversity in thought and perspective, providing critical tools for becoming an educated person; therefore, including the voices and worldviews of Black males will only help solidify these approaches. In the end, if our goal is to promote meritocratic education in our nation's schools, then we must get past exclusionary rhetoric to ensure that what we mean by this term in the future is not what it has meant in the past.

REFERENCES

Ascher, C. (1991). School Programs for African-American Male Students. New York: Teachers College, Columbia University. (ERIC/CUE Trends and Issues, No. 15, ERIC Clearinghouse on Urban Education).

Bennett, W. J. (1992). *The de-valuing of America: The fight for our culture and our children.* New York: Touchstone.

Bonner, F. (1999). *Extraordinary gifts often come in plain brown wrappers.* Retrieved February 15, 2005, from http://www.sp.uconn.edu/'~nrcgt/news/fall99/fall995.html.

Bonner, F. A. (2000). African American giftedness: Our nation's deferred dream. *Journal of Black Studies*, 30(5), 643–663.

Bourdieu, P. (1997). The forms of social capital. In A. H. Halsey, P. Brown, & A. S. Wells (Eds.), *Education, culture, economy, society* (pp. 46–58). Oxford, England: Oxford University Press. (First published in Richardson, J. E. (Ed.). (1986). *Handbook of Theory for Research in the Sociology of Education.* Westport, CT: Greenwood Press)

Brownstein, A. (2000). Are male students in short supply, or is this "crisis" exaggerated? *Chronicle of Higher Education, 47*(10).

Bruner, J. (1996). *The Culture of Education.* Cambridge, MA: Harvard University Press.

Chemers, M. M., & Murphy, S. E. (1995). Leadership for diversity in groups and organizations. In M. M. Chemers, S. Oskamp, and M. A. Costanzo (Eds.), *Diversity in Organizations* (pp. 157–190). Newbury Hills, CA: Sage.

Children's Defense Fund (2003, May 28). Analysis: Number of Black children in extreme poverty hits record high. Retrieved November 23, 2009, from http://cdf.convio.net/site/DocServer/extremepoverty.pdf?docID=464.

Cose, E. (1997). *Color-blind: Seeing beyond race in a race obsessed world.* New York: Harper-Collins.

Davis, J. E. (2002). Race, gender, and sexuality: (Un)doing identity categories. *Educational Researcher. 31*(4), 29–32.

Dee, T. (2004), The race connection. *Education Next, 4,* 52–59.

Delgado, R. (Ed.). (1995). *Critical race theory: The cutting edge.* Philadelphia: Temple University Press.

Delpit, L. (2003). Dewitt Wallace–Reader's Digest Distinguished Lecture: Educators as "seed people" growing a new future. *Educational Researcher, 32*(7), 14–21.

D'Souza, D. (1996). *The end of racism.* New York: Free Press Paperbacks.

Dunbar, C. (2001). *Alternative schooling for African American youth: Does anyone know we're here?* New York: Peter Lang.

Dunn, R., & Dunn, K. (1992). *Teaching elementary students through their individual learning styles.* Boston: Allyn & Bacon.

Economic Policy Institute. (2005). *Economic snapshots 2005 April.* Retrieved October 14, 2005, from http://www.epinet.org/content.cfm/webfeatures_snapshots_20050406.

Essay staff. (2003). Girls get extra school while boys get Ritalin. *USA Today.*

Ferguson, A. (2000). *Bad boys: Public schools in the making of Black masculinity.* Ann Arbor: University of Michigan Press.

Ferguson, A. (2001). *Bad Boys: Public school in the making of Black masculinity.* Ann Arbor: University of Michigan Press.

Ferguson, R. F. (1998). Teachers' perceptions and expectations and the black-white test score gap. In C. Jencks & M. Phillips (Eds.), *The black-white test score gap* (pp. 273–317). Washington, DC: Brookings Institution.

Ford, D. Y. (1992). Determinants of underachievement as perceived by gifted, above-average, and average Black students. *Roeper Review, 14*(3), 130–136.

Ford, D. Y. (1994). *The recruitment and retention of African-American students in gifted education programs: Implications and recommendations.* Storrs: University of Connecticut, The National Research Center on the Gifted and Talented.

Freire, P. (1993). *Pedagogy of the oppressed.* Translated by Myra Bergman Ramos. New York: Continuum.

Fuentes, A. (2003). Discipline and punish: Zero Tolerance policies have created a "Lockdown Environment" in schools. *The Nation 277,* 17–20.

Gewertz, C. (2004, December 18). Foundation tackles Black males' school woes. *Education Week, 4*(24), 6.

Gordon, E. (1999). *Education and justice: A view from the back of the bus*. New York: Teachers College Press.

Hannushek, Kain, D. O'Brien, & Rivkin, S. E. (2005). *The market for teacher quality*. Retrieved October 17, 2005, from http://www.nber.org/papers/w11154.

Harry, B., & Anderson, M. (1994). The disproportionate placement of African American males in special education programs: A critique of the process. *Journal of Negro Education 63*(4), 602–619.

Herrera, J. (1998). The disproportionate placement of African Americans in special education: An analysis of ten cities. (ERIC Document Reproduction Service No. ED423324).

Herring, C. (1995) *African Americans and disadvantage in the U.S. labor market*. Retrieved February 3, 2005, from http://www.rcgd.isr.umich.edu/prba/perspectives/#spr95.

Herrnstein, R. J., and Murray, C. (1994). *The bell curve*. New York: Free Press.

Hilliard, A. G. (1976). *Alternatives to IQ testing: An approach to the identification of gifted "minority" children* (Report No. PS 009 639). Sacramento: California Department of Education, Special Education Division. (ERIC Document Reproduction Service No. ED147009).

Hoff-Sommers, C. (2000). *The war against boys: How misguided feminism is harming our young men*. New York: Simon & Schuster.

Hollins, E. R. (1996). *Culture in school learning: Revealing the deep meaning*. Mahwah, NJ: Erlbaum.

hooks, b. (2004). *We real cool: Black men and masculinity*. New York: Routledge.

Horn, L., & Kojaku, L. (2001). High school academic curriculum and the persistence path through: Persistence and transfer behavior of undergraduates 3 years after entering 4-year institutions. *Education Statistics Quarterly, 3*(3). Retrieved October 17, 2005, from http://nces.ed.gov/programs/quarterly/vol_3/3_3/q4–1.asp.

Irvine, J. J. (1990). *Black students and school failure*. New York: Greenwood Press.

King, J. E. (2000). *Gender equity in higher education: Are male students at a disadvantage?* Washington, DC: American Council of Education, Center for Policy Analysis.

King, J. (2002). *Gender equity in higher education: Are male students at a disadvantage?* Washington, DC: American Council on Education Center for Policy Analysis.

Kunjufu, J. (2005). *Keeping Black boys out of special education*. Chicago: African American Images.

Lee, C. C. (1996). *Saving the native son: Empowerment strategies for young Black males*. Greensboro, NC: ERIC Counseling and Student Services Clearinghouse.

Lopez, N. (2003). Hopeful girls, troubled boys: *Race and gender disparity in urban education*. New York: Routledge.

Losen, D. J., & Orfield, G. (2002). *Racial inequality in special education*. Cambridge, MA: Civil Rights Project and Harvard Education Press.

Lowe, L.A. (2002, November 2). *Color blindness: Anti-discrimination doctrine or hegemonic reproduction of racial inequality?* Retrieved October 14, 2005, from http://employment.education.uiowa.edu/lalowe/07b154_ePortfolio/COLOR_BLIND_PAPER.htm.

McNally, J. (2003). *A ghetto within a ghetto: African American students are overrepresented in special education programs*. [Electronic Version]. Rethinking Schools. Retrieved September 23, 2005, from http://rethinkingschools.org/archive/17_03/ght179.shtml.

Mincy, R. B. (1994). *Nurturing young Black males*. Washington, DC: Urban Institute Press.

Murrell, P. C. (2002). *African-centered pedagogy: Developing schools of achievement for African American Children*. Albany: State University of New York Press.

Orfield, G., & Losen, D. (2002). *Racial inequity in special education.* Cambridge, MA: Harvard Education Publishing Group.

Parham, T. A., White, J. L., & Ajamu, A. (2000). *The psychology of Blacks: An African centered perspective* (3rd ed.). Upper Saddle River, NJ: Prentice Hall.

Shade, B. J. (1982). Afro-American cognitive style: A variable in school success? *Review of Educational Research, 52,* 219–244.

Simpson, A. W., & Erickson, M. T. (1983). Teachers' verbal and nonverbal communication patterns as a function of teacher race, student gender, and student race. *American Educational Research Journal, 20*(2), 183–198.

Skiba, R., Michael, R., Nardo, A., & Peterson, R. (2002). The color of discipline: Sources of racial and gender disproportionality in school punishment. *Urban Review, 34*(4), 317–342.

Smith, Rosa A.(2005). Building a positive future for black boys. *American School Board Journal, 192*(9), 26–28.

U.S. Department of Education. (2003). *National Center for Education Statistics mini-digest of education statistics.* Retrieved October 17, 2005, from http://www.aacte.org/programs/multicultural/enrollment_ethnicity_yr93–94.htm.

Warburton, E., Bugarin, R., & Nuñez, A. (2001). Bridging the gap: Academic preparation and postsecondary success of first-generation students. *Education Statistics Quarterly, (3)*3. Retrieved October 14, 2005, from http://nces.ed.gov/programs/quarterly/Vol_3/3_3/q4–2.asp#H4.

Witkin, H. A., & Moore, C. A. (1975). *Field-dependent and field-independent cognitive styles and their educational implications.* Princeton, NJ: Educational Testing Service.

Woodson, C. G. (1990). *The mis-education of the Negro.* Trenton, NJ: Africa World Press. (Reprinted from *The Negro in Our History,* 5th edition, by C. G. Woodson, 1933, Washington, DC: Associated Publishers)

References

INTRODUCTION

Bonner, F. A., II. (2000). African American giftedness: Our nation's deferred dream. *Journal of Black Studies, 30*(5), 643–663.

Bonner, F. A. II. (2001). Academically gifted African American male college students: A phenomenological study. Monograph of the National Research Center for the Gifted and Talented (in conjunction with Yale University, University of Connecticut, and University of Georgia, and the U.S. Department of Education).

Bonner, F. A., II, & Evans, M. (2004). Can you hear me? Voices and experiences of African American students in higher education. In D. Cleveland (Ed.), *Broken silence: Conversations about race by African American faculty and students on the journey to the professorate* (pp. 3–18). New York: Peter Lang.

Bonner, F. A., II, & Jennings, M. (2007). Never too young to lead: Gifted African American males in elementary school. *Gifted Child Today, 38*(2), 30–36.

Bonner, F. A., II, Jennings, M., Marbley, A. F., & Brown, L. (2008). Capitalizing on leadership capacity: Gifted African American males in high school. *Roeper Review, 30*(2), 93–103.

Colangelo, N., & Davis, G. A. (Eds.). (2003). *Handbook of gifted education.* Boston: Allyn & Bacon.

Cuyjet, M. J., & Associates. (2006). *African American men in college.* San Francisco: Jossey-Bass.

Fashola, O. (2005). *Educating African American males: Voices from the field.* Thousand Oaks, CA: Corwin Press.

Ford, D. Y. (1994). The recruitment and retention of African-American students in gifted education programs: Implications and recommendations. Storrs: University of Connecticut, The National Research Center on the Gifted and Talented.

Ford, D. Y. (1995). Desegregating gifted education: A need unmet. *Journal of Negro Education, 64*(1), 52–62.

Ford, D. Y., Grantham, T. C., & Harris III, J. J. (1998). Multicultural gifted education: A wakeup call to the profession. *Roeper Review, 19,* 72–78.

Ford, D. Y., Harris, J. J., III, Tyson, C. A., & Frazier-Trotman, M. (2002). Beyond deficit thinking: Providing access for gifted African American students. *Roeper Review, 24*(2), 52–58.

Ford, D. Y., Webb, K. S., & Sandidge, R. F. (1994). When gifted kids grow up. *Gifted Child Today*, 34–42.

Fries-Britt, S. (1998). Moving beyond Black achiever isolation: Experiences of gifted Black collegians. *Journal of Higher Education, 69*(5), 556–576.

Fries-Britt, S. L., & Turner, B., (2002). Uneven stories: The experiences of Black collegians at a historically Black and a traditionally White campus. *Review of Higher Education, 25*(3), 315–350.

Ginwright, S. A. (2004). *Black in school: Afrocentric reform, urban reform, and the promise of hip-hop culture.* New York: Teachers College Press.

Harper, S. R. (2005). Leading the way: Inside the experiences of high-achieving African American male students. *About Campus, 10*(1), 8–15.

Hebert, T. P. (1997). Jamison's story: Talent nurtured in troubled times. *Roeper Review, 19*, 142–148.

Hebert, T. P. (2002). Gifted black males in a predominantly white university: Portraits of high achievement. *Journal for the Education of the Gifted, 26*(1), 25–64.

Hughes, R., & Bonner, F. A., II. (2006). Leaving Black males behind: Debunking the myths of meritocratic education. *Journal of Race and Policy, 2*(1), 76–87.

Kershaw, T. (2001). African American national leadership: A model for complementarity. *Western Journal of Black Studies, 25*(4), 211–219.

Kunjufu, J. (1991, November 20). Detroit's male academies: What the real issue is. *Education Week*, p. 29.

Kunjufu, J. (2005). *Hip hop street curriculum.* Chicago: African American Images.

Renzulli, J. S., Smith, L. H., & Reis, S. M. (1981). The revolving door model: A new way of identifying the gifted. *Phi Delta Kappan, 62*, 648–649.

Shujaa, M. (Ed.). (1994). *Too much schooling, too little education: A paradox of Black life in White societies.* Baltimore: Africa World Press.

White, J. L., & Cones, J. H., III. (1999). *Black man emerging: Facing the past and seizing a future in America.* New York: W. H. Freeman.

CHAPTER ONE

Colangelo, N., & Davis, G. A. (Eds.). (2003). *Handbook of gifted education.* Boston: Allyn & Bacon.

Davis, G., & Rimm, S. (1989). *Education of the gifted and talented* (2nd ed.). Englewood Cliffs, NJ: Prentice Hall.

Davis, G., & Rimm, S. (Eds.). (2003). *Education of the gifted and talented* (5th ed.). Boston: Allyn & Bacon.

First Official U.S. Education Mission to the USSR. (1959). Soviet commitment to education, Bulletin 1959, No. 16. Washington, DC: Office of Education, Department of Health, Education, and Welfare.

Ford, D. Y. (1994). *The recruitment and retention of African-American students in gifted education programs: Implications and recommendations.* Storrs: University of Connecticut, National Research Center for the Gifted and Talented.

Gagné, F. (1990). Toward a differentiated model of giftedness and talent. In N. Colangelo & G. Davis (Eds.), *Handbook of gifted education* (pp. 65–81). Needham Heights, MA: Allyn & Bacon.

Gagné, F. (1993). Constructs and models pertaining to exceptional human abilities. In K. A. Heller, F. J. Monks, & A. H. Passow (Eds.), *International handbook for research on giftedness and talent.* London: Pergamon Press.

Gardner, H. (1983). *Frames of mind: The theory of multiple intelligences.* New York: Basic Books.

Hollingworth, Leta Stetter. (1975). *Children Above 180 IQ.* New York: Arno Press.

Marland, S. P. (1972). *Education of the gifted and talented, Volume 1: A report to the Congress of the United States by the U.S. Commissioner of Education.* Washington, DC: U.S. Government Printing Office.

Meyer, A. E. (1965). *An educational history of the western world.* New York: McGraw-Hill.

Parentpals.com. (n.d.). Definition of gifted. http://www.parentpals.com/gossamer/pages/Detailed/686.html.

Piirto, J. (1994). *Talented children and adults: Their development and education.* New York: Macmillan College Publishing Company.

Piirto, J. (1999). *Talented children and adults: Their development and education.* (2nd ed.). Upper Saddle River, NJ: Merrill.

Plucker, J. A. (Ed.). (2003). Human intelligence: Historical influences, current controversies, teaching resources. Retrieved February 13, 2009, from http://www.indiana.edu/~intell.

Renzulli, J. S. (1986). The three-ring conception of giftedness: A developmental model for creative productivity. In R. J. Sternberg & J. E. Davidson (Eds.), *Conceptions of Giftedness.* New York: Cambridge University Press.

Renzulli, J. S. (2005). The three-ring conception of giftedness: A developmental model for promoting creative productivity. In R. J. Sternberg & J. Davidson (Eds.), *Conceptions of giftedness* (2nd ed.) (pp. 217–245). Boston, MA: Cambridge University Press.

Robinson, A., & Clinkenbeard, P. R. (2008). History of giftedness: Perspectives from the past presage modern scholarship. In S. Pfeiffer (Ed.), *Handbook of giftedness in children: Psycho-educational theory, research, and best practices.* New York: Springer.

Sternberg, R. J. (1985). *Beyond IQ: A triarchic theory of human intelligence.* Cambridge, England: Cambridge University Press.

Sternberg, R. J. (2007). Cultural concepts of giftedness. *Roeper Review, 29*(3), 160–166.

Tannenbaum, A. (1979). Pre-sputnik to post-Watergate concern about the gifted. In A. H. Passow (Ed.), *The gifted and the talented.* Chicago: National Society for the Study of Education.

U.S. Department of Education. (1993). *National excellence: A case for developing America's talent.* Washington, DC: Office of Educational Research and Improvement, U.S. Department of Education.

Whitmore, J. R. (1980). *Giftedness, conflict, and underachievement.* Boston: Allyn & Bacon.

Witty, P. A., & Jenkins, M. D. (1935). The case of 'B'—a gifted Negro girl. *Journal of Social Psychology, 6,* 117–124.

CHAPTER TWO

Arnez, N. (1993). Equity and access in instruction. *Journal of Black Studies, 23*(4), 500–514.

Bonner, F. A., II. (2000). African American giftedness. *Journal of Black Studies, 30,* 643–664.

Carnegie Corporation of New York. (1984–1985). Renegotiating society's contract with the public schools. *Carnegie Quarterly, 29–30,* 1–4, 6–11.

Dunn, R., & Dunn, K. (1992). *Teaching elementary students through their individual learning styles.* Boston: Allyn & Bacon.

Hammond, L. (1985). *Equality and Excellence: Educational Status of Black Americans.* New York, The College Board.

Horner, M. (1972). Toward an understanding of achievement-related conflicts in women. *Journal of Social Issues, 28,* 157–176.

Gardner, H. (1983). *Frames of mind: The theory of multiple intelligences.* New York: Basic Books.

Gollnick, D. M., & Chinn, P. C. (1990). *Multiculturalism education in a pluralistic society.* (3rd ed.). Columbus, OH: Merrill.

Gouldner, H. (1978). *Teachers' pets, troublemakers, and nobodies: Black children in elementary school.* Westport, CT: Greenwood.

Feshbach, N. D. (1969). Student teacher preferences for elementary pupils varying in personality characteristics. *Journal of Educational Psychology, 60,* 126–132.

Ford, D. Y. (1994). *The recruitment and retention of African-American students in gifted education programs: Implications and recommendations.* Storrs: University of Connecticut, The National Research Center on the Gifted and Talented.

Hilliard, A. G. (1976). *Alternatives to IQ testing. An approach to the identification of gifted "minority" children* (Report No. PS 009 639). Sacramento, CA: State Department of Education, Special Education Division. (ERIC Document Reproduction Service No. ED 147 009)

Hudley C, Graham, S. (2002). Stereotypes of achievement striving among early adolescents. *Social Psychology Education, 5,* 201–224.

Irvine, J. J. (1990). *Black students and school failure.* New York: Greenwood Press.

King, J. E. (2000). *Gender equity in higher education: Are male students at a disadvantage?* Washington, DC: American Council on Education, Center for Policy Analysis.

Kofsky, G. E. (1992). *Increasing the number of minority elementary students found eligible for placement in a gifted program by enhancing the quality of screening instruments and inservice training provided to school staff* (Report No. HE-301–312). Nova University. (ERIC Document Reproduction Service No. ED 346 697)

Lightfoot, S. L. (1978). World apart: Relationships between families and schools. In J. J. Irvine (Ed.), *Black students and school failure.* New York: Greenwood Press.

McCarthy, B. (1990). Using the 4MAT system to bring learning styles to schools. *Educational Leadership, 48,* 31–37.

Office of Civil Rights. (2002). Minority students in special and gifted education. Washington, DC: National Academy of Sciences Report.

Pegnato, C. W., & Birch, J. W. (1959). Locating gifted children in junior high school: A comparison of methods. *Exceptional Children, 25,* 300–304.

Peter, K., Horn, L. (2005). Gender differences in participation and completion of undergraduate education and how they have changed over time (NCES 2005–169). U.S. Department of Education, National Center for Education Statistics. Washington, DC: U.S. Government Printing Office.

Peters, M. F. (1981). "Making it" Black family style: Building on the strengths of the Black family. In N. Stinnett, J. DeFrain, K. King, P. Knaub, & G. Rowe (Eds.), *Family strengths three: Roots of well-being* (pp. 73–91). Lincoln: University of Nebraska Press.

Renzulli, J. S. (1986). The three-ring conception of giftedness: A developmental model for creative productivity. In R. J. Sternberg & J. E. Davidson (Eds.), *Conceptions of giftedness*. New York: Cambridge University Press.

Rhodes, L. (1992). Focusing attention on the individual in identification of gifted Black students. *Roeper Review, 14*(3), 108–110.

Shade, B. J. (1982). Afro-American cognitive style: A variable in school success? *Review of Educational Research, 52,* 219–244.

Sternberg, R. J. (1985). *Beyond IQ: A triarchic theory of human intelligence.* Cambridge, England: Cambridge University Press.

Sternberg, R. J., & Davidson, J. (1986). *Conceptions of giftedness.* New York: Cambridge University Press.

Torrance, E. P. (1973, September). *Emergent concepts concerning culturally different gifted children.* Paper presented at the Work Conference on the Culturally Different Gifted Child, Rougemont, NC.

Torrance, E. P. (1977). *Discovery and nurturance of giftedness in the culturally different.* Reston, VA: Council for Exceptional Children.

Torrance, E. P., & Reynolds, C. R. (1978). Images of the future of gifted adolescents: Effects of alienation and specialized cerebral functioning. In J. C. Gowan, J. Khatena, & E. P. Torrance (Eds.), *Educating the ablest.* Itaska, IL: Peacock. (Reprinted from *Gifted Child Quarterly, 22,* 40–54)

Whiting, Gilman W. (2006). From at risk to at promise: Developing scholar identities among black males. *The Journal of Secondary Gifted Education, 17,* 222–229.

Whitmore, J. R. (1986). Understanding a lack of motivation to excel. *Gifted Child Quarterly, 30,* 66–69.

Whitten, L. (1992). Survival conflict and survival guilt in African-American college students. In M. Lang & C. A. Ford (Eds.), *Strategies for retaining minority students in higher education.* Springfield, IL: Charles C. Thomas.

Witkin, H. A., & Moore, C. A. (1975). *Field-dependent and field-independent cognitive styles and their educational implications.* Princeton, NJ: Educational Testing Service.

Wood, D., Kaplan, R., & McLoyd, V. C. (2007). Gender differences in the educational expectations of urban, low-income African American youth: The role of parents and the school. *Journal of Youth and Adolescence, 36,* 417–427.

CHAPTER THREE

Astin, A. W. (1977). *Four critical years.* San Francisco: Jossey-Bass.

Astin, A. W. (1985). *Achieving academic excellence.* San Francisco: Jossey-Bass.

Astin, A. W. (1993). What matters in college. *Liberal Education, 79*(4), 4–15.

Attinasi, L. C., Jr. (1989). Mexican Americans' perceptions of university attendance and the implications for freshman year persistence. *Journal of Higher Education, 60*(3), 247–277.

Berger, J. B., & Milem, J. F. (2000). Promoting undergraduate self-concept: Differences between historically Black and predominantly White colleges. *Journal of College Student Development, 41*(4), 381–394.

Bonner, F. A. II. (2001). Academically gifted African American male college students: A phenomenological study. Monograph of the National Research Center for the Gifted and Talented (in conjunction with Yale University, University of Connecticut, and University of Georgia, and the U.S. Department of Education).

Bonner, F. A. II & Bailey, K. (2006). Assessing the academic climate for African American men. In M. Cuyjet (Ed.) *African American Men in College* (pp. 24–46). San Francisco: Jossey-Bass.

Bonner, F. A. II & Evans, M. (2004). Can you hear me?: Voices and experiences of African American students in higher education. In D. Cleveland (Ed.), *Broken silence: Conversations about race by African American faculty and students on the journey to the professorate* (pp. 3–18). New York: Peter Lang.

Carroll, J. (1988). Freshman retention and attrition factors at a predominantly Black urban community college. *Journal of College Student Development, 29,* 52–59.

Cuyjet, M. J., & Associates. (2006). *African American men in college.* San Francisco: Jossey-Bass.

Daniel, N. (1985). School and college: The need for articulation. *Roeper Review, 7*(4), 235–237.

D'Augelli, A. R., & Hershberger, S. L. (1993). African American undergraduates on a predominantly White campus: Academic factors, social networks, and campus climate. *Journal of Negro Education, 62*(1), 67–81.

Fleming, J. (1984). *Blacks in college.* San Francisco: Jossey-Bass.

Ford, D. Y. (1994). *The recruitment and retention of African-American students in gifted education programs: Implications and recommendations.* Storrs: University of Connecticut, National Research Center for the Gifted and Talented.

Ford, D. Y., Webb, K. S., & Sandidge, R. F. (1994). When gifted kids grow up. *Gifted Child Today, 17,* 34–42.

Fries-Britt, S. L., & Turner, B. (2002). Uneven stories: The Experiences of successful Black collegians at a historically Black and a traditionally White campus. *Review of Higher Education, 25*(3), 315–330.

hooks, b. (2004). *We real cool: Black men and masculinity.* New York: Routledge.

Lewin, K. (1936). *Principles of topological psychology.* New York: McGraw-Hill.

Piirto, J. (1994). *Talented children and adults: Their development and education.* New York: Macmillan College Publishing Company.

Schlossberg, N. K. (1989). Marginality and mattering: Key issues in building community. *New Directions for Student Services, 48,* 5–15.

Sedlacek, W. E. (1993). Employing noncognitive variables in the admission and retention of nontraditional students. In *Achieving diversity: Issues in the recruitment and retention of traditionally underrepresented students* (pp. 33–39). Alexandria, VA: National Association of College Admissions Counselors.

Smith, D., & Associates. (1997). *Diversity works: The emerging picture of how students benefit.* Washington, DC: Association of American Colleges and Universities.

White, J. L. & Cones, J. H., III. (1999). *Black man emerging: Facing the past and seizing a future in America.* New York: W. H. Freeman.

CHAPTER FOUR

Ford, D. Y. (1992). Determinants of underachievement as perceived by gifted, above-average, and average Black students. *Roeper Review, 14*(3), 130–136.

Rodenhouse, M. P., & Torregrosa, C. H. (1995). *1996 higher education directory.* Reston, VA: Higher Education Publications.

Straughn, C. T., & Straughn, B. L. (1995). *Lovejoy's college guide* (23rd ed.). New York: Arco.

CHAPTER FIVE

Allen, W. R. (1986). *Gender and campus race differences in Black student academic performance, racial attitudes and college satisfaction.* Atlanta: Southern Education Foundation.
Baxter Magolda, M. B. (1992). *Knowing and reasoning in college: Gender related patterns in students' intellectual development.* San Francisco: Jossey-Bass.
Miles, M. B., & Huberman, A. M. (1994). *Qualitative data analysis* (2nd ed.). Thousand Oaks, CA: Sage.
Nettles, M. T., & Johnson, J. R. (1987). Race, sex and other factors as determinants of college students' socialization. *Journal of College Student Personnel, 28,* 512–524.

CHAPTER SIX

Davis, G. A. (2003). Identifying creative students, teaching for growth. In N. Colangelo & G. A. Davis (Eds.), *Handbook of gifted education* 3rd ed. (pp. 268–281). Boston: Allyn & Bacon.
Fleith, D., Renzulli, J. S. & Westberg, K. L. (2002). Effects of a creativity training program on creative abilities and self-concept in monolingual and bilingual classrooms. *Creativity Research Journal, 14.*
Hughes, M. S. (1987). Black students' participation in higher education. *Journal of College Student Personnel, 28,* 532–545.
Jackson, K. W., & Swan, L. A. (1991). Institutional and individual factors affecting Black undergraduate student performance: Campus race and student gender. In W. R. Allen, E. G. Epps, & N. Z. Haniff (Eds.), *College in Black and White: African American students in predominantly White and in historically Black Public Universities.* Albany: State University of New York Press.
Sutton, E. M. (2006). Developmental mentoring of African American college men. In M. Cuyjet (Ed.) *African American Men in College* (pp. 95–112). San Francisco: Jossey-Bass.

CHAPTER SEVEN

Davis, R. (1986). *Social support networks and undergraduate student academic success related outcomes: A comparison of Black students on Black and White campuses.* Paper presented at the meeting of the American Educational Research Association.
Hanks, M., & Eckland, B. (1976). Athletics and social participation in the educational attainment process. *Sociology of Education, 49,* 271–294.
Roebuck, J. B., & Murty, K. S. (1993). *Historically Black colleges and universities: Their place in American higher education.* Westport, CT: Praeger.
Sewell, W., & Hauser, R. (1975). *Education, occupation, and earnings: Achievement in the early career.* New York: Academic Press.

CHAPTER EIGHT

Davis, R. B. (1991). Social support networks and trader- graduate student academic success-related outcomes: A comparison of black students on black and white campuses. In W. R. Allen, (Eds.), *College in black and white* (pp.143–157). Albany: State University of New York Press.

Gurin, P., & Epps, E. (1975). *Black consciousness, identity, and achievement: A study of students in historically black colleges.* New York: John Wiley & Sons.

Harvey, W. B., & Williams, L .E. (1996). Historically Black colleges and universities: Models for increasing minority. In C. Turner, M. Garcia, A. Nora, & L. I. Rendon (Eds.), *Racial and ethnic diversity in higher education, ASHE Reader Series* (pp. 233–240). Needham Heights, MA: Simon & Schuster.

Kannerstein, G. (1978). Black colleges: Self concept. In C. Willie and R. Edmonds (Eds.), *Black colleges in America: Challenge, development, survival.* New York: Teachers College Press.

Pascarella, E. T. (1980). Student-faculty informal contact and college outcomes. *Review of Educational Research, 50,* 545–595.

U.S. Department of Education. (1993). *National excellence: A case for developing America's talent.* Washington, DC: Office of Educational Research and Improvement, U.S. Department of Education.

CHAPTER NINE

Allen, W. R. (1986). *Gender and campus race differences in Black student academic performance, racial attitudes and college satisfaction.* Atlanta, GA: Southern Education Foundation.

Allen, W. R., Spencer, M. B., & O'Connor, C. (2002). *African American education: Race community, inequality and achievement—A tribute to Edgar G. Epps.* Oxford, England: Elsevier Science.

Barthelemy, S. J. (1984). The role of Black colleges in nurturing leadership. In A. Garibaldi (Ed.), *Black colleges and universities: Challenges for the future.* New York: Praeger.

Boyer, E. L. (1987). *College: The undergraduate experience in America.* New York: Harper & Row.

Du Bois, W.E.B. (1961). *Souls of Black folk.* (Reprint). Greenwich, CT: Fawcett.

Fleming, J. (1984). *Blacks in college.* San Francisco: Jossey-Bass.

Friedlander, S. R., & Watkins, C. E. (1984). Facilitating the development of gifted college students: A support group approach. *Journal of College Student Personnel, 25,* 559–560.

Gurin, P., & Epps, E. (1975). *Black consciousness, identity, and achievement: A study of students in historically black colleges.* New York: John Wiley & Sons.

Hemmons, W. M. (1982). From the halls of Hough and Halstedt: A comparison of Black students on predominantly White and predominantly Black campuses. *Journal of Black Studies, 12,* 383–402.

Kannerstein, G. (1978). Black colleges: Self concept. In C. Willie and R. Edmonds (Eds.), *Black colleges in America: Challenge, development, survival.* New York: Teachers College Press.

Mays, B. E. (1971). *Born to rebel: An autobiography.* New York: Scribner's.

Roebuck, J. B., & Murty, K. S. (1993). *Historically Black colleges and universities: Their place in American higher education.* Westport, CT: Praeger.

Shade, B. J. (1982). Afro-American cognitive style: A variable in school success? *Review of Educational Research, 52,* 219–244.

Shade, B. J. (1997). *Culture, style and the educative process.* Springfield, IL: Charles C. Thomas.

Solomon, R. C., & Solomon, J. (1993). *Up the university: Re-creating higher education in America.* MA: Addison-Wesley.

Willie, C. V., & Edmonds, R. (Eds.). (1978). *Black colleges in America.* New York: Teachers College Press.

Index

Black Manhood Training (Lee), 178
Black Nationalist Movement, 177
Blacks in College (Fleming), 30
Black Students and School Failure (Irvine), 12
Black tax, 173–74
Bodily-kinesthetic intelligence, 5
Bonner II, Fred A., 111, 127, 137, 147, 167, 188
Bowling Green State University, 111
Bowman-Perrott, Lisa, 147
Boyer, Ernest, 81
Boys and Girls Club, 89, 179
Boy Scouts of America, 140, 176
Bridging school, 127
Brown, Lesley-Ann, 167
Brown 1954, 196
Brown *vs.* Board of Education, 109
Bruner, Jerome, 197

CalTech, 102
Carnegie Corporation, 10, 111
Carroll, J., 25
Cascade Independent School (CISD), 157; African American male high school students in, 159–60; African American male middle school students in, 157–59
"The Case of B—A Gifted Negro Girl" (Jenkins), 8
"Catch-22" scenario, 10
Children above 180 IQ (Hollingsworth), 4
Children's Defense Fund, 195
Chinese people, 1–2
Chinn, Peter C., 21
Chronicle of Higher Education (Brownstein), 188
Classroom action research recommendations, 135
Clinkenbeard, 8
Cognitive style, 13, 115
Colangelo, 3
College Board, 10, 111
College selection, 28–29
"Color Blindness: Anti-Discrimination Doctrine or Hegemonic Reproduction of Racial Inequality?" (Lowe), 195

Colorblind philosophy, 195–96
Componential theory, 6
Conceptually clustered matrix, 39, 60
Concerned Black Men, 140
Confident populations, 153, 155
Contextual theory, 6
Control, 133
Conventional populations, 153, 155
Council of the State Directors of Programs for the Gifted, 170
Counterstories, 190
Creative gifts, 7
Creative-productive giftedness, 6
Creativity, 131
Creativity trait, 6
Critical race theory (CRT), 189
Cross, Jr., William E., 152, 172
Cultural pluralism, 21, 121
Cultural rejection, 193–95
Culture, 21, 121
The Culture of Education (Bruner), 197
"Cut-off" scores, 11
Cuyjet, Michael, 24m 27

Dallas-Fort Worth Section Scholar Award, 33
Daniel, Neil, 28
Darwin, Charles, 2–3
D'Augelli, Anthony, 24
Davidson, Carol, 11, 113, 118
Davidson Institute, 170
Davis, Gary, 1, 3
Deferred dream, 111–23
Dell Labs, 101
Determination, 131
Differentiated model of giftedness, 7
Doctorial University I, 32
Du Bois, W.E.B., 85, 139, 171
Dunn, Kenneth, 13
Dunn, Rita, 13

Earl Lester Cole University Honors College, 38
East Texas State University (ETSU). *See* Texas A&M University—Commerce (TAMUC)
Eckland, Bruce, 68

ABOUT THE AUTHOR

Fred A. Bonner II is professor of higher education administration and student affairs in the Department of Educational Administration and Human Resource Development and associate dean of faculties at Texas A&M University in College Station, TX.